1971

FOUR GENERATIONS

Population, Land, and Family
in Colonial Andover, Massachusetts

FOUR GENERATIONS

Population, Land, and Family
in Colonial Andover, Massachusetts

Philip J. Greven, Jr.

Cornell University Press
ITHACA AND LONDON

First published 1970

Standard Book Number 8014-0539-4
Library of Congress Catalog Card Number 76-87018
PRINTED IN THE UNITED STATES OF AMERICA
BY KINGSPORT PRESS, INC.

For Helen

Preface

History is subject to generational changes; our perspectives and our understanding of the past tend to shift as successive generations of historians come to maturity. The changing circumstances of society alter the formative experiences of historians, whose subsequent work often reflects their changing assumptions and values. The particular questions asked, the particular types of research undertaken, the particular forms of evidence used, also have much to do with ways in which approaches to the past are transformed. The choices and decisions that individual historians make about their researches may seem to reflect only their private interests and predispositions; yet when it becomes evident that such choices have much in common with the choices being made by other historians as well, one can begin to speak meaningfully about the emergence of a generation.

The appearance of a number of studies by younger historians, sharing many premises similar to my own and providing new and distinctive perspectives upon early American history and society, suggests that a significant change in the way historians study the past may now be taking place.[1] Although our particular studies differ in many respects, it is becoming apparent that we hold certain convictions in common. Our

[1] In particular, see the following: John Demos, *A Little Commonwealth: Family Life in Plymouth Colony* (New York, 1970);

works reflect the belief that historians must seek to explore the
basic structure and character of society through close, detailed examinations of the experiences of individuals, families,
and groups in particular communities and localities. We share
the assumption that historians must use the techniques and
questions of other disciplines, including historical demography, sociology, and psychology, whenever they are pertinent
to an analysis and an understanding of the past. We share a
common conviction that social historians in the past have
made too many unfounded assumptions about many basic
elements of experience and behavior. In seeking more reliable
answers to questions about the nature of early American social
experience, we have become aware of the value and the importance of quantifiable data. Yet none of us would be in-
clined to underestimate the importance of subjective factors
in recreating the past. For our generation, at least, the old
argument over History as an art or as a science has little
relevance to what we are actually trying to do. We have come
to believe that the historian must count and quantify data
whenever possible and use them as fully as he can; at the same
time, we believe that the historian must also use imagination

Kenneth A. Lockridge, "Dedham, 1636–1736: The Anatomy of a
Puritan Utopia" (Ph.D. diss., Princeton University, 1965), which is
to appear in a revised form as *A New England Town: The First
Hundred Years, Dedham, Massachusetts, 1636–1736* (New York,
1970); Sumner Chilton Powell, *Puritan Village: The Formation
of a New England Town* (Middletown, Conn., 1963); Darrett B.
Rutman, *Winthrop's Boston: Portrait of a Puritan Town, 1630–1649*
(Chapel Hill, 1965); Stephan Thernstrom, *Poverty and Progress:
Social Mobility in a Nineteenth Century City* (Cambridge, Mass.,
1964); and John J. Waters, Jr., *The Otis Family in Provincial and
Revolutionary Massachusetts* (Chapel Hill, 1968). I was fortunate to
be able to read Demos' study in manuscript, thanks to the kindness of
John Demos and Arthur Pyle, of Plimoth Plantation, Inc.

and intuition continuously in the reconstruction of the past. In this study, at least, I have tried to do both.

Younger generations are always influenced by the generations which precede them, as this study itself amply demonstrates. My own work has been profoundly influenced at every stage by the teaching and the scholarship of Bernard Bailyn, who guided my initial research and directed the writing of my doctoral dissertation. The stimulating hypotheses first sketched out in Bailyn's essay, *Education in the Forming of American Society: Needs and Opportunities for Study* (Chapel Hill, 1960), shaped the direction of my research and exerted a considerable influence upon my growing awareness of the central role which the family has played in molding American experience and society. The earlier pioneering study by Edmund S. Morgan, *The Puritan Family: Religion & Domestic Relations in Seventeenth-Century New England* (rev. ed., New York, 1966), also had an impact upon my awareness of the family as a subject for historical inquiry. Oscar Handlin's course in American social history transformed my awareness of the nature and the potential importance of social history, just as Bailyn's course on colonial America converted me to a field which had previously held no interest for me. Teaching and scholarship serve different purposes, no doubt, but both can exert an extraordinary influence upon the directions which are to be followed by younger generations.

During the past decade, I have become indebted to many people who have contributed in many different ways to the work which I have done. Among those who criticized and commented upon an earlier version of the manuscript or upon portions of it which have been published, I wish to thank William W. Abbot, Bernard Bailyn, John Demos, Oscar Handlin, Thomas Leavitt, H. Roy Merrens, Margaret

Ormsby, and Walter Whitehill, for their many helpful suggestions. I also owe a particular debt to P. M. G. Harris for his acute and thorough commentary. In addition, my former colleagues in the History Department at the University of British Columbia raised many cogent questions about the chapter on the seventeenth-century family. I am also most grateful to Darrett B. Rutman and to Richard P. McCormick, for the comments, criticisms, and suggestions which they provided for an earlier draft of the manuscript for this book, and to the staff of Cornell University Press. Their efforts made this a better book, and any deficiencies or errors which remain are entirely my own responsibility.

The research for this book would not have been possible without the kind cooperation of many people. Irving Piper, Town Clerk of Andover, and his secretary, Annetta Wrigley, provided me with ready access to the original town records, and working-space in their office, courtesies for which I have always been most grateful. I also appreciated the hospitality of the staff of the Merrimack Valley Textile Museum in North Andover, and of Bruce Sinclair and Rex Parody in particular. Over the years, the staff at the Essex Institute in Salem has been unfailingly helpful and gracious in permitting me to explore and to use their superb collection of manuscripts. Leo Flaherty was also most helpful in finding manuscripts in the Massachusetts Archives in Boston. The staffs at the New England Historic Genealogical Society in Boston, Widener Library at Harvard University, and the Memorial Library in Andover provided access to the countless local histories and genealogies which were so essential to me. Mrs. Sessions, of the Andover Historical Society, made accessible to me the typescripts of the Abbott genealogies as well as the manuscript collections of the Society. I am particularly indebted to the custodians of the seventeenth- and eighteenth-century records of Essex County—the Clerk of the County Courts, the Clerk of the Registry of Deeds, and the Clerk of the Probate Records, and their staffs—for their generous assistance and for providing me with the opportunity to use these historically invaluable records.

I have also appreciated the financial assistance which I received during the course of my work on Andover. The North Andover Historical Society provided funds for typing; the University of British Columbia Research Council and the American Association for State and Local History both provided funds for research; and the Charles Warren Center, Harvard University, provided funds for microfilms.

For permission to draw upon portions of earlier versions of chapters in this book, I wish to thank the Essex Institute for the use of "Old Patterns in the New World: The Distribution of Land in 17th Century Andover," *Essex Institute Historical Collections*, CI (1965), and the Editor of the *William and Mary Quarterly*, for the use of "Family Structure in Seventeenth-Century Andover, Massachusetts," *WMQ*, XXIII (1966). For their courteous permission to quote from the following books, I wish to thank: Little, Brown and Company (The Atlantic Monthly Press), and Collins-Knowlton-Wing, Inc., for Oscar Handlin's *The Americans: A New History of the People of the United States* (copyright © 1963 by Oscar Handlin); Charles Scribner's Sons, for Peter Laslett's *The World We Have Lost*; Routledge & Kegan Paul Ltd. (London), and Humanities Press Inc. (New York), for W. M. Williams' *A West Country Village, Ashworthy: Family, Kinship and Land*.

Debts of another, but no less important, kind are owed to friends and to members of my family. Lawrence Bonaguidi, Thomas Condon, Thomas Davis III, John Demos, Jane and Wendell Garrett, Kenneth MacRae, Preston Munter, Grady

McWhiney, Harold Poor, John Schott, and William Slottman provided over the years friendship, counsel, and encouragement which I have greatly appreciated. My parents, Sarah H. and Philip J. Greven; my grandparents, Julia O. and Harry H. Hawkins; and my parents-in-law, Gurney F. and J. Tyson Stokes, have all provided me with countless reasons to acknowledge my indebtedness to them. Above all, though, it is my wife, Helen Stokes Greven, who has made this book possible. The extent of my debt to her is immeasurable; but it can be acknowledged, as I have done in dedicating this book to her.

Throughout the book, I have retained all dates as they appeared in the original records, except that I have assumed that the year began on January 1 rather than on March 25 for the period prior to 1752. Accordingly, I have altered all double dates, so that a date such as February 5, 1722/3, becomes February 5, 1723, in the text. I have also retained the highly individualistic spellings of the original documents, except for altering the archaic "u" to "v" and "f" to "s." Otherwise the citations are as they appeared in their original forms.

In order to avoid the necessity for including long lists of citations of probate records and deeds for each of the four generations studied, I have deposited a fully annotated copy of the manuscript for this book in the library of the Merrimack Valley Textile Museum, North Andover, Massachusetts, where it will be accessible to anyone who may wish to use it.

P. J. G., Jr.

Highland Park, New Jersey
June 1969

Contents

Map

Graphs

Tables

Abbreviations

AHR	*American Historical Review.*
AQ	*American Quarterly.*
EHR	*Economic History Review*, second series.
EIHC	*Essex Institute Historical Collections.*
Essex Deeds	MSS transcripts of Essex County, Massachusetts, deeds. Located in the Registry of Deeds and Probate Court Building, Salem, Mass.
Essex Quarterly Court	*Records and Files of the Quarterly Courts of Essex County Massachusetts*, ed. George F. Dow. 8 vols. Salem, Mass., 1911–1921.
JEH	*Journal of Economic History.*
Mass. Archives	Massachusetts Archives. Located in the State House, Boston, Mass.
NEHGR	*New England Historical and Genealogical Register.*
PR	Files of original MSS Probate Records of Essex County, Massachusetts. Located in the Probate Record Office, Registry of Deeds and Probate Court Building, Salem, Mass.
Vital Records	*Vital Records of Andover Massachusetts to the End of the Year 1849.* 2 vols. Topsfield, Mass., 1912.
WMQ	*William and Mary Quarterly*, third series.

FOUR GENERATIONS

Population, Land, and Family
in Colonial Andover, Massachusetts

"Such as Families are, such at last the Church and Common-wealth must be."

JAMES FITCH
Boston, 1683

"Father says he has been much distressed for land, for his children, too much—one is taken away and needs none. Bewails that he took so much care."

SAMUEL CHANDLER
Andover, December 23, 1745

"I was told by the 40 year old man he was not a child to be controuled; but I answered 40 ought to hear reasons. Another said every [man] ought to do as they pleased."

LANDON CARTER
Sabine Hall, Virginia, March 15, 1776

"Mr Sparks said to me today: 'Landed estates in Massachusetts are no longer being divided up. The eldest almost always inherits the whole of the land.'

'And what happens to the other children?' I asked.

'They emigrate to the West.'

Note: the bearings of this fact are immense."

ALEXIS DE TOCQUEVILLE
Boston, October 2, 1831

I

Introduction: Problems, Sources, and Methods

The basic questions that I have chosen to ask and to answer in this book involve three interrelated subjects—population, land, and the family—as they affected the lives of four successive generations in one New England town—Andover, Massachusetts—during the seventeenth and eighteenth centuries. Accordingly, this is a case study in demographic, economic, and familial history which focuses upon certain central, but almost totally neglected, aspects of life in an early American community: the fundamental events of birth, marriage, and death as they affected both individual families and the population of the community as a whole; the relationship of families to the land, which is of crucial importance in shaping the character of family life in an agrarian society and of basic importance for the character of the society as a whole as well; the relationships of fathers and sons in successive generations, particularly as they reflected the extent of paternal authority and control over the lives of sons and the extent to which sons succeeded in establishing their own autonomy when they reached maturity; the structures of families and the variations in structure which resulted from the changing economic and demographic circumstances within the town in successive generations; and, finally, the extent to which families remained permanently rooted to this particular community or emigrated to other places.

Although each of these aspects of experience within this particular town can be considered separately, it is only when all of them are studied together and interwoven into a reasonably coherent picture that the basic characteristics of the lives of successive generations of families can be established and understood. And only by seeing the changing circumstances of life in a town such as Andover and by studying successive generations of people living in one particular community can the slow, subtle, yet critically important changes which occurred be examined and assessed.

For the most part, the demographic and economic circumstances that affected the lives and molded the families of inhabitants of towns like Andover have received little attention from historians. Even genealogists have noted them only obliquely. This is not surprising, in view of the surviving sources for the history of the family. On the whole, these are disparate, intractable, tedious to acquire, difficult to decipher, and only partially intact. Their story is not revealed easily, and certainly not from their surface. They must be pieced together into collections of data and evidence, from which certain patterns can be ascertained and some aspects of the total picture revealed. The experience often is like trying to put together a complex picture puzzle when no directions exist and many of the crucial pieces are missing. Had the farmers and craftsmen of Andover and their wives and children written something about their lives and thoughts in letters, diaries, or autobiographies, this task would be somewhat simplified. Almost nothing of the sort has survived for the seventeenth century, however, and very little for the eighteenth century. Literary evidence, therefore, scarcely exists for the families studied in this community, and even when it does, it rarely tells what a modern historian wants to know.

Fortunately, however, an abundance of evidence of a very different sort has survived and does provide answers to many, if not all, of the questions which can be asked about the lives and families of these early New Englanders. This evidence, in the form of probate records, deeds, town records, and vital records, has been neglected by historians or used by them for illustrative rather than for analytical purposes. If such evidence is examined with care and imagination, however, it actually reveals more about the lives and actions of ordinary individuals and families than has been ascertained from studies of literary sources alone. Collectively, these sources form the basis for this study of population, land, and families in early Andover.

The demographic history of Andover during the colonial period can be described and analyzed because of the preservation of the original manuscript records of the vital events which occurred in the community from 1650 to 1800.[1] In addition, there are two printed volumes of vital records for Andover, one containing information arranged alphabetically by families for births and the other arranged similarly for marriages and deaths.[2] These two published volumes are not only based upon the manuscript town records but also draw upon the records for the churches of the North and South

[1] A Record of Births, Deaths, & Marriages, begun 1651 Ended 1700; Births, Marriages, Deaths, and Intentions, 1701–1800, located in the Town Clerk's Office, Andover.

[2] Vital Records of Andover Massachusetts to the End of the Year 1849, 2 vols. (Topsfield, Mass., 1912). This work is part of a series of volumes of vital records for Massachusetts towns, published under the auspices of the Topsfield Historical Society. The transcriptions, on the whole, are remarkably accurate.

Parishes, gravestone records, court records, and family records, particularly as recorded in bibles. These volumes are an indispensable supplement to the town records, and they facilitate the process of genealogical research and the reconstitution of family histories. The published records were used in conjunction with the genealogies compiled for early settler families by Charlotte Helen Abbott, an indefatigable genealogist and local historian, whose researches still provide a basis for the initial task of putting together the demographic history of this community in its early period.[3] I have relied also upon the numerous published genealogies of Andover families collected by the New England Historic Genealogical Society in Boston, thus using and building upon the labors of several generations of diligent genealogists and antiquarians, whose researches, often very thorough and impressive, have been almost entirely neglected as historical sources. Collectively, these genealogies are storehouses of elusive but essential information about the origins, lives, and migrations of many successive generations of Americans.

This study is built around the genealogical histories of 28 separate families—the first generation of permanent settlers who arrived and settled during the 1640's and 1650's, and who received house lots and accommodation lands from the town —and their progeny for three successive generations. I collected genealogical data for more than 247 families, and for more than 2,000 individuals bearing these family names, most of whom were born in Andover and many of whom continued to live there. I gathered the data for these families by generations on family reconstitution forms, adapted from those used in England by The Cambridge Group for the

_____

[3] Copies of her typed genealogies are located in the Memorial Library, Andover, and in the Andover Historical Society.

Study of Population and Social Structure.[4] The information on my forms was a composite of data drawn partly from genealogies, partly from the *Vital Records*, and partly from the original manuscript records themselves. By using these varied sources of information, the demographic histories of these families, as far as they can be known from the surviving records, have been reconstituted.

The demographic analysis which I have undertaken involves two quite different perspectives upon the vital events which occurred in Andover since it focuses upon two separate, though overlapping, groups: the families of early settlers through four generations, and the entire population of Andover. Generally, the two perspectives form a unified picture of the demographic history of the community, which suggests that the demographic histories of other families in Andover —those which settled in the late seventeenth and during the eighteenth centuries, and which formed between one-quarter and one-half of the population during the eighteenth century —were not very different from the histories of the settler families. But I have not reconstructed a demographic account of the lives and families of the latecomers since my concern throughout this study has been with the first settlers and their progeny. The data for the entire town do serve, however, as a useful check upon the specific data for these particular families.

The reconstruction of the demographic history of the community as a whole is based upon the method of aggregative analysis and the use of only the manuscript vital records for

[4] For sample forms, and for further details on methodology, see E. A. Wrigley, ed., *An Introduction to English Historical Demography from the Sixteenth to the Nineteenth Century* (New York, 1966), pp. 126, 146, and ch. 4; also see Philip J. Greven, Jr., "Historical Demography and Colonial America," *WMQ*, XXIV (1967), 438–454.

the period from 1651 to 1799, which provide the data for the study of Andover's population.[5] Births, marriages, and deaths are recorded separately, in most instances, and are recorded in chronological sequence, which facilitated the process of counting vital events. Except for a brief period in the early eighteenth century when the records were mutilated, there appear to be no obvious gaps in the recording of vital data until the 1770's, when a persistent underrecording is evident.[6]

The problem of the reliability of vital records, particularly in terms of the underrecording of births and deaths, is one which confronts everyone who attempts to study demographic phenomena prior to the modern period.[7] Demographic studies based upon seventeenth- and eighteenth-cen-

[5] For a discussion of methodology, see Wrigley, ed., *Introduction to English Historical Demography*, ch. 3. I have also drawn upon a number of demographic studies for models, particularly two articles by E. A. Wrigley, "Family Limitation in Pre-industrial England," *EHR*, XIX (1966), 82–109, and "Mortality in Pre-industrial England: The Example of Colyton, Devon, over Three Centuries," *Daedalus*, Spring 1968, pp. 546–580, and the collection of essays edited by D. V. Glass and D. E. C. Eversley, *Population in History: Essays in Historical Demography* (Chicago, 1965). For a discussion of French techniques, see Roland Pressat, *L'analyse démographique: Méthodes, résultats, applications* (Paris, 1961).

[6] The opening pages in the MS volume of vital records for the period 1701 to 1800 are torn, and some are incomplete. In some instances, only half of a name is extant; in others, names are missing altogether. For the purposes of counting births, however, only the entries for the years 1706–1709 are too incomplete to be used with assurance. For these years, I have had to estimate the probable number of missing entries on particular pages, adding them to the entries which survive. For this reason, the data on births from 1706 to 1709 are estimates only.

[7] For a general discussion, see Robert Gutman, "Birth and Death Registration in Massachusetts, I: The Colonial Background, 1639–1800," *Millbank Memorial Fund Quarterly*, XXXVI (1958), 58–74. Also see Wrigley, ed., *Introduction to English Historical Demography, passim.*

tury vital records cannot be as accurate and as reliable as those based upon modern records. Studies such as mine are approximations, at best, of reality. The reader ought to bear this limitation in mind, since statistics have a way of appearing more reliable and authoritative than they actually are. Nevertheless, I am confident that the data for the families that were reconstituted in this study are reasonably reliable and usually represent most of the vital events which occurred in these families. There are gaps, of course, particularly in the records of births and deaths. But evidence from the last testaments of Andover men nearly always confirms the evidence from the vital records, since children mentioned in wills are usually present on the family reconstitution forms. This indicates, I think, that the data for children who survived infancy are generally trustworthy. What cannot be known, of course, is the number of vital events which went unrecorded. Gaps in the series of births, indicated by more than about thirty-six months intervening between known births, may indicate miscarriages, stillbirths, or unrecorded births. The gaps are observable in the family forms, but their causes cannot be determined. Similarly, the underrecording of deaths is a recurrent problem in this period; but I found that many of the people whose deaths were unrecorded in Andover had lived to adulthood (wills and marriage records often confirm this) and moved away, dying elsewhere.[8] On the whole, I found that most children who survived early infancy and most adults who lived in Andover were recorded at their deaths in the town records. Without pretending that the records which have survived represent all of the vital events in families of

[8] For a discussion of underrecorded deaths in Colyton, see Wrigley, "Mortality in Pre-industrial England," pp. 548–551, 562. In addition, see Kenneth A. Lockridge, "The Population of Dedham, Massachusetts, 1636–1736," *EHR*, XIX (1966), pp. 319, 332–333.

this community, I am certain that they provide us with a tremendous amount of essential information about the lives of Andover's inhabitants. Rather than being distressed by the lacunae in the records, historians must be grateful that men in the seventeenth- and eighteenth-century New England towns like Andover bothered to keep records at all, and that those which they did keep were as complete as they were.

By using all of the available demographic data for Andover's population as a whole and for specific families as well, I have attempted to establish as reliable answers as possible for questions such as these: What was the probable size of Andover's population during the seventeenth and the eighteenth centuries? How many births, marriages, and deaths occurred? What changes were there in the magnitude of probable birth rates, fertility rates, and mortality rates for the population as a whole? What patterns of growth were apparent in the population during the period between 1650 and 1800? Did the rate of population growth vary over time? More particularly, how many children were born to families and how many of these children survived to adulthood and old age? How large were families, and did the sizes of families vary significantly over time? At what ages did people marry, and how often did they remarry? How long were the lives of men and women who survived at least to the age of twenty-one years, and what were the basic characteristics of longevity in this community? More generally, how reliable are the common assumptions about birth, marriage, and death that are found in many general accounts of early American society? To what extent did the demographic experiences of Andover's inhabitants resemble or differ from the demographic experiences of Englishmen during the seventeenth and the eighteenth centuries? And, very importantly, to what extent did the demographic experience of Andover change during the course of time?

Such questions are fundamental to the study of the history of Andover's population. The answers very often prove to be quite unexpected.

Along with demographic factors, the relationship of men to the land played a role of overwhelming importance in the lives of people during the seventeenth and eighteenth centuries, when Andover was still essentially an agricultural community. Questions concerning the land—its distribution, its ownership, its uses, and the ways in which it was passed from generation to generation—have begun to be asked by historians in recent years, yet much remains to be discovered about the economic basis of life in the agricultural towns of New England.[9]

[9] Until relatively recently the history of agriculture and of farming communities in colonial New England has been generally ignored by historians, apart from a few old studies, such as Percy Wells Bidwell and John I. Falconer, *History of Agriculture in the Northern United States, 1620–1860* (Washington, 1925), Roy H. Akagi, *The Town Proprietors of the New England Colonies* (Philadelphia, 1924), Charles M. Andrews, *The River Towns of Connecticut: A Study of Wethersfield, Hartford, and Windsor* (Baltimore, 1889), and Robert Walcott, "Husbandry in Colonial New England," *New England Quarterly*, IX (1936), 218–252. Sumner Chilton Powell's *Puritan Village: The Formation of a New England Town* (Middletown, Connecticut, 1963), Charles S. Grant's *Democracy in the Connecticut Frontier Town of Kent* (New York, 1961), Darrett B. Rutman's *Husbandmen of Plymouth: Farms and Villages in the Old Colony, 1620–1692* (Boston, 1967), Harry Roy Merrens' *Colonial North Carolina in the Eighteenth Century: A Study in Historical Geography* (Chapel Hill, 1964), and Jackson Turner Main's *The Social Structure of Revolutionary America* (Princeton, 1965) have made important contributions to an understanding of the role which land played in early American society. English historians often have been acutely conscious of their agrarian past. In particular, see W. G. Hoskins' *The Midland Peasant: The Economic and Social History of a Leicestershire Village* (London, 1957), *Essays in Leicestershire History* (Liverpool, 1950), and *Provincial England: Essays in*

There is no dearth of evidence with which to answer questions about the land and its effects upon mens' lives. In Andover, as in most New England towns, there are three principal types of records which provide essential data: the town records, which contain information about particular grants of land to the inhabitants; probate records, containing both wills and inventories of estates; and deeds for the transference of land. Each of these provides invaluable information for the reconstruction of patterns of land ownership and land transmission in seventeenth- and eighteenth-century Andover, as well as valuable data on wealth and economic status in general. The manuscript town records for Andover are complete from 1656 to the present, and there are also two manuscript volumes of proprietors' records for the period from 1714 to 1824. The probate records for Essex County are located in Salem, where the manuscript files have been carefully preserved from the seventeenth century.[10] I have made extensive use of the probate records (most of them original manuscripts although a few have been lost, with only a photostatic record surviving) for a total of 273 estates, including 30 first-generation settlers, 57 second-generation sons of these settlers, 103 third-generation grandsons, and 83 fourth-generation greatgrandsons. In addition, probate records for more than 100

Social and Economic History (London, 1963); Mildred Campbell, The English Yeoman Under Elizabeth and the Early Stuarts (New Haven, 1942); and Joan Thirsk, ed., The Agrarian History of England and Wales, 1500–1640 (Cambridge, 1967), vol. IV.

[10] A series of the earliest probate records have been published in The Probate Records of Essex County Massachusetts (1635–1681), 3 vols. (Salem, Mass., 1916–1920). Some probate records are scattered in George F. Dow, ed., Records and Files of the Quarterly Courts of Essex County Massachusetts, 8 vols. (Salem, Mass., 1911–1921), which covers the period 1656–1683; others are to be found in the Essex County Court Papers, in the Office of the Clerk of the County Court, Salem, Mass.

other men who settled in Andover later in the seventeenth and throughout the eighteenth century provided useful perspectives upon the estates of the settler families and their heirs. Equally important for the study of the transmission of land from one generation to the next were the transcriptions of deeds of gift and deeds of sale recorded in more than 100 volumes of Essex County deeds which have been kept at the Registry of Deeds in Salem. These Essex County probate records and deeds constitute an extensive body of source material for economic and social history in the colonial period, yet they have scarcely been touched by modern historians.

The value of such abundant source materials depends almost entirely upon the uses to which they are put, of course, and much depends upon the questions and the methods employed by the historian. My own focus has been principally upon the problem of inheritance and the methods of transmission of estates, especially of land, from one generation to the next.[11] By examining patterns of inheritance from generation to generation, it is possible to see how men used their land for the purpose of perpetuating their families and providing for the settlements of their offspring. Through a careful reconstruction of many specific cases involving the transference of

[11] The study of inheritance has been almost entirely neglected by American historians, despite the profound importance of inheritances in social and economic history. Alexis de Tocqueville's observations on the role of inheritances in shaping the character of American society have gone unheeded; see *Democracy in America,* ed. Phillips Bradley (New York, 1956), I, pp. 47–51, and *Journey to America,* ed. J. P. Mayer (New Haven, 1962), pp. 19, 66, 77. See also C. Ray Keim, "Primogeniture and Entail in Colonial Virginia," *WMQ,* XXV (1968), 545–586. George C. Homans' *English Villagers of the Thirteenth Century* (1941; reprint ed., New York, 1960) is a classic study based upon an analysis of inheritance patterns, family structure, and field systems.

land from fathers to sons—an extremely detailed process, but virtually the only way to reconstitute the actual facts about the actions of particular men and their families—a remarkably complex and extensive picture of their economic life emerges. Most important of all, though, is the fact that what men did with their land had immensely important implications for the character of their families. The study of the land is thus of critical importance for the study of the family in an agricultural community.

The overarching concern of this study, and the subject which brings together both the demographic and the economic data and justifies the concern with the welter of details which form the basis of this book, is the history of the family in colonial Andover.[12] Since there is little literary evidence of any value, it is only by the collation of disparate types of data and the careful reconstruction of case histories of particular people and families that anything of significance can be discovered about either the structures or the functioning of these early American families in this particular community. Embedded in this demographic and economic evidence is information about the probable composition of households and the

---

[12] The question about the nature of early American families was formulated most clearly by Bernard Bailyn in his brilliant, and immensely influential, essay in hypothetical history, *Education in the Forming of American Society: Needs and Opportunities for Study* (Chapel Hill, 1960), esp. pp. 15–29, 75–78. The earlier study by Edmund S. Morgan, *The Puritan Family: Religion & Domestic Relations in Seventeenth-Century New England* (rev. ed., New York, 1966), remains the indispensable introduction to the history of the family in early America. It is based essentially upon literary sources, and represents a definitive study of the family from this point of view. The pioneering work by Arthur W. Calhoun, *A Social History of the American Family*, 3 vols. (Cleveland, Ohio, 1917), is still useful, but it tends to be too impressionistic and unreliable.

structures of kinship networks and families in general.[13] This evidence also permits us to reconstruct the actions that can reveal the subtle, yet vitally important, relationships between fathers and sons, a matter of critical importance in establishing whether or not families were patriarchal.[14] By observing at what point in their lives sons were able to establish their own autonomy and economic independence, indicated both by the ownership of property and by marriage, and by observing the extent to which sons followed their fathers' occupations and shared their fathers' economic burdens and responsibilities, it ought to be possible to determine whether or not there really were patriarchal families in colonial Andover, and whether or

[13] Very little is known as yet about family structure in either England or America during the seventeenth, eighteenth, and nineteenth centuries. The pioneering article by Peter Laslett and John Harrison, "Clayworth and Cogenhoe" (in H. E. Bell and R. L. Ollard eds., *Historical Essays, 1600–1750, Presented to David Ogg* [London, 1963], pp. 157–184), which demonstrated the presence of mobile nuclear families in two seventeenth-century villages, has not yet been supplemented by other comparable studies. H. J. Habakkuk's "Family Structure and Economic Change in Nineteenth-Century Europe," *JEH*, XV (1955), pp. 1–12, is very suggestive about the relationship of family structure and inheritance. For colonial America, see John Demos, "Notes on Life in Plymouth Colony," *WMQ*, XXII (1965), esp. pp. 279–286, and "Families in Colonial Bristol, Rhode Island: An Exercise in Historical Demography," *WMQ*, XXV (1968), 40–57; and Richard S. Dunn, "The Barbados Census of 1680: Profile of the Richest Colony in English America," *WMQ*, XXVI (1969), 21–24. The extent of our ignorance about the nature of family structure is evident from the paucity of such studies. We do not yet have an analysis comparable to Philippe Ariès' brilliant study of French and Dutch families, *Centuries of Childhood: A Social History of Family Life*, trans. Robert Baldick (New York, 1962).

[14] Peter Laslett has vigorously, if not always persuasively, argued the case for patriarchalism in English families in the seventeenth century in *The World We Have Lost* (New York, 1965), esp. pp. 3–4, 18–21, 78–79, 90, 150–151, 173. Most historians, however, have ignored the entire question.

not particular forms of family relationships could be perpetuated, for how long, and under what circumstances. In addition, it is also possible to probe the economic and demographic
basis for familial stability or mobility by establishing the extent to which sons in successive generations remained settled
in the same community as their parents or chose to leave
Andover to resettle somewhere else, and by discovering the
circumstances which either inhibited or fostered their mobility.[15]

The term "family" has proven to be immensely elastic in its
meanings, and the attempts to refine its definitions and to
establish some basic consensus on terminology have not yet
been fully successful.[16] For the purposes of this book, my own
conceptions regarding the family ought to be made as clear as

[15] The extent, character, and influence of geographical mobility in
early America have yet to receive the attention their importance
warrants. Suggestive essays by Rowland Berthoff, "The American
Social Order: A Conservative Hypothesis," AHR, LXV (1960),
495–514; Everett S. Lee, "The Turner Thesis Re-examined," AQ,
XIII (1961), pp. 77–83; Demos, "Life in Plymouth," pp. 265–268; and
Lockridge, "Population of Dedham," esp. pp. 320–324, all consider
the problem of mobility in America. For English population mobility, see: E. E. Rich, "The Population of Elizabethan England," EHR,
II (1950), 247–265; Lawrence Stone, "Social Mobility in England,
1500–1700," Past and Present, April 1966, esp. 29–33, 49–50; and
Laslett and Harrison, "Clayworth and Cogenhoe," pp. 174–180.

[16] One of the best analyses of the complexities of definition and
terminology, particularly in terms of the extended family, is by
Colin Rosser and Christopher Harris, in The Family and Social
Change: A Study of Family and Kinship in a South Wales Town
(London, 1965), ch. 1, esp. pp. 18–32. Sidney M. Greenfield, "Industrialization and the Family in Sociological Theory," American
Journal of Sociology, LXVII (1961), 312–322, reprinted in Bernard
Farber, ed., Kinship and Family Organization (New York, 1966), pp.
408–417, is suggestive. For a classic definition of modern American
family structure, see Talcott Parsons, "The Kinship System of the
Contemporary United States," American Anthropologist, XLV
(1943), pp. 22–38. Most American sociologists have accepted Parsons'
assumptions about modern family structure.

possible here, with the reservation that the documentation and, indeed, the very basis of my conceptions are to be found in the histories of these Andover families themselves. For purposes of analysis, a family can be considered either a household of kindred or a group of kindred who usually, but not always, reside in the same community or in relatively close proximity. Most studies of modern American and European families have observed that the most frequently found household consists of the nuclear family—husband, wife, and their own children. When households include other kindred, especially grandparents, but possibly uncles, aunts or cousins as well, they form an extended family, which most often is defined in terms of a trigenerational household.[17] Such a definition of an extended family necessarily focuses attention upon a single household, thereby narrowing the concept of "the family" to a relatively small number of people.

In the course of my reconstruction of the households and kinship networks of Andover, however, I found such a conception too narrow to be particularly useful. It became evident that the extended family actually consisted most frequently of a kinship network of separate, but related, households. An analysis that concentrates on households cannot appreciate the complexities of structure that emerge from the expansion and the contraction of the kinship group within a given community and within a given social setting.

My own definition of the extended family equates it with a kinship network consisting, for the most part, of separate households.[18] Throughout the colonial period in Andover, as

[17] An example is Bailyn's, *Education*, pp. 15–16. Two of Demos' articles, "Life in Plymouth," p. 279, and "Families in Colonial Bristol," p. 40, also focus upon the household when defining an extended family.

[18] My definition coincides with those used by Rosser and Harris in *Family and Social Change*, pp. 13–16, 32, and ch. 6, pp. 193–235, and by Michael Young and Peter Willmott in *Family and Kinship*

probably elsewhere in the New England colonies and in England as well, the basic household most often was nuclear in structure. The principal variable, then, is not the structure of the household (although it could and did vary) but the structure and extent of the extended kin group residing within the community. What matters most in determining the structures of families, therefore, are the factors of residence, mobility, and interrelationship of kindred. This accounts for the great importance which I have attached to these factors throughout this study; they are central to any attempt to delineate the structures and the characters of families in the past.

By studying the families of four successive generations of residents in Andover, I have sought to answer one of the most

---

in East London (London, 1957), pp. 31–32. In an earlier version of Chapter 4, published as "Family Structure in Seventeenth-Century Andover, Massachusetts," *WMQ*, XXIII (1966), p. 255, I used the phrase *"modified* extended family" to describe this form of structure. This simply adds to the confusion of terms, and I now prefer to define my use of the term "extended family" carefully, rather than creating a new term. The potential confusion is evident from the fact that Eugene Litwak also uses the term "modified extended family," but defines it differently, in "Occupational Mobility and Extended Family Cohesion," *American Sociological Review*, XXV (1960), pp. 9–21, and "Geographical Mobility and Extended Family Cohesion," *American Sociological Review*, XXV (1960), pp. 385–394. Marvin B. Sussman and Lee G. Burchinal discuss extended families in "Kin Family Network: Unheralded Structure in Current Conceptualizations of Family Functioning," *Marriage and Family Living*, XXIV (1962), 231–240, and "Parental Aid to Married Children: Implications for Family Functioning," *Marriage and Family Living*, XXIV (1962), 320–332, both of which are reprinted in Farber, ed., *Kinship and Family Organization*, pp. 123–133, 240–254. Edmund Morgan assesses the functioning of the extended kinship network in seventeenth-century New England in *Puritan Family*, pp. 150–160. Peter Laslett discusses the extended kinship network among gentry families in mid-seventeenth-century England in "The Gentry of Kent in 1640," *Cambridge Historical Journal*, IX (1948), 148–164.

crucially important questions that can be asked about the nature and history of the family: Did the structure and the character of families change through time and from place to place? The answer, as this entire study demonstrates, is affirmative; families did change, and patterns of family structure, patterns of relationships between fathers and sons, patterns in the transmission of land, and patterns in demographic experience all gradually altered in the course of the seventeenth and the eighteenth centuries. Because of these complex and almost continuous changes, many of them very subtle and difficult to detect—particularly from the sources which have survived—one can describe the family as having a history. The nature of the family was as mutable as the circumstances shaping the lives of the men, women, and children who were born, matured, and died in this community and in others. To a considerable degree, these changes corresponded closely with the generational cycles that underlay some of the most fundamental rhythms of life in agricultural communities like Andover.[19] The surface of life in such towns seems to be

[19] The presence of generational cycles has also been detected in Dedham, Mass., and Kent, Conn. (Lockridge, "Population of Dedham," p. 328, and Grant, *Kent*, pp. 97–103.) Generational cycles are evident in some European communities, too, as noted in D. E. C. Eversley, "Population, Economy and Society," and Pierre Goubert, "Recent Theories and Research in French Population between 1500 and 1700," both in Glass and Eversley, eds., *Population in History*, pp. 50, 472. Anthony Esler based his study upon the concept of a "social generation": *The Aspiring Mind of the Elizabethan Younger Generation* (Durham, N.C., 1966). Studies of successive generations of particular families also are suggestive: Richard S. Dunn, *Puritans and Yankees: The Winthrop Dynasty of New England, 1630–1717* (Princeton, 1962); Byron Fairchild, *Messrs. William Pepperrell: Merchants of Piscataqua* (Ithaca, 1954); Philip L. White, *The Beekman Family of New York in Politics and Commerce, 1647–1877* (New York, 1956); and John J. Waters, Jr., *The Otis Family in Provincial and Revolutionary Massachusetts* (Chapel Hill, 1968).

unbroken in its continuity, but beneath the surface, changes gradually altered both the landscape and the lives of the inhabitants.

Many questions cannot be answered by using such sources as local records, probate records, land records, and vital records. Questions involving the innermost workings of families —their emotional life, their methods of child nurture, discipline, and acculturation, their motivations, personal viewpoints, and values—are particularly difficult to answer or to document from such records. What can be done with the records we have is basically to determine what men did, what actions they took, and how they behaved—to answer, in effect, the questions which have been outlined in this introductory chapter in extraordinary detail. Since very few of these people left records of their thoughts, their actions must speak for them. It may not be possible, by undertaking the time-consuming process of demographic and familial reconstitution, to recover the complete secular reality of human experience in a community like Andover, but it is remarkable, nevertheless, how much can be discovered by such a method about the lives and actions of ordinary people in an early American community.

The importance of generational patterns is also evident in Bernard Bailyn's *The New England Merchants in the Seventeenth Century* (Cambridge, Mass., 1955), and Perry Miller's, *The New England Mind from Colony to Province* (Cambridge, Mass., 1953).

PART I

THE FIRST AND SECOND GENERATIONS

2

Life and Death in a Wilderness Settlement

By the time Andover was founded in 1646, all of the early settlers had successfully withstood the arduous process of transplantation from the old country to the new. Few had yet actually encountered the difficult circumstances inherent in an entirely new settlement, however, since most had been late-comers to the communities in which they first settled.[1] The environment which was to shape most of the remainder of their lives was still a wilderness when they first arrived during the 1640's and 1650's; Andover was rather remote from Boston, twenty miles or so to the south, and from Newbury, fifteen miles away on the coast. As an inland plantation, Andover was less marshy than a town like Ipswich or Newbury, but it was not clear at the outset whether it would prove to be a healthful place in which to live and raise children. The records which have survived, however, do provide a means of assessing some aspects of the quality of the environment and of the circumstances shaping the lives of the settlers. By examining the demographic experiences of the first two

[1] For a detailed discussion of the process of settlement in Andover, see Philip J. Greven, Jr., "Four Generations: A Study of Family Structure, Inheritance, and Mobility in Andover, Massachusetts, 1630–1750" (Ph.D. diss., Harvard University, 1964), ch. 1, pp. 1–53.

generations, it is possible to establish the fact, which few historians have been willing to consider likely, that this new community proved to be a remarkably healthful place, conducive to the preservation of life and to the fecundity of the inhabitants.[2]

Unlike the settlers themselves, all of whom had been born in England, the majority of the children of first-generation families were born in the New World, either in the towns in which their parents first settled or in Andover itself. Fewer than one-third of the children were born prior to 1650, when the Andover records began to be kept. Of these, at least 20 were born prior to 1640, and at least 42 were born during the 1640's, with a probable maximum of about 82 children being born prior to 1650. The births of 201 children occurred after 1650, with nearly half (47.3 per cent) taking place during the 1650's and 1660's. Thereafter the number of second-generation births declined, with 47 births in the 1670's, 19 in the 1680's, and only one in the 1690's. In effect, the generational profile of births demonstrates that the critical decades of the 1650's and 1660's, when decisions were made regarding the distribution of town land, also happened to be years in which large numbers of the next generation were being born.

The distribution of births of the second generation must be distinguished from the total births recorded in the town records for the period, which include births of later-comers during the 1660's and 1670's as well as some births for the next generation. From 1650 to 1654, the town recorded the births of 28 infants; from 1655 to 1659, 32; from 1660 to 1664, 43; from 1665 to 1669, 44; between 1670 and 1674 the figure rose

[2] For a discussion of sources and methods used in this study of the demographic history of Andover, see Chapter 1. For a complete series of data from 1650 to 1799 for births, marriages, and deaths, see the Appendix.

to 78, and to 90 between 1675 and 1679. This persistent increase in the numbers of births recorded suggests a growing population, but, unfortunately, the birth rate (the number of births per thousand of the population) cannot be estimated for this early period since neither a census nor tax lists survive to indicate the approximate total population.

It is possible, however, to determine the proportion of births to marriages during this period; this provides a useful index to fertility and thus indirectly indicates whether the birth rate itself was high or low. If the number of births for a decade are divided by the number of marriages for the decade which began five years earlier, the marriages during the dec-

Table 1. Births per marriage, 1650–1684

Marriages		Births		
Years	Number	Years	Number	B/M
1650–1659	13	1655–1664	75	5.8
1660–1669	23	1665–1674	122	5.3
1670–1679	38	1675–1684	215	5.7

ade 1650–1659 produced 5.8 births per marriage, and for 1660–1669 produced 5.3 births per marriage (see Table 1).[3] Since the proportion of births to marriages in Dedham, Massa-

[3] Several different methods have been used by historical demographers, this being the one suggested by J. D. Chambers, in his essay "The Course of Population Change," in D. V. Glass and D. E. C. Eversley, eds., *Population in History: Essays in Historical Demography* (Chicago, 1965), p. 333. For a different method, see D. E. C. Eversley, "A Survey of Population in an Area of Worcestershire from 1660 to 1850 on the Basis of Parish Registers," in Glass and Eversley, eds., *Population in History*, p. 403 (originally published in *Population Studies*, X, [1957], pp. 253–279). One can also divide births and marriages recorded during exactly the same periods, but this method does not seem to be as useful as Chambers'.

chusetts, during the period 1636–1668 was 4.8, the relative height of the figures for Andover during the 1650's and 1660's would indicate that the birth rate itself was higher than normal during the early period following the settlement of the town.[4]

The growth of the population depended not only upon the birth rate, of course, but upon the death rate as well, since the proportion of infants surviving to adulthood was of critical importance in determining the growth of the town's population. During various periods of their history many communities in England and Europe had suffered from an excess of deaths over births, and throughout the seventeenth century the surplus of births over deaths was rarely sufficient to permit a significant increase in the total population.[5] By contrast, the

[4] Kenneth Lockridge, "The Population of Dedham, Massachusetts, 1636–1736," *EHR*, XIX (1966), 330. The relative height of the fertility index in Andover is also indicated by comparisons with the index of 5.8 births per marriage in Clayworth, Nottinghamshire, during the period 1676–1688, when the birth rate was "very high indeed"; see Peter Laslett and John Harrison, "Clayworth and Cogenhoe," in H. E. Bell and R. L. Ollard, eds., *Historical Essays, 1600–1750, Presented to David Ogg* (London, 1963), p. 173, and the Addendum, Table 2, which contains the data I used to determine the ratio of births to marriages. During the seventeenth century, the number of births per marriage in French villages around Beauvais ranged from 4.44 to 5.75, with the mean being 5.04 (Pierre Goubert, *Beauvais et le Beauvaisis de 1600 à 1730: Contribution à l'histoire sociale de la France du XVIIe siècle* [Paris, 1960], p. 37, table).

[5] For discussions of mortality in seventeenth-century England, see W. G. Hoskins, "The Population of an English Village, 1086–1801: A Study of Wigston Magna," in Hoskins, *Provincial England: Essays in Social and Economic History* (London, 1963), ch. 10, pp. 196–197. In Clayworth, deaths exceeded births during the period 1676–1688, with 190 baptisms and 197 burials (Laslett and Harrison, "Clayworth," Table 2, p. 182). In Colyton, the period from the 1640's to the 1730's was one "with burials normally more numerous than baptisms and population apparently falling" (E. A. Wrigley, "Mor-

experience of Andover during the early period of settlement and, indeed, throughout the entire seventeenth century fostered the rapid expansion of the population because of the remarkably low death rate during this period.

Few deaths were recorded in Andover during the early decades following its settlement. During the 1650's, seven deaths were recorded, five of them being children; during the 1660's, eighteen deaths were recorded, twelve of them children. Using data drawn from the family reconstitution forms, a total of nineteen deaths can be determined to have occurred between birth and nineteen years of age during these decades. This gives a mortality rate for children born to the settler families during the period 1640–1669 of 123 per thousand dying before nineteen years of age out of a group of 155 children whose ages at death can be determined with relative certainty, and a rate of 93 per thousand dying before nineteen years of age out of a total group of 204 children. This means that between 877 and 907 children out of every thousand born between 1640 and 1669 survived to the age of twenty, and between 890 and 917 children out of every thousand survived at least to the age of ten; these rates are astonishingly high. Even assuming that the mortality rates were double those found for these Andover families, about 754 out of every thousand children—three-quarters of those born in Andover during this period—would still have survived to the age of twenty years. Actually, though, the evidence seems to indicate that an even higher proportion of children survived to become adults. Given the fact that the deaths which were recorded during the 1650's were only 11.6 per cent of the births recorded during that decade, and the deaths during the 1660's were only 20.6 per cent of the births, the mortality

tality in Pre-industrial England: The Example of Colyton, Devon, over Three Centuries," *Daedalus*, Spring 1968, p. 556).

rates computed for the settler families appear to correspond rather closely to the proportion of deaths to births recorded in the town records.

The initial period following the settlement of Andover thus seems to have been one of exceptional healthiness. Even with allowances made for gaps in the records and underrecording of deaths, the fact remains that in Andover during the 1650's and 1660's there was an unusually high proportion of survivors among the infants and children born in the wilderness community. The second generation began its life auspiciously. Circumstances evidently combined to encourage a high birth rate and an exceptionally low death rate, a combination which produced a population that grew at a rapid pace. The numbers, of course, were still small, but the growth potential was immense. The chances of raising most of one's children to adulthood were far greater in Andover than in many similar villages in the Old World or some of the older communities in the New.

A study of deaths in Andover also suggests that those who did survive to adulthood could anticipate long and healthy lives. The average age of twenty-nine first-generation men at the time of their deaths was 71.8 years, and the average age at death of twenty first-generation wives was 70.8 years. Twenty-two of the men who settled permanently in Andover died after reaching their sixtieth year, five of them in their seventies, six in their eighties, three in their nineties, and one, according to the town records, at the remarkable age of 106. Similarly, fifteen of their wives also lived to be at least sixty years old, with four dying in their seventies, five in their eighties, one in her nineties, and one at the age of 100 years. The lifespans of their children were also impressively high, the average age at death of 111 second-generation men who had survived at least to the age of twenty-one being 64.2

years, and the average age of 58 second-generation women
being 61.6 years.

The age distribution at death for ninety-two men born
between 1640 and 1669 and surviving at least to the age of
twenty also indicates the longevity of the men born in
Andover during its early period (see Table 2): nearly four-

Table 2. Age at death of persons born between 1640 and 1669 and surviving
to age 20

Age	Male		Female	
	No.	%	No.	%
20–29	13	14.1	2	4.5
30–39	4	4.3	5	11.4
40–49	2	2.2	5	11.4
50–59	10	10.9	9	20.5
60–69	16	17.4	6	13.6
70–79	25	27.2	9	20.5
80–89	19	20.6	4	9.1
90–99	3	3.3	4	9.1
100 and over	0	0.0	0	0.0
Total	92	100.0	44	100.1

fifths lived to be at least fifty years old (79.4 per cent) and
slightly more than half (51.1 per cent) reached the age of
seventy. Although the age at death can be determined for
only forty-four women born between 1640 and 1669 and
surviving to the age of twenty, the distribution of their
ages at death as shown in Table 2 nevertheless suggests that
women also tended to reach advanced ages in appreciable
proportions during this period: nearly three-quarters of these
women lived to be at least fifty years old (72.8 per cent),
more than half reached sixty years (52.3 per cent), and more
than one-third reached seventy years (38.7 per cent). It is also
suggestive that only 15.9 per cent of these women died be-

tween the ages of 20 and 39—years of childbearing and high risk for life; this figure was higher among the men, 18.4 per cent of whom died during their twenties and thirties. If the lifespans of this sample group of women are at all representative of those of the entire group born during this period, then it appears likely that both men and women born in Andover during the early decades following its settlement enjoyed longer lives after surviving the normal hazards of childhood and youth than previous studies of colonial America have indicated.[6]

[6] Perry Miller and Thomas Johnson, for instance, stated baldly that "the death rate was very high" during the Puritan era in New England (*The Puritans* [New York, 1938], p. 389). Perhaps Arthur W. Calhoun's views in *A Social History of the American Family* (Cleveland, Ohio, 1917), I, 105–106, have shaped most modern assumptions about the colonial family. According to Calhoun: "It was difficult at first to rear children in the new country. In the bareness and cold of Massachusetts, mortality of infants was frightful." More recently, Oscar Handlin has reasserted these assumptions, stating that "a high death rate remained constant and throughout the [seventeenth] century embittered the personal relationships of the colonists" ("The Significance of the Seventeenth Century," in James Morton Smith, ed., *Seventeenth-Century America: Essays in Colonial History* [Chapel Hill, 1959], p. 8).

The few recent demographic studies of Massachusetts towns point toward conclusions similar to those for Andover. John Demos, for example, found that the inhabitants of seventeenth-century Plymouth were healthy and long-lived, and that "the rate of infant mortality in Plymouth seems to have been relatively low" ("Notes on Life in Plymouth Colony," *WMQ*, XXII [1965], 270–272). In Dedham, Lockridge found that the probable death rate was low ("Population of Dedham," pp. 332–333). In Hingham, too, the life expectancy for the inhabitants in the seventeenth century was high, with 105 out of 827 people living to the age of 80, with the "average life of the married women of Hingham" being about 61.4 years, and with the average age at death for 818 of their children being 65.5 years—very similar to the data for Andover during the second generation (Thomas Jefferson Wertenbaker, *The First Americans, 1607–1690*

Further confirmation of the longevity of Andover's women is to be found in the evidence on remarriage. The data for the first generation obviously are unreliable for the period before their settlement in Andover, although genealogists have tried to determine as much as possible about some of them prior to the 1650's. Out of thirty-four first-generation men, twenty-three or 67.6 per cent appear to have had only one wife during their lifetimes, with nine or 26.5 per cent marrying twice, and two marrying three times. None are known to have married more than three times. The proportion of second-generation males marrying only once proved even higher, with sixty-six out of a total of eighty-nine marrying only once (74.2 per cent). If the four whose remarriages are uncertain are excluded, a total of 77.6 per cent of these second-generation men had only one wife during their lifetimes. Of the second-generation men who married more than once, sixteen married twice, two married three times, and one married four times. Marriages broken by premature deaths clearly were the exceptions, not the general rule, since both men and women lived much longer than many of us have realized.[7]

The combination of circumstances which tended to prolong life and those which evidently fostered an unusually high birth rate had very important implications for the families

---

[New York, 1929], pp. 184–186). Barbados in the 1670's, experienced an "appallingly high mortality rate" (Richard S. Dunn, "The Barbados Census of 1680: Profile of the Richest Colony in English America," *WMQ*, XXVI [1969], 24).

[7] In view of the Andover evidence, there is reason to doubt Oscar Handlin's generalization: "It was rare in this century that a husband and wife should live into old age together. The frequency of remarriages by widowers and widows showed how familiar a factor in life was death" ("Significance of the Seventeenth Century," p. 8). In England during this period the high rate of mortality evidently did cause a high rate of remarriages (Peter Laslett, *The World We Have Lost* [New York, 1965], pp. 99–100).

which settled in this new frontier community. In particular, families tended to be very large. The average number of children known to have been born to all of the wives of thirty-four first-generation fathers is 8.3, with an average of 7.2 children known to have survived to at least the age of twenty-one years. An analysis of twenty-seven completed families (those in which the wife in a first marriage survived at least to the age of forty-five years) produces exactly the same averages: 8.3 children born and 7.2 children surviving at least to twenty-one years of age. In terms of the children known to have been born to complete first-generation families, one-quarter had families ranging from one to six children in size, and three-quarters had between seven and thirteen children; none had more than thirteen children. The reason for this is that the birth intervals of children produced in this period by families begun between 1647 and 1669 and completed averaged twenty-eight months, thus making the probable maximum number of children born to a woman marrying about the age of eighteen and surviving to at least forty-five, about twelve children.

Although the size of families varied considerably, and some were very large, the common assumptions about extremely large families must be brought into correspondence with the average sizes actually encountered during any particular period. In Andover, the first-generation families were large, even after the winnowing process of death for infants, children, and adolescents. However, not one of twenty-seven completed first-generation families had more than twelve children surviving to the age of twenty-one years: 40.7 per cent of the completed families ranged in size from none to six children, and 59.3 per cent of these families ranged in size from seven to eleven children. That nearly 60 per cent of the completed first-generation families raised seven or more children to adulthood is as strong an indication as one can get that families in early Andover were relatively large in size and reflected the favorable conditions of life in this new frontier village.[8] In the long run, it meant that families would have a considerable number of children to nurture and to settle in callings and livelihoods when they reached maturity.

The ages at which men and women mature and become adults in their own eyes and in the eyes of their elders have varied considerably in the past, reflecting not only legal practices but also—and more importantly—the effects of custom, parental influence, and the varied social and economic circumstances of a given period. The most sensitive register of maturity is the age at marriage, since the responsibilities and

---

[8] Calhoun stated that "large families were the rule," with ten or twelve children being "very common," and families with twenty to twenty-five children not being too rare (*American Family*, I, 87). Plymouth families during this period were about the same as those in Andover, ranging from 7.8 to 9.3 children born to the first three generations in that colony, and ranging from 7.2 to 7.9 children living to the age of twenty-one years (Demos, "Life in Plymouth," p. 270). Wertenbaker's analysis of Hingham yielded an average of 7.8 children for each family (*First Americans*, p. 184). In contrast, Laslett and Harrison found that "the average number of children in a household was 2.45 and 2.61" in 1676 and 1688 in Clayworth, with the result that the size of the household was "surprisingly small," a conclusion which must be modified, however, by the fact that it represents a single point in time, rather than completed family size (Laslett and Harrison, "Clayworth," pp. 166, 170). In Bridgetown, Barbados, families were very small, with few couples having more than two children and the largest English family having "only seven children" (Dunn, "Barbados Census of 1680," pp. 22–24). For comparison, see John Demos, "Families in Colonial Bristol, Rhode Island: An Exercise in Historical Demography," *WMQ*, XXV (1968), 51–53. E. A. Wrigley notes that "very large families . . . were rare at any time in Colyton, the largest during the full three centuries being only 13" ("Family Limitation in Pre-industrial England," *EHR*, XIX [1966], esp. pp. 97–98).

duties involved in the establishment of a new family suggest
the recognition that the married couple were ready to function as adults. The age at marriage also can provide clues to
circumstances affecting family life and to patterns of family
relationships which otherwise might be impossible to determine or even to imagine.[9]

Despite the significance of the age at marriage, however,
historians rarely have been concerned about it, with the result
that very little is known about marriage and marriage ages in
the American colonies. More often than not, historians have
made the assumption that men and women in the seventeenth
and the eighteenth centuries married very young, thus assuming the roles of adults while still in their teens or very early

[9] The most sophisticated analyses of marriage ages and their relationship to the social structure, family life, and economic conditions
of various communities have been made by English historians and
sociologists. Two exceptionally useful studies of contemporary English villages are by W. M. Williams: *The Sociology of An English
Village: Gosforth* (London, 1956), esp. pp. 45–49, and *A West
Country Village, Ashworthy: Family, Kinship, and Land* (London,
1963), esp. pp. 85–91. The study by J. Hajnal, "European Marriage
Patterns in Perspective," in Glass and Eversley, eds., *Population in
History*, pp. 101–143, is invaluable for comparative studies of marriage ages in Europe and America. K. H. Connell remarks that "the
age at marriage is at the heart of Irish population history before the
Famine as well as in the twentieth century" ("Land and Population
in Ireland, 1780–1845," *EHR*, II [1950], p. 280, reprinted in Glass and
Eversley, eds., *Population in History*, pp. 423–433). Irish studies also
include K. H. Connell, "Peasant Marriage in Ireland: Its Structure
and Development since the Famine," *EHR*, XIV (1962), 502–523;
Michael Drake, "Marriage and Population Growth in Ireland,
1750–1845," *EHR*, XIV (1963), 301–313; and the suggestive general
study by Conrad M. Arensberg and Solon T. Kimball, *Family and
Community in Ireland* (1940; reprint ed., Gloucester, Mass., 1961).
For the fullest statistical and historiographical account of marriage
ages in the United States, see Thomas P. Monahan, *The Pattern of
Age at Marriage in the United States*, 2 vols. (Philadelphia, 1951).

twenties.[10] Like so many unexamined assumptions, this proves either to be false or to require significant qualifications. What becomes most striking about the experiences of many men and women in Andover during the decades following its settlement is the fact that the patterns of relatively high ages at marriage characteristic of seventeenth-century England persisted in this New World village as well. The ages at first marriage of both men and women in the second generation in Andover proved to be much higher than most historians would expect (see Table 3).

The average ages of women at the time of their first marriages in seventeenth-century Andover were somewhat higher than has been assumed, but they were still relatively low, nevertheless. The average age at first marriage for fourteen first-generation wives was only 19.0 years, whereas the average age at first marriage for eighty-one second-generation females was 22.3 years. Three-quarters of the second-generation females married before reaching age 25, and an overwhelming majority (92.7 per cent) married before age 30. The mean age at marriage for women marrying for the first

[10] Curtis P. Nettels, in *The Roots of American Civilization* (New York, 1938), p. 442, assumes the prevalence of "the custom of early marriage," which implies an early adulthood for the colonists. Similarly, Oscar Handlin wrote: "Boys no sooner emerged from adolescence than they insisted on being off to fend for themselves; and the abundance of land permitted them to break away easily" (*The Americans: A New History of the People of the United States* [Boston, 1963], p. 41). Perhaps the common assumption about early marriages and early maturity originated with Arthur W. Calhoun, who stated categorically that "the early Puritans married young" (*American Family*, I, 67). Perry Miller and Thomas H. Johnson qualified this assumption by stating that "Puritans were married young, though by no means so young as we often suppose" (*The Puritans*, p. 389), but the impression of youthful marriages still remained.

Table 3. Age at marriage of second-generation males and females

Age	Male		Female	
	No.	%	No.	%
Under 21	5	4.8	29	35.8
21–24	36	34.6	32	39.5
25–29	39	37.5	14	17.3
30–34	17	16.3	3	3.7
35–39	4	3.8	2	2.5
40 and over	3	2.9	1	1.2
Total	104	99.9	81	100.0
24 and under		39.4		75.3
25 and over		60.5		24.7
Total, all ages		99.9		100.0
29 and under		76.9		92.7
30 and over		23.0		7.3
Total, all ages		99.9		100.0

time in successive five-year intervals in Andover from 1650 to 1699 was as follows: 18.0, 21.2, 18.8, 22.7, 20.4, 22.1, 21.6, 22.5, 21.6, 22.0, thus ranging between the averages of 18 and 22.7 years throughout the second half of the century. These mean ages at first marriage for Andover women are comparable to those found for women in both Plymouth Colony and in Dedham, Massachusetts: in Plymouth between 1650 and 1675 the average age was 21.3 years, and from 1675 to 1700 was 22.3 years; in Dedham, the average age for women married between 1640 and 1690 was 22.5 years.[11] The contrast between mean ages in these Massachusetts towns and those found in the English parish of Colyton, in Devon, is startling confirmation of the assumption that the marriage ages for seventeenth-century New England women in these specific

[11] Demos, "Life in Plymouth," p. 275, Table 4, and Lockridge, "Population of Dedham," p. 330.

places were much lower than in parts of England. In Colyton, the mean age at first marriage for women during the period 1560–1646 was 27.0 years, rising to a high mean of 29.6 years for the period 1647–1719.[12] On the whole, the assumption seems justified that women tended to marry younger in seventeenth-century Andover than was common in England during the same period.

An examination of marriage ages for men reveals that the patterns commonly found in England and throughout much of Europe during this period continued to be found in Andover as well. The age of 19 first-generation male settlers at the time of their first marriages can be estimated with approximate accuracy and averaged about 26.8 years. The average age at first marriage of 104 second-generation males in Andover was 26.7 years; only five married before the age of twenty-one, approximately 40 per cent married before the age of twenty-five, and slightly more than three-quarters married before the age of thirty (see Table 3). The average ages of men marrying in successive five-year intervals between 1660 and 1699 are as follows: 22.9, 26.0, 26.1, 26.9, 26.7, 26.4, 23.5, and 27.0; this suggests that only two short periods, 1660–1664 and 1690–1694, were conducive to early marriages for men during the latter half of the seventeenth century. In general, these averages are slightly higher than the average of 25.5 years found for men in Dedham between 1640 and 1690,

---

[12] Wrigley, "Family Limitation," pp. 86–88, esp. Table 1. However, the average ages at which European women married varied considerably more than did the ages at marriage of men, and sometimes they were about the same as for Andover; more often, though, they seem to have ranged between twenty-four and twenty-eight years (Hajnal, "European Marriage Patterns in Perspective," *passim*). Laslett's *World We Have Lost*, p. 82, provides some data from Canterbury, England, where women married on the average at about twenty-four years.

and for men in Plymouth during the second half of the seventeenth century, where the average age at marriage was 26.1 years for those born between 1625 and 1650, 25.4 years for those born between 1650 and 1675, and 24.6 years for those born between 1675 and 1700.[13] In England during the seventeenth century the average marriage age for men appears to have ranged between 26 and 28 years. In Colyton, the mean age was 27.2 years between 1560 and 1646, and 27.7 years between 1647 and 1719.[14] In Canterbury, the mean age for men marrying between 1619 and 1660 was about 27.75.[15] In general, second-generation Andover men married at ages comparable to those of countless men in the old country during the seventeenth century, thus maintaining the pattern of late marriage ages characteristic of Europe from at least the sixteenth through the nineteenth centuries.[16] Whatever the particular reasons behind such characteristic delays in male marriages—whether custom, parental influence, the vagaries of a restrictive economy, or insufficient land—the general phenomenon persisted in seventeenth-century Andover just as it had in many English villages.

[13] Lockridge, "Population of Dedham," p. 330, and Demos, "Life in Plymouth," p. 275.

[14] Wrigley, "Family Limitation," pp. 86–87.

[15] Laslett, *World We Have Lost*, p. 82.

[16] See the data in Hajnal, "European Marriage Patterns in Perspective," *passim*. Hajnal states (p. 101): "The distinctive marks of the 'European pattern' are (1) a high age at marriage and (2) a high proprotion of people who never marry at all. The 'European' pattern pervaded the whole of Europe except for the eastern and south-eastern portion." High ages at marriage are still to be found in some English rural villages, such as Ashworthy, where "the average age at which farmers' sons married in the period 1880–1960 was 27.5" and "the average age for farmers' daughters in Ashworthy was 23.8" (Williams, *Ashworthy*, p. 89). In this respect, at least, the experiences of farmers' sons in twentieth-century Ashworthy and seventeenth-century Andover are analogous, and this is why Williams' study is so suggestive.

Contrary to common assumptions, Andover men in the seventeenth century did not marry as youths and therefore did not begin to mature as adults establishing their own families until they had reached at least their middle twenties. Until then, they remained for the most part as members of their fathers' families, dependent and dutiful sons. In Andover throughout the seventeenth century, a son's marriage often depended upon the willingness of the settler father to allow the marriage to take place and to provide for the new couple's economic subsistence, most generally in the form of land. Without the means to support a wife, marriage was virtually impossible. Perhaps this might account for the fact that eldest sons married younger than second sons, with the average age for twenty-eight eldest sons being an unusually low 25.2 years, compared with an average of 28.6 years for twenty-one second sons. The average age for twenty-eight youngest sons was 27.3 years, and the average age for twenty-five sons known to have followed trades was 26.4 years. Although the first generation thus appears to have favored eldest sons in their earlier marriages, for the majority of sons in Andover, as in England, effective maturity and marriage very often were long delayed.

The second generation began to appear upon the village scene as mature married men in appreciable numbers after 1670, rising to a peak between 1685 and 1689. An earlier peak between 1660 and 1664, the last period in which second-generation sons might have obtained abundant land from the town itself, was echoed by a later peak between 1705 and 1709, perhaps a reflection of the delayed marriages of so many men in this generation. The result was a generational profile of marriages which was less regular in its pyramidal shape than successive generations were to be, but indicative nevertheless of the emergence of this generation during the years between 1670 and 1694 in particular. In terms of the total

number of marriages recorded in the town during this period,
a comparable peak in numbers occurred during the 1680's,
with a slight fall in numbers occurring during the next decade
and a half (see Graph 1). Whether measured in terms of the
marriages of second-generation men alone or in terms of marriages of all of Andover's inhabitants, it was clear that the
1680's was a period in which more people than before were
reaching maturity. And with their marriages, a new genera-

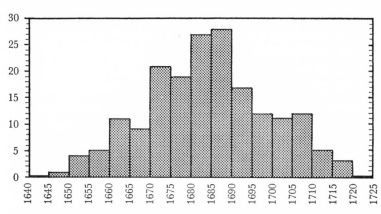

Graph 1. Second-generation marriages in consecutive five-year intervals

tional cycle was beginning to shape the characteristics of life
in Andover.[17]

By 1685, the transition between the first and second generation had become evident in the town records, as an analysis of
the town rate list of September 28, 1685, indicates. Of the 120
men who paid taxes in the town, 75 were second-generation
sons of settler families, 15 were first-generation settlers, one
was a third-generation son, and 29 were men who had settled
in Andover after 1662. The average age of 103 of these men

[17] A similar generational pattern is evident in Dedham (Lockridge, "Population of Dedham," p. 328).

was 38.3 years, indicative of the relative youthfulness of the adult male population of the town, with 26 men in their twenties, 33 in their thirties, 22 in their forties, 16 in their fifties, and 6 over sixty. Equally impressive, however, is the fact that so many of the original settlers were still alive and present in Andover, although not all appeared on the tax list. Of the original 34 permanent settlers, 26 were still in Andover in 1685, 10 of them in their fifties, 5 in their sixties, 3 in their seventies, and 3 in their eighties. Nine of the first-generation men died between 1685 and 1689, 7 between 1690 and 1694, 4 between 1695 and 1699, and 6 after 1700. The longevity of so many of the first-generation settlers and the relatively late marriages of so many of their sons assured that the community would be dominated throughout the second half of the seventeenth century by the lives and actions of only two generations: those who settled and those who inherited from the settlers.

Equally significant for the structures of families and the nature of community life in seventeenth-century Andover was the fact that the overwhelming majority of the second generation remained permanently settled in the town which their fathers had established. Nearly four-fifths of the second-generation men (78.3 per cent) spent their entire lives in Andover, with only 28 out of a total of 129 men eventually departing for other communities. Of those who left, 18 had resided in the North Parish (64.3 per cent) and 10 had resided in the South Parish (35.7 per cent). The majority of those who left Andover departed after 1690, since only 5 second-generation men are known to have left Andover prior to 1690.[18] Whether compared with English villages such as Clay-

[18] The five men who departed prior to 1690 settled in Boston, Roxbury, Newbury, and Topsfield, Mass., and in New London, Conn.; those who left after 1690 moved to towns in Massachusetts

worth, with American villages in Plymouth Colony, or with later generations in Andover itself, the second generation in Andover appears to have been remarkably rooted.[19] Their immobility, taken in conjunction with the demographic and economic characteristics of Andover during this period, helped to shape the distinctive forms of family life and family structure which emerged during the second half of the seventeenth century.

(including Amesbury, Marblehead, Methuen, Mendon, Salem, and Westford) and Connecticut (including Abington, Ashford, Enfield, Plainfield, and Pomfret, four of these being in the newly opened territory of Windham County).

[19] Dedham's population was almost completely immobile during this period (Lockridge, "Population of Dedham," pp. 322–324), whereas the population of Plymouth Colony appears to have been highly mobile throughout the seventeenth century (Demos, "Life in Plymouth," pp. 264–269). I suspect, however, that Demos has overemphasized the mobility of Plymouth's inhabitants. It seems more likely that many of the emigrants from the original settlement of Plymouth would have resettled permanently in one of the newer towns in the colony, just as people did in Andover and Dedham. Population mobility in sixteenth- and seventeenth-century England has been discussed by Laslett and Harrison ("Clayworth," pp. 174–180), E. E. Rich ("The Population of Elizabethan England," *EHR*, II [1950], 247–265), and Lawrence Stone ("Social Mobility in England, 1500–1700," *Past and Present*, April 1966, pp. 16–55).

3

Land for Families: The Formative Decades

In any farming community, the distribution and use of the land are of fundamental importance in shaping both the community itself and the character of family life for those who reside there. In Andover, as in all new plantations, the first generation was responsible for deciding how to divide the abundant land which had been given to the townsmen by the General Court. The cumulative effects of their decisions regarding such matters as the locations of residences, the allotments of land, the locations, proportions, and extent of these allotments, and the number of persons to whom such allotments were to be granted were decisive in determining many of the most basic characteristics of life for themselves, for their children, and for future generations as well. No written record has survived, however, which might reveal something explicit about the original intentions, the assumptions, and the wishes which probably shaped the settlers' actions regarding their town's land during the first two or three decades after settlement—a period in which they were fashioning the character of the community in which they and their families were to live.[1] Only by reconstructing their actions in sequence can

[1] The earliest surviving volume of town records, the Ancient Town Records, located in the Andover Town Clerk's Office, covers the period from 1656 to 1708 and is actually the second volume of

we see how their original plans for their community changed, thereby altering, in many essential ways, the character of farming and of family life in early Andover.[2]

The leadership of the initial group of eighteen men who settled in the new plantation during the early 1640's was dominated by men originally from Hampshire, Lincolnshire, and Wiltshire counties in England. Their influence must have weighed heavily in the early deliberations and decisions of the planters, since the initial distribution of land within the town reflected traditional patterns of agricultural life in the open-field areas of England.[3] One of the principal characteristics of

town records. The first was already tattered and torn when the second was begun, and it vanished long ago. The principal source for the study of land distribution is a handwritten seventeenth-century collection of records for individual grants of land, which includes not only all of the early settlers and house-lot owners, but also many of the later-comers who bought smaller parcels of land from the town, without rights to accommodation land. A complete set of these records is to be found in the misleadingly titled volume, Record of Town Roads and Town Bounds, and a partial set is to be found in the Ancient Town Records, which also contains town meeting records that deal with the giving and selling of land and a list of the early house lots.

[2] For comparisons, see: Sumner Powell's study of seventeenth-century Sudbury, Mass., *Puritan Village: The Formation of a New England Town* (Middletown, Conn., 1963); Charles Grant's study of eighteenth-century Kent, Conn., *Democracy in the Connecticut Frontier Town of Kent* (New York, 1961); and Kenneth A. Lockridge, "Dedham, 1636–1736: The Anatomy of a Puritan Utopia" (Ph.D. diss., Princeton University, 1965), esp. pp. 18–33. Lockridge's study of Dedham complements my study of Andover in many important respects; these two towns had much in common during the seventeenth century. Edward S. Perzel, "Landholding in Ipswich," *EIHC*, CIV (1968), 303–328, provides important data for seventeenth-century Ipswich. An earlier version of this chapter was published as "Old Patterns in the New World: The Distribution of Land in 17th Century Andover," *EIHC*, CI (1965), 133–148.

[3] The fact that Andover was originally fashioned upon the pattern of English open-field villages eluded earlier historians of Andover.

open-field villages in England was the nuclear structure of the towns, with all of the inhabitants residing side by side along the streets of the villages rather than dwelling on separate and distant farms outside the village center. In addition, the land was distributed in large open fields in which all of the inhabitants possessed pieces of land, sometimes in strips, sometimes in parcels of varying size and shape. The open-field villages prevalent through large areas of England since the middle ages were in marked contrast to the enclosed-farm areas, in which people owned relatively consolidated farms and lived at a distance from each other on their own lands. Lincolnshire had been the birthplace of Simon Bradstreet, a magistrate and

---

See Abiel Abbot, *History of Andover from its Settlement to 1829* (Andover, 1829), p. 12; Sarah Loring Bailey, *Historical Sketches of Andover . . . Massachusetts* (Boston, 1880), pp. 27–33; Claude M. Fuess, *Andover—Symbol of New England: The Evolution of a Town* (Andover, 1959), pp. 33–35. Further information on the open-field systems of England can be found in Howard Levi Gray's classic study, *English Field Systems* (Cambridge, Mass., 1915), C. S. Orwin, *The Open Fields* (rev. ed., Oxford, 1954), and Joan Thirsk, ed., *The Agrarian History of England and Wales, 1500–1640* (Cambridge, 1967), vol. IV, esp. Thirsk's ch. 1. George Caspar Homans' study, *English Villagers of the Thirteenth Century* (1941; reprint ed. New York, 1960), esp. chs. 2, 5, 8, and 9, is very suggestive, particularly for the relationship between family structure, inheritance patterns, and open- and enclosed-field farming practices. The history of the open-field system in England has yet to be fully explored. What is apparent already, however, is the variability and the flexibility of the system in those areas in which it was used, and the gradual process of change towards enclosed fields in many parts of England during the seventeenth and the eighteenth centuries. One of the best studies of an open-field village which was resistant to change is W. G. Hoskins, *The Midland Peasant: The Economic and Social History of a Leicestershire Village* (London, 1957). In view of the extraordinary variety of forms and customs of agriculture in England, it should not surprise us to find a great variety in the use of land in America. See Powell's *Puritan Village*, and Darrett B. Rutman's *Husbandmen of Plymouth: Farms and Villages in the Old Colony, 1620–1692* (Boston, 1967).

the most prominent leader of the Andover group; it was largely an area of two-field villages. Stanton had been the Wiltshire home of the Reverend John Woodbridge, his brother, Benjamin, and Henry Jaques; John Osgood, who stood second only to Bradstreet in rank in Andover, had come from Wherwell, in Hampshire; both had been two-field villages.[4] The fact that Osgood had been a yeoman both in England and in Newbury suggests that his own experiences, combined with his new influence, may have carried considerable weight in the decision of the planters to recreate the familiar patterns of open-field villages in this new plantation. Since relatively few of the settlers are known to have been farmers by training, and since those who had been craftsmen or servants would have had little to say from personal experience about the agricultural pattern which was to characterize Andover, it is not surprising that the planters initially agreed to make Andover a nucleated, open-field village.[5]

The village center was established in the northeastern section of the plantation between the Cochicawick and the Shawsheen rivers, a short distance south of the Great Pond. In the area presently forming the green in the older section of North Andover, two roughly parallel streets were laid out, separated by open land, and house lots were assigned to the

[4] See Gray, *English Field Systems*, pp. 70, 466–468, 501. For a general discussion of the open-field system in Hampshire, see Barbara Carpenter Turner, *A History of Hampshire* (London, 1963), p. 34. The field system was flexible, but many villages used either a two-field or a three-field system.

[5] One of the initial settlers, John Stevens, came from the village of Caversham, Oxfordshire, which evidently was largely an enclosed-field village at this time. His preference thus might have been for an enclosed farm, and he might possibly have been among the men whose influence, after the death of John Osgood, fostered the changes in the original field system. For Caversham, see Gray, *English Field Systems*, p. 386.

men and the families who had been accepted as townsmen.[6]
The original agreement, taken at the time of settlement, was
recalled at a general town meeting held on January 18, 1663,
in which the settlers noted that

y͏ᵉ persons impowred by the Genll. Court wᵗʰ such others as
they associated to themselves, did Covenant and agre at their first
planting of this towne [to] give every Inhabitant whome they
received as a Townsman an house lott proportionable to his
estate, or otherwise as he should reasonably desire, with suteable
accomodations thereunto of meadow, and all other divisions of
upland & plouging ground, that should afterwards be divided.[7]

The assignment of house lots (see Table 4) was a matter of
the utmost importance since their size reflected the initial
economic and social standing of the settlers and governed the
extent of all subsequent allotments of land. From the beginning, there was to be a hierarchy of rank and wealth among
Andover families rather than an equal sharing in the land.
What is most striking in retrospect, though, is the relative
narrowness of the range of landholdings actually established
by the decision to limit the largest house lots to twenty acres
and the smallest to four acres.[8] In practice, this meant that a
man as wealthy and prestigious as Simon Bradstreet, a gentle-

[6] I am indebted to Mr. Forbes Rockwell, of North Andover, for
permitting me to see the meticulous maps which he has drawn,
reconstructing in minute detail the nucleus of the village in the
seventeenth century and tracing each successive alteration in the
ownership of this land through the eighteenth century.

[7] *Essex Quarterly Court*, VIII, 81.

[8] Perhaps Andover followed the precedent of neighboring Haverhill, which voted, November 6, 1643, "that there shall be three
hundred acres laid out for house lotts & no more, and that he that was
worth two hundred pounds should have twenty acres for his house
lott, and none to exceed that number, and so every one under that
sum" (Haverhill Town Book Number 3, p. 5 [located in the vault of
the City Clerk's Office, Haverhill, Mass.]).

Table 4. The settlers to whom house lots were given prior to 1662 and the sizes of their lots

Settler	Original size (in acres)	Final size (in acres)
Bradstreet, Simon	20	31
Osgood, John	20	20
Holt, Nicholas	15	15
Parker, Joseph	10	10
Frye, John, Sr.	8	8
Stevens, John	8	12
Woodbridge, Benjamin	8	8
Aslett, John	7	7
Barker, Richard	7	10
Dane, Francis	6	6
Faulkner, Edmund	6	6
Remington, John	6	6
Tyler, Job	6	6
Allen, Andrew	5	5
Ballard, William	5	5
Barnard, Robert	5	5
Chandler, Thomas	5	8
Foster, Andrew, Sr.	5	5
Jaques, Henry	5	5
Lovejoy, John	5	7
Martin, Solomon	5	5
Poor, Thomas	5	5
Rowell, Thomas	5	5
Abbot, George, Sr.	4	4
Abbot, George, Jr.	4	4
Chandler, William	4	4
Farnum, Ralph	4	4
Farnum, Thomas	4	4
Foster, Andrew, Jr.	4	4
Fry, John, Deacon	4	4
Graves, Mark	4	4
Johnson, John	4	4
Johnson, Stephen	4	4
Johnson, Thomas	4	4
Parker, Nathan	4	7
Poor, Daniel	4	7
Russ, John	4	4
Russell, Robert	4	4
Sherman, Thomas	4	4
Stevens, Timothy	4	4

Source: Based upon evidence in Town Roads and Town Bounds, *passim.*

man, would receive a house lot which was no larger than that of John Osgood, a yeoman, whose estate was modest in comparison with Bradstreet's although greater than anyone else's in the new plantation. Both men, though, were active leaders in the settlement and both thus shared the top positions in the new ordering of status in the town. The third largest house lot, fifteen acres, was granted to Nicholas Holt, a tanner, who had had less land before coming to Andover than Osgood had. Another tanner, Joseph Parker, received a ten-acre lot. Three men received eight-acre lots, two received seven-acre lots, and four received six-acre lots. Interestingly enough, Edmund Faulkner, the only man other than Bradstreet to be called "Mister" in the town records, undoubtedly in acknowledgment of his status as the younger son of an English gentry family, received only a six-acre lot. Social status alone was not enough to place him among the top men in the town, although it may have served to distinguish him from the majority of the householders who received four- or five-acre lots. For the most part, these initial allotments provided the basis for the Andover land which was to be owned by the families of the early settlers. Several, however, added to their lots either by grants from the town, as in the case of Richard Barker, who received an additional three acres, or by purchasing the rights of men such as Henry Jaques, John Remington, Thomas Sherman, and Benjamin Woodbridge, who decided not to stay in Andover.[9]

[9] Town Roads and Bounds, pp. 2, 32–33, 38, 78, 144–145. In addition, two other first-generation settlers purchased their house lots and accommodation lands from men who had settled previously. Samuel Blanchard purchased Henry Jaques' rights sometime prior to 1654 (Town Roads and Bounds, pp. 78, 270–272). Henry Ingalls purchased Thomas Chandler's original five-acre house lot and accommodations, and some land from Nicholas Holt as well (Town Roads and Bounds, pp. 84, 132, and the list of house lots in Ancient

For about a decade and a half after the initial settlement of the town, the townsmen apparently were prepared to provide house lots and rights to accommodation land to newcomers who proved acceptable and who wished to settle. By about 1660, forty house lots had been laid out. Since there is no evidence of any additional lots being distributed later, it is highly probable that the townsmen had decided to limit the number of inhabitants in Andover with rights to town land. By 1662, therefore, the group of inhabitants who were to constitute the first generation of householders in Andover and the core of the community for generations to come had been formed.[10]

After the initial decisions were made about the ranking of men by their house lots, the next step involved the distribution of the remaining land itself. With nearly sixty square miles of land at their disposal, Andover's settlers might have chosen to divide it among themselves, leaving some for commons and some for newcomers, but giving to all who settled a gentlemanly estate of hundreds or perhaps even as much as a thousand acres apiece.[11] But this proved not to be their decision,

---

Town Records). Thomas Chandler, in turn, took up Benjamin Woodbridge's eight-acre lot (Town Roads and Bounds, pp. 38, 132–134).

[10] Similar considerations evidently governed the actions of Dedham's settlers as well, where limits upon expansion also were established and a clearly defined group of first-generation settlers, with an effective monopoly upon the land, emerged. See Lockridge, "Dedham," pp. 83–85.

[11] This, in fact, was to be done in eighteenth-century Kent, Conn., where the proprietors, with about 50,000 acres at their disposal, granted themselves about 32,000 acres within only two years, giving to each about 1,000 acres. Speculation rather than farming was their chief interest, since they could certainly subsist upon farms of 50 to 100 acres in size (Grant, *Kent*, pp. 14–15). Richard L. Bushman's study of land, community-building, and trade in eighteenth-century

for they distributed their land hesitantly, perhaps reluctant to break with the scale of traditional agricultural life in England, where men were used to holdings of relatively small size, and where land was scarce and valuable.[12] It seems very likely that their English experience was one of the major reasons why Andover's settlers found it impossible to take immediate advantage of the undivided land which was theirs. Perhaps, too, their evident intention to establish an open-field village also inhibited their desires for great quantities of private land.

Other factors, too, may account for the settlers' reluctance to parcel out the land in great tracts. As a group, they were young, their average age in 1645 being thirty-two, and only about half of the initial group were married prior to settling in the new plantation. Six families brought children into the wilderness, but the oldest boy known to be in the settlement in 1645 was only fifteen years old. The lack of mature children to share the tasks of physical labor placed the principal burdens of building houses, clearing the land, and breaking the soil upon the settlers themselves. Few evidently brought servants, for as a group they were men of limited means and humble social backgrounds. For these men perhaps the acceptance of small initial holdings was reinforced by the scarcity of labor in the new plantation. Whatever their reasons, they took sparingly of their land at the outset.[13]

The first allotment of land among the initial settlers created

----

Connecticut provides a striking contrast to the limited desires and expectations of Andover's settlers in the seventeenth century (*From Puritan to Yankee: Character and the Social Order in Connecticut, 1690–1765* [Cambridge, Mass., 1967]).

[12] See Mildred Campbell's study of *The English Yeoman under Elizabeth and the Early Stuarts* (New Haven, 1942); and Hoskins, *Midland Peasant*, esp. pp. 198–200, 242–244.

[13] A similar hesitancy to distribute the land was evident in Dedham (Lockridge, "Dedham," p. 18).

the first open field, called the Shawsheen Field, located on the west side of the river and containing approximately 160 acres. The land was divided among the holders of twenty-one house lots on the basis of one acre in the field for each acre of an inhabitant's house lot, providing the inhabitants with a minimum of four and a maximum of twenty acres in the field, with allowance made for differences in the quality of the land. Because many of the holdings in the field were scattered, relatively few field allotments were located in a single consolidated parcel. Such fragmentation of individual holdings had been characteristic of open fields in England, and it remained typical of landholdings in Andover long after the open-field system had been abandoned.[14]

The second division of upland was located in another field equal in size to the first and called, appropriately if unimaginatively, the Newfield. The date of the establishment of the second open field is not known, but it evidently was some time after the Shawsheen Field had been laid out. In the Newfield, too, some grants were consolidated but most were scattered about in small parcels. Its exact location is unknown, but it was probably north of the Shawsheen Field, beside the Merrimack River. The inhabitant's decision to allot only one acre in the Newfield for each acre of a house lot, as in the first field, suggests an attempt to recreate in Andover patterns of land allotment and farming familiar in open-field villages in England, where a "fundamental trait" of both two- and

[14] Abiel Abbot noted in 1829 that the early "method of laying off land has rendered farms inconvenient; and much of the inconvenience remains to this day. Very few farms of considerable size are compact" (*Andover*, p. 12). The inventories of the first four generations of Andover men confirms the persistence of fragmentation. In spite of consolidations made by each successive generation, the use of partible inheritances also fostered the continued dispersion of individual holdings.

three-field systems was "that the arable acres of a holding were divided with approximate equality between the two or three fields."[15] Although each householder in the village now had ploughing ground in each of the two fields, none had yet received an appreciable amount of land in this new plantation, since even a twenty-acre house lot entitled its owner to only forty acres of land in the fields. Such relatively small grants could, conceivably, be augmented by following the pattern of land distribution being used in towns like Sudbury, where open fields were established as they were needed by the town.[16] Certainly there was nothing to prevent the addition of more fields to the original two in Andover, should the inhabitants desire more land. The pattern of open-field farming was sufficiently flexible to permit as much growth as the community might wish to provide. Relatively rapidly, however, signs of changes in the method of land distribution became apparent, indicating that the open-field system was being abandoned.

Although it is impossible now to know why Andover altered its initial commitment to the open-field system of farming, several factors are likely to have influenced the change. The community lost two of the important leaders of its early years: The Reverend John Woodbridge departed for England in 1647 with his brother; then, on October 24, 1651, John Osgood died, leaving only Simon Bradstreet to carry on the influence of the original leaders of the plantation. These men had been from two-field villages originally, and their disappearance from the community might conceivably have altered the balance of sentiments within it to a significant

[15] Gray, *English Field Systems*, p. 40.
[16] Powell, *Puritan Village*, p. 95. In Dedham there were twenty-nine separate divisions of town land between 1636 and 1718 (Lockridge, "Dedham," p. 23).

degree. During the same period, four newcomers from the town of Bishops-Stortford, Hertfordshire, arrived, including Francis Dane, Andover's second minister; these men were unlikely to be committed to a system of open-field farming. The other members of the community undoubtedly were divided among themselves, some feeling very strongly about the need for a closely-knit, nucleated village with open fields about it, and others possibly seeing advantages in independent farms for themselves. The changes in the character of the distribution of land during the 1650's and 1660's do suggest, however, that those who favored the open-field system were becoming a minority.

The first indication of a shift away from the perpetuation of the open-field system came with the third division of upland, granted by vote of the townsmen sometime before 1658.[17] In terms of land, the division was more generous than

---

[17] The evidence available for Haverhill suggests that a similar development was taking place there, too, at approximately the same pace and during the same period. The first grants, made in 1643, three years after the initial settlement, consisted of house lots and the first division of ploughing land, given at the rate of one acre of upland for each acre of house lot. The second division of ploughing ground was not made until 1651 and was not laid out until June 1652, twelve years after the initial settlement of the town, with four acres being given for every acre of house lot. In 1653 the third division was ordered, apparently using the ratio of twenty to one. Six years later, in 1659, the fourth and final division during the lifetimes of the settlers was made, also at twenty acres to each acre of a house lot. The next division of town land was not made until 1721. See the Haverhill Town Book Number 2 for details of individual grants and the Haverhill Town Book Number 3 for the chronological sequence of land grants by the town. A useful but limited discussion of these early grants can be found in George Wingate Chase, *The History of Haverhill, Massachusetts* . . . (Haverhill, 1861), pp. 74–92. The development of Andover, and evidently of Haverhill as well, contrasts sharply with that of Sudbury, which split apart because of a controversy among the inhabitants over the retention of the open-field system (Powell, *Puritan Village*, pp. 118–138).

either of the first two, with an allotment of four acres of upland being granted for each acre of a house lot. This meant that owners of all four-acre house lots received a division grant of 16 acres, which would provide each man with a total of 24 acres of upland from the first three divisions. Similarly, holders of an eight-acre house lot received a third division grant of 32 acres, bringing their total upland acreage to 48. For the two owners of twenty-acre house lots, the third division provided 80 acres, bringing their total upland grants to 120 acres. The third division thus provided an appreciable augmentation to the lands divided among the inhabitants, although all of the estates of the settlers were still well within the normal limits prevalent in many villages of England.[18]

In terms of the nature of the community and the pattern of agricultural life which was being imposed upon the landscape, however, the third division was more significant for its failure to provide the townsmen with an additional open field than it was for the acreages granted to them as individuals. This division was not consolidated within a single field, as had been the earlier two, but rather consisted of grants evidently dispersed fairly widely about the town. And, suggestively, no name was ever given to the third grant, which is known in the records of the town simply as the third division of upland. The original pattern of an open-field village was changing. There were to be no more fields.

The disintegration of the original field system was evident also in the grants of land given by the town to newcomers

[18] Taking the forty original house lots as an example, the total acreage granted in Andover by the first three divisions of upland would have provided each lot owner with an average of about thirty-seven acres. In Weyhill, Hampshire, between 1601 and 1639, the average acreage held by thirty-eight people was only about thirty-five acres per person (Powell, *Puritan Village*, Appendix II, p. 173). Thus far, the scale of landholding in Andover was very similar to that of an English village.

arriving during the 1650's. Those who were given house lots by the town—and thereby accepted as inhabitants and proprietors—also received rights to accommodation lands equal in acreage to those already granted to the earlier settlers. The locations of these first-, second-, and third-division grants proved to be different, however, from those of the original settlers. The equivalent grants for the first two divisions were not located in either the Shawsheen Field or the Newfield, nor were they located in any other field established for this purpose. Instead, they tended to be either consolidated in a single piece adjoining the house lots or scattered about the town. Thomas Rowell, for example, who settled in Andover by 1654 and received a "ffyve acre house lott, with all accommodations thereunto belonging" from the town, had his Newfield-division land located next to his house lot rather than in the original field, and his first- and third-division land was located together on the Indian Plain in a parcel of 25 acres. Ralph Farnum's first-, second-, and third-division land was consolidated into a single parcel adjacent to his house lot.[19] The alteration in the distribution of the town's land during the 1650's affected the holdings of all who settled in the town in this period.

Although the open-field system had been abandoned by the time most of the later settlers arrived, Andover continued for some time to be a compact, nucleated village, with all of its inhabitants residing in houses built upon the house lots granted to them by the town while they farmed the lands located outside the village. When Richard Sutton, formerly of Roxbury, arrived in Andover in 1658, the house lot and

[19] Town Roads and Bounds, pp. 220–221, 186–187. Only the first twenty-one settlers had land in the two original fields. The nineteen who settled afterward had their division land outside the fields. Their various grants are recorded in Town Roads and Bounds.

dwelling house which he purchased from Simon Bradstreet were located in the town, whereas the "forty and eight acres of upland belonging to the sayd house lott" lay "on the farr side" of the Shawsheen River.[20] But although the village center persisted through successive generations and many of the inhabitants preferred to reside in close proximity to their neighbors, during the late 1650's and early 1660's even this traditional pattern of community life began to disintegrate.

By the early 1660's, the signs of change within the structure of the original open-field village became evident as villagers began to desire to live upon their division farming lands. The third division of upland already had provided many of the townsmen with sizable parcels of land at a considerable distance from the village, rendering them inconvenient for daily farming. Their dispersal would weaken the closely-knit community settled together in the village, and it would profoundly alter the character of life in this predominantly agricultural community. That the majority of Andover's inhabitants intuitively sensed the significance of such a change is reflected in initial efforts to condemn such removals and to keep the inhabitants together in the original village center. "Att a generall Towne meeting March 1660," the townsmen

[took] into consideration the great damage that may come to the Town by persons living remote from the Towne upon such lands as were given them for ploughing or planting and soe, by their hoggs & cattle destroy the meadows adjoyning thereunto

Accordingly, they ordered

that whosoever, inhabitant or other shall build any dwelling-house in any part of the towne but upon such house lott or other place granted for that end without express leave from the Towne

[20] Essex **Deeds**, II, p. 372; quoted in Bailey, *Historical Sketches*, pp. 9–10.

shall forfeit twenty shillings a month for the time he shall soe live in any such p'hibited place

The townsmen added that they did not intend

to restrain any p'son from building any shede for himself or cattle that shall be necessary for the ploughing of his ground or hoeing of his corne, but to restraine only from their constant abode there, the towne having given house lotts to build on to all such as they regard as inhabitants of the towne.[21]

The stiff fine imposed by the town evidently had little effect in halting the ultimate dispersal of the inhabitants. Within twenty years, nearly half of the inhabitants of Andover had moved their residences to the south end of the town, remote from the original village center.[22] The disper-

[21] Ancient Town Records, March 1660; quoted in full in Bailey, *Historical Sketches*, p. 33.

[22] See the town rate list for December 27, 1680, in the Old Tax and Record Book, 1670–1716 (located in the Town Clerk's Office, Andover). The process of dispersal from the old village center eventually necessitated the division of the town into two parishes, which was accomplished in 1709 after a protracted quarrel. In 1855 the two parishes became two separate towns, Andover and North Andover. The South Parish, larger and more populous than the original center of the town, took for itself the name which formerly had joined the two halves together.

In Haverhill, a similar dispersal from the original village occurred during the same period. George W. Chase noted that the town meeting votes of February 28, 1661, indicated "the change already taking place in the town. The settlers were fast approaching the present individuality in property." By 1661: "The settlers had already begun to form their lands into farms, by 'laying down,' 'taking up,' buying, selling, and exchanging lots; many had built themselves houses, and removed their families on to their farms; and the best part of the town's territory was fast becoming dotted with the cottages of the settlers" (*History of Haverhill*, p. 92). The Andover town records from 1660 on are filled with similar transactions as men strove to consolidate their scattered holdings in the town as well as they could, mostly by exchanging them for more conveniently located places.

sion of so many of the inhabitants to their distant farming lands radically altered the character of the community and transformed the original patterns of life reminiscent of an English open-field village into a more complex arrangement of social and familial relationships. In effect, these changes diminished the cohesive force of the community and augmented the significance of the individual family, settled on its own lands at an appreciable distance from other neighbors. The reality of this new development was made possible by the decision of the town to distribute the fourth and, for the seventeenth century, final allotment of ploughing land.

At a general town meeting in Andover on November 24, 1662, the inhabitants "ordered and Granted That for every acre of houselott There shall be laid out to it Twentie acres of upland to be Taken up and chosen the same way and order that hath been used in the divisions of Land according to the Time of mens comming to the Town." These fourth-division grants could be taken up in any place beyond the Shawsheen River to the west of the village center or any place on the eastern side of the river, provided only that no part of the division land "be within four miles of the meeting house."[23] With allotments at such a distance and dispersed in such a manner, it was evident that the open-field system of the first two divisions was permanently abandoned. From the magnitude of this division it was evident also that the inhabitants of Andover had decided to take advantage of the land which belonged to them in common for their private interests. By a single vote, the householders of the town gave themselves five times as much land as they had received in the third division and twenty times as much land as they had received in either of the first two divisions. The minimum grant allotted by the division of 1662 was 80 acres; the largest allotments were 400

[23] Ancient Town Records, November 24, 1662.

acres in extent. The total acreage of upland allotted to owners of forty house lots amounted to approximately 5,160 acres, an average of 129 acres each.

When the fourth division was added to the previous grants of house lots, the three divisions of upland, two divisions of meadow, and a division of swampland, each of the townsmen possessed a sizable estate in Andover. The meadow divisions, voted sometime prior to 1662, had provided an acre and a half for each acre of a house lot in the first division, and an acre for the second. The swamp division, voted in 1661, had granted one and a half acres to the men who had been among the initial settlers of the community and who had borne the major costs of settling the plantation, whereas later-comers received only one acre for each acre of their house lots. Cumulatively, these divisions of town land gave the owners of four- and five-acre house lots—the majority of Andover's inhabitants —total landholdings of between 122 acres and 152.5 acres. Owners of six-, seven-, and eight-acre house lots had 183, 213.5, and 244 acres respectively, and those with lots ranging in size between 10 and 20 acres ultimately acquired between 305 and 610 acres of land in the town (see Table 5). The total

Table 5. Allotment of land in successive divisions to 1662 (in acres)

House lot	Upland				Meadow		Swamp	Total
	First	Second	Third	Fourth	First	Second		
4	4	4	16	80	6	4	4	122
5	5	5	20	100	7.5	5	5	152.5
6	6	6	24	120	9	6	6	183
7	7	7	28	140	10.5	7	7	213.5
8	8	8	32	160	12	8	8	244
10	10	10	40	200	15	10	10	305
12	12	12	48	240	18	12	12	366
15	15	15	60	300	22.5	15	15	457.5
20	20	20	80	400	30	20	20	610

acreage of town land allotted to owners of forty original house lots or those who had purchased them privately from their original owners, including later additions by the town to their lots during the first two decades of Andover's history, was approximately 7,869 acres, with an average holding of 196.7 acres.[24] This represents a striking jump in the magnitude of the landholdings in Andover, compared both to earlier allotments and to the average holdings of villagers in England during this period.

The fourth division of upland thus marked a decisive break with past experience in Andover. Above all, it provided those families which had chosen to settle and establish themselves in Andover with land on a scale impossible for most of them to have anticipated possessing either in England or in the towns in which they had first settled in the New World. Nathan Parker, for instance, who had arrived in 1638 as a young indentured servant received more than 213.5 acres from the town and left an estate of more than 225 acres at his death in 1685. Daniel Poor, also a servant originally, received the same amount of land from the town. Others, like George Abbot, who settled as young landless men, received at least 122 acres. Men such as Nicholas Holt and John Osgood, both of whom had owned land in Newbury before settling in Andover, increased their landholdings appreciably: Holt's increased

---

[24] According to Lockridge, the average holding of Dedham's first settlers was about 210 acres apiece, with the average holding of about 200 individuals receiving land there between 1636 and 1690 being 150 acres. In Watertown, the average holding was between 125 and 150 acres. He also suggests "that an estimate of 150 acres for the typical early inhabitant of an eastern Massachusetts town is a reasonable one" ("Land, Population and the Evolution of New England Society, 1630–1790," *Past and Present* [April 1968], pp. 64–66). Land allotments in early Andover thus appear to be comparable in magnitude to allotments in other towns.

from 110 acres in Newbury to at least 457 in Andover, and Osgood's increased from 163 acres in Newbury to 610 in Andover.[25] With the creation of such estates as these, the land, for all practical purposes, had been distributed. The division of 1662 proved to be the last collective division of town land during the lifetimes of the first generation. The first formative twenty years of the town's history were over, having served to establish, for generations to come, the basis for family life in this essentially agricultural village. The first generation's economic futures in Andover were secure. Those who arrived after 1662 were to discover why it paid to be among the pioneers. Thenceforth, the generation of first settlers would

[25] For Parker's estate, see Town Roads and Bounds, pp. 66–68, and the inventory, July 17, 1685, PR 20536. For Poor, see Town Roads and Bounds, pp. 138–139. At his death in 1689, Poor left an estate of about 240 acres, including 140 acres of "wildernesse land." See the inventory of his estate, September 23, 1689, in Essex County Probate Records, vol. 302, p. 198 (photostat copy) (located in the Registry of Deeds and Probate Court Building, Salem, Mass.). For Abbot, see Town Roads and Bounds, pp. 108–109. At the time of his death in 1681, Abbot left real estate, including buildings, worth £350, which indicates that he probably owned between 150 and 200 acres in all. See the inventory, January 18, 1682, PR 43. For Holt, see Town Roads and Bounds, pp. 17–19. For Osgood, see Town Roads and Bounds, pp. 7–9. John Osgood died in 1650, age 55, leaving his entire real estate to the eldest of his two sons, John, Jr. His real estate, including house and land, was valued at only £80, but unfortunately no acreage was given, although it almost certainly consisted entirely of his house lot, his Shawsheen field, and his Newfield land. Had it included the third-division land, it would have been worth much more than it was. This indicates that the division occurred after his death, which must have made a significant difference to the way the community was being organized. See his will, April 12, 1650, and his inventory, 1651, in Essex Quarterly Court, I, 239–240. For the land allotments of Holt, Osgood, and other Andover men while residents of Newbury, see Newbury Proprietors' Records from 1635 (located in Town Hall, Newbury, Mass.).

control most of the land in this community, with far-reaching consequences for their children and families.

Indicative of the crystallization of the economic and social structure of the community after the division of 1662 was the heightened concern over legal titles to private property within Andover. In early 1664, concern over the establishment of authoritative property titles was voiced at the general town meeting which passed the following resolution:

Now whereas the sd Inhabitants, att their first settling here, & since, hath not been soe carefull and exact, as they might and should have been, for ye due & true recording of all such graunts, as have been made to pticular psons, some being lost, some not entered, others imperfectly, which in time to come may prove troublesome and pjuditiall to ye owners thereof. Upon serious Consideration whereof, and that all mens proprieties & inheritances may be made clear and Certaine, whilst things are fresh in memory, & all disputes & questions about ye same may be prevented, and avoyded for time to Come, the sd Inhabitants did agree to nominate & chose seaven of ye Townsmen . . . imporing them to view & examine all gifts and graunts made to pticular psons, from ye begining of this plantation, until this psent, with other claimes by purchase or otherwise, and such as they finde clear & certaine to allow and Confirme undr their hands, . . . which being done are to be recorded in ye Towne booke and to be esteemed & accounted as valid & authentick, as if they had been entered and recorded at ye time when they were graunted, though ye day & year of such graunts be not mentioned nor remembered.[26]

Memory and collective experience no longer sufficed to determine the extent and the location of land as they evidently had during the earlier years of small holdings and open

[26] Although this resolution was not recorded in the town records themselves, a copy survived among the court records. See *Essex Quarterly Court*, VIII, 82. The meeting was held January 18, 1664.

fields. For the new land system, with its extensive and dispersed farms, permanent boundaries and precise records were essential. For men principally concerned with their own lands, to be used by their own families and to become the inheritances of their children, clear, permanent, legal titles to their acquisitions were indispensable.

The first generation further ensured its economic and social status after 1662 by decisively altering the previous method of granting land to prospective Andover settlers, whether children of the inhabitants themselves or newcomers from outside. Hitherto, only five second-generation sons of men who had been among the early settlers had been provided with estates comparable to those of many first-generation inhabitants through grants of house lots with appropriate accommodation lands.[27] Although such grants might have been continued, providing land in ample quantities to the children of the settlers, the townsmen evidently decided against such a policy. Instead, by the late 1660's, the town began to offer twenty-acre plots of land for sale to anyone wishing to settle in Andover.[28] No more house lots, and no further divisions of accommodation land, were granted. The town thus drastically reduced the amount of land available to individuals seeking town land. The cost of the twenty-acre lots was not great, however; the purchasers were to pay the town "for ever" the sum of ten shillings a year, half in wheat and half in Indian corn—a nominal sum, considering that a bushel of wheat was worth about five shillings and a bushel of Indian corn was worth about three shillings during this period.

[27] These included Andrew Foster, Jr., John Frye, Jr., Stephen Johnson, Thomas Johnson, and Timothy Stevens. See their grants in Town Roads and Bounds.
[28] See the town meeting, March 22, 1669, and subsequent meetings for the grants of twenty-acre lots, in Ancient Town Records.

Such terms seem as though they ought to have been attractive to some husbandman and many craftsmen. On the whole, however, judging by those who actually took advantage of the town's offer, the appeal was largely to men from outside the town.[29] Out of forty lots sold between 1668 and 1686, only thirteen were taken by men from Andover, all of them being second-generation sons of the settlers themselves.[30] In an agricultural community in which status was largely determined by wealth in land, men who acquired these town lots generally would be at the bottom of the social and economic scale. Under the circumstances, most second-generation sons

[29] A high proportion of these latecomers to Andover chose to stay as permanent settlers, since twenty-one out of the twenty-seven (about 78 per cent) of those becoming townsmen with twenty-acre lots remained in the town. These men and their families represent the second phase in the emigration into Andover during the seventeenth century, and their arrival and settlement indicate that Andover was still attractive to outsiders even without the appeal of rights to the division land granted to the early settlers. Few were able to achieve the economic status of the first settlers, however. For instance, John Ayres, "of Andover" at the time of his death in 1683 (apparently the son of John Ayres, of Ipswich, and brother of Zachariah Ayres, who became an Andover townsman in 1677), left a frame for a house and about twenty acres of upland, valued at £10 in all, and some meadow which he had bought, valued at £10, together with one bed and a few personal items. He owed his father £18 and his brother about £8 and was unmarried at the time of his death. Evidently he preferred the prospect of life in Andover on a small farm of his own to life with his father in Ipswich. See the inventory to his estate in Essex County Probate Records, vol. 304, p. 33 (photostat).

[30] The second-generation sons who took up twenty-acre lots included the following: William Barker, husbandman; Joseph Parker, Jr., carpenter; Francis Faulkner, husbandman; Joseph Abbot; George Abbot, shoemaker; John Abbot, husbandman; Nathan Stevens; John Abbot, husbandman; Henry Ingalls; Samuel Ingalls, husbandman; Thomas Osgood; Christopher Osgood, tanner; Hope Tyler, blacksmith.

recognized the advantages of waiting to be settled by their own fathers upon a part of the family lands. The restrictions placed by the town as a whole upon the distribution of town land had the effect, whether consciously designed or not, of strengthening the positions of the first-generation settlers themselves.

Not all of Andover's inhabitants evidently concurred with the restrictive land policy, however, and some were prepared to depart in order to acquire more land for themselves or their children. Only one brief, tantalizing entry in the town records reveals the existence of a dispute within the town and the agitation which accompanied it. After the town meeting of January 4, 1675, the town clerk noted: "Whereas there is a great Controversie in y° towne, about giving out of Land," the inhabitants had chosen a committee of eleven prominent men "to se if it be convenient to give away any more land, or how, & to whome." Although the committee was instructed to "consider about y° same and bring in y° result against y° next meeting day," no further record was entered in the town book.[31] Since nothing was altered in the town's practice of selling twenty-acre lots, the majority of the committee and of the town's inhabitants evidently continued to favor the current policy. A minority, however, apparently sent a petition to the General Court at Boston, requesting the Court to grant them a tract of land between Haverhill and Exeter, New Hampshire, for their settlement, noting that many of the petitioners were "much straitened in their p'sonall acommodations and most of their children grown up and many others of y° petitioners wholly destitute of land for settlement and soe under a necessity to look out for inlargment and places of habitation." Undoubtedly, the outbreak of warfare in Octo-

[31] Ancient Town Records, January 4, 1675.

ber 1675 intervened to halt action by the General Court on such petitions since nothing came of it.[32] Controversy may also have evaporated in the face of a series of Indian raids which killed a number of the inhabitants and brought fear to all. Whatever the reason, when the war was over a year later, life in the village resumed its old course. The town kept its policy of land distribution and ceased to discuss the question of land from the town for the younger generation. For the most part, the inhabitants took measures themselves to provide land for the settlement of their sons.

First-generation families in Andover often were unable to make use of an appreciable portion of their lands, much of which remained uncleared wilderness for several decades. Transforming the wilderness into farming land—chopping down trees, breaking up the land, growing crops—was a constant process engaging the energies and the time of most families in this community. Many proved to be in no hurry to take up the large allotments granted to them by the town in

---

[32] Mass. Archives, vol. 112, p. 202, reprinted in Bailey, *Historical Sketches*, pp. 147–148. Bailey suggested that the petition had been made within "the first fifty years," but internal evidence makes it certainly before 1678, when one of the men who signed it died, and very likely either in 1674 or 1675. Eight of the eleven men appointed to the town committee in 1675 had no familial involvement in the petition to the General Court, since no Bradstreet, Barker, Chandler, Abbot, Frye, Lovejoy, or Poor was among the signers, although there were three Johnsons, one Osgood, and two Stevenses among the petitioners. Twelve of the twenty-three men who signed the petition were members of five families, and four of the remaining eleven were related to these families by marriage. This indicates that the demand for outside land was limited to relatively few Andover families. Bailey provides a thorough discussion of the impact of Indian warfare upon Andover in *Historical Sketches*, pp. 162–193. Douglas Edward Leach's *Flintlock and Tomahawk: New England in King Philip's War* (New York, 1958) is a detailed study of King Philip's War.

1662, a division which continued to serve families as a sort of land bank which could be drawn upon when needed for several decades.

The fourth division often was more than families could use until their sons matured and wanted land for settlements of their own. John Johnson, for instance, waited until November 3, 1675, to have 40 acres of his fourth division laid out, and his son, Lieutenant Thomas Johnson, waited until October 7, 1696, to take up another 40 acres of division land. Similarly, Thomas Chandler took up 80 acres of division land from the town in March 1685, but the remaining 80 acres of the 1662 grant were not laid out to him until November 1696, thirty-four years after the original allotment had been voted. George Abbot took up only 20 acres of his fourth-division land before his death in 1681, leaving the remaining 60 acres to be taken up by his widow on March 19, 1686, together with four acres of swamp land owed to Abbot by the town since 1661. Another settler, Daniel Poor, waited fifteen years before taking up his great division land from the town, which laid out his 140 acres on March 12, 1677. Twelve years later, at the time of Poor's death, the inventory of his estate revealed that he still possessed 140 acres "of wildernesse land," his original division allotment. The following year, 1691, his second son, John Poor, who inherited this division land, died unmarried at the age of thirty-two, leaving as his own estate the same 140 acres of wilderness, together with a small parcel of meadow and a dwelling house. This land had never yielded a crop or a profit.[33]

[33] For Johnson, see Town Roads and Bounds, pp. 157, 208; for Chandler, pp. 133, 134; for Abbot, pp. 108–109; for Poor, p. 139; and Daniel Poor, inventory, September 23, 1689, Essex County Probate Records, vol. 302, p. 198 (photostat copy, the original being lost); John Poor, inventory, March 26, 1691, PR 22352.

Similarly, the Allen family found its land more than sufficient for its needs and left much of it as wilderness during the
lifetimes of the first and second generations. Andrew Allen,
Sr., had had his great division grant of 100 acres laid out by
the town on May 5, 1663, within a year after the division had
been voted.[34] But most of this land continued to be forested
and unbroken for the next three decades. All but twenty acres
of this fourth-division land were inherited by the second of
Allen's two sons, John, providing him with nearly all of his
estate in Andover. Yet the inventory taken in 1691, shortly
after his death from smallpox at the age of twenty-eight,
revealed that he had only "8 acres broke up land" in his
possession, together with "72 acres unbroken up land."[35] Although married four years, John Allen had managed to break
up only about two acres a year for cultivation. Few of the
extant inventories of the seventeenth century are as explicit as
Allen's in distinguishing between broken and unbroken land,
between wilderness and cultivated land, but the slowness with
which many families took up their allotments of land does
suggest that much of the land granted in Andover during the
first two decades following its settlement remained unused
throughout the lifetimes of the first generation.

It took time for a town to emerge from the crude conditions characteristic of every frontier and for farmers to clear
their land and to make the wilderness productive.[36] It is evi-

[34] Town Roads and Bounds, p. 120.
[35] See Andrew Allen, Sr., will, October 6, 1690, PR 370; and John
Allen, photostat of inventory, January 21, 1691, Essex County Probate Records, vol. 304, p. 351.
[36] For a discussion of the economy of Essex County between 1640
and 1682, see William I. Davisson, "Essex County Price Trends:
Money and Markets in 17th Century Massachusetts," *EIHC*, CIII
(1967), 144–185, and "Essex County Wealth Trends: Wealth and
Economic Growth in 17th Century Massachusetts," *EIHC*, CIII

dent, however, both from the account books of Salem merchants and from inventories of estates probated during the seventeenth century, that Andover farmers did make at least some of their land productive shortly after the settlement began. As early as 1653, grains, particularly wheat, Indian corn, and rye, were being grown and formed staple crops, and both grain and livestock were being used in lieu of cash in exchanges for hard goods from Salem merchants.[37] Throughout the century, Andover men relied upon the produce of their land to pay for items such as cloth, paper, tobacco, salt, pins, powder, nails, knives, and other products which could be obtained only through merchants in Salem or Boston. Their produce, known collectively as "country pay," was thus used to supplement the necessities for subsistence which their own lands could produce. Their dependence upon the land was obviously a fundamental fact of life.

Equally important is the fact that Andover families were also dependent upon each other, for the subsistence economy and the scarcity of labor fostered the interdependence of families as each obtained goods and services from others and provided them in turn. This is suggested by the one extant account book from seventeenth-century Andover kept by the Reverend Thomas Barnard, the third minister, between 1688

(1967), 291–342. It is evident that Andover does not fit Davisson's conclusions—raising a question about the general applicability of his theses. Undoubtedly they are accurate for the coastal towns, particularly Salem, Ipswich, and Newbury, but I doubt that they can be used for inland agricultural communities without considerable caution.

[37] For details, see George Corwin Papers, 8 vols., and especially his account books for 1653–1655, 1658–1663, 1663–1668. Jonathan Corwin's ledger, 1685–1691, contains additional Andover accounts. These MSS volumes are located in the Essex Institute, Salem, Mass.

and 1707.[38] Particularly interesting are the relationships between Barnard and the numerous Andover families which paid their annual minister's rates by their physical labor rather than by produce or cash. Labor itself was a commodity frequently used in Andover instead of cash, and probably served as one of the principal means for families to acquire the additional labor which they needed for the work on their lands.

Ralph Farnum, for instance, paid his rate in 1703 by "carying corn to market" for Barnard and "by 2 days of himself & one day of his son" working for Barnard. Nicholas Holt II paid his rates by the labors of his sons, who mowed hay for Barnard and did other work as well. Abraham Foster's rates were paid "by sowing Barley & wheat & his boy 1 day to harrow it." Deacon Joseph Stevens paid his rates in 1701 "by himself & boy & Teem ½ day sowing and harrowing," "by breaking up the pasture," "by plowing part of Lott," "by carting 1 Load of Hay," and "by taking [Barnard's] horse to market & selling y° Load." Such activities were typical, and nearly everyone in the town, at some time or other, either worked or had their sons work for Barnard.

Among other things, such patterns of activity reveal clearly that parents often used the labors of adolescent sons for their own interests. Sons were not paid directly; their parents received credit for their wages. Since several of the sons who worked for Barnard in behalf of their families were twenty-one years old, it is evident that sons were considered to be an integral part of their families' domestic economy until their early twenties. As a result, despite the sums which they earned

[38] Thomas Barnard, Personal Account Book, 1688–1707, Essex Institute, Salem, Mass. This is the only Andover account book for the period which I have located.

by their labors for Barnard and for others, sons presumably remained without money of their own until at least their early twenties. This helps to account for their prolonged economic dependence upon their parents.

Barnard's account book also reveals the inadequacy of wage labor as a means for young men to acquire capital during this period. If the experience of Barnard's "man," who worked for an annual wage, is representative, it is clear that hired laborers in Andover would have worked hard with little real monetary gain. Stephen Barnard (no apparent relation to the Reverend Barnard) worked for the minister at least from 1702 to 1707, when the account ends. He was a bachelor of thirty in 1702 when he agreed to work for Thomas Barnard, who noted that he had "Agreed & Bargained with Stephen Barnard to serve me one year from the Date hereof for which I am to give him Ten Pounds in money. He came to Live with me the Seventh Day of December 1702." Previously, he had worked on a daily basis, at a daily wage of two shillings, standard throughout this period. Since he might be able to make at least £30 a year working 300 days at a wage of two shillings a day, his willingness to work for only £10 suggests that such a decision was reasonable and desirable. He continued to work for an annual wage for at least five years, during which time he was completely at the disposal of the minister, who often sent him to work for others to whom he owed money.

Stephen Barnard's labors brought him little actual profit. At the beginning of 1704, for instance, his total profit, after the Reverend Barnard deducted expenses incurred during the year for clothing and other items, came to only £1.15.2. The following year he actually *owed* his employer eight shillings and two pence. In 1706 he made a profit of £2.3.3, but in 1707 it was only fourteen shillings. After 1705 he had agreed to accept an annual wage only partly paid in money, but he gained very little from his labors in any event. He remained, for all his work, a poor man, as his marriage in 1714 at the advanced age of forty-two testifies. Others must have known how unprofitable physical labor was. It served to heighten their dependence upon their fathers and upon their families' lands if they themselves were to escape similar fates.

4

Patriarchalism and the Family

The decisions made by the first generation with regard to the distribution of the town's land before the end of 1662 and their use and transmission of the land after 1662 had profound effects upon the character of family life and family structure. The demographic characteristics of families and of the population of the town as a whole also had important effects upon family development. It is clear that the patterns of familial experience characteristic of many families prior to their settlement in Andover had been altered significantly before the end of the lifetimes of the first generation and during the period in which their second-generation offspring were coming to maturity and establishing families of their own in Andover.

Most of the first-generation settlers had immigrated to Massachusetts either alone or in the company of their own immediate families. Some came with other relatives; none, however, brought an extensive group of kindred with them from England to America. The common experience of migration evidently limited the degree to which families were likely to be extended in structure during their early years in the New World. After their arrival, though, some men began to form kinship connections with other immigrants through their marriages, and many of the settlers established either personal or familial connections with each other before or soon after the settlement in Andover began. Kinship often served as an influential factor in bringing additional settlers to Andover as well. From the outset, there were several embryonic kinship groups settled together in Andover.[1]

It is evident that the structures of families were being extended rapidly by the time the second generation began to reach adulthood, and that the character of families was being reshaped by the circumstances of life in the new community. The combination of relatively abundant land, large families, a proclivity to remain permanently settled in Andover, and long delays in the actual transmission of land from the first to the second generation fostered the development of families which were extended in their structures, patriarchal in character, and rooted to this one community.[2]

[1] An earlier version of this chapter appeared as "Family Structure in Seventeenth-Century Andover, Massachusetts," *WMQ*, XXIII (1966), pp. 234–256. The process of immigration and resettlement in coastal towns prior to coming to Andover is discussed in detail in Philip J. Greven, Jr., "Four Generations: A Study of Family Structure, Inheritance, and Mobility in Andover, Massachusetts, 1630–1750," (Ph.D. diss., Harvard University, 1964), pp. 1–53.

[2] In the last analysis, my argument about patriarchalism in Andover rests upon inferences based upon the scattered data drawn from wills and deeds. Since no literary evidence of consequence has survived, I believe that actions must reveal the design of intention and behavior. I also believe that the actions of men living in the modern world can be used to illuminate the meaning of actions of men in the past. Forms of behavior and attitudes closely resembling those which I have found in Andover are *still* to be found in farming communities in *modern* England, Canada, and, I suspect, the United States.

My understanding of the complex relationships of men to the land, and of fathers to sons, and of the critically important role of the transference of control of the land from one generation to the next has been greatly increased by two studies of modern English farming communities by W. M. Williams: *The Sociology of an English*

The intimate relationship between paternal authority over children and the possession of land is revealed with some clarity in the marriage negotiations of the sons and daughters of New England families.[3] Marriage in the seventeenth century was often as much an economic as an emotional affair, involving the transference of property from one generation to another and from one family to another. Although relatively few records of such marriage negotiations have survived, either for Andover or for other communities, enough do exist to serve as models for actions which almost certainly were commonplace at most levels of society during the seventeenth century. The implications of such negotiations over the disposition of properties to children are far more significant than is sometimes realized, revealing vividly the expected and the fulfilled roles of fathers in the marriages of their children. The marriages themselves depended not only upon obtaining parental consent but, equally importantly, upon obtaining pa-

---

Village: Gosforth (London, 1956), and *A West Country Village, Ashworthy: Family, Kinship and Land* (London, 1963). The study of Ashworthy, in particular, provides a model for understanding the role of the land in the creation of patriarchal families. In Ashworthy, the average age at marriage of farmer's sons was high—27.5 during the years between 1880 and 1960—and many sons waited many years before taking over the control of their fathers' farming land. Williams also found that delay in the transference of the land "allows young men to achieve adult status as married men and fathers long before they obtain economic independence and the status of farmers in their own right" (*Ashworthy*, pp. 97–98). His most significant observation was that "the length of time which the transference of control takes is broadly a reflection of the degree of patriarchalism within the family: the more authoritarian the father, the longer the son has to wait to become master" (p. 91).

[3] For a general discussion, see Edmund S. Morgan, *The Puritan Family: Religion & Domestic Relations in Seventeenth-Century New England*, rev. ed. (New York, 1966), pp. 78–86.

rental support in the form of a marriage portion, customary and necessary throughout this period.[4]

The marriage of sons, in particular, depended upon parental, especially paternal, consent and support. Until a son had been given the means to support a wife, or had acquired them on his own, marriage was virtually impossible. In effect, marriages of second-generation sons in seventeenth-century Andover depended upon the willingness of fathers to permit sons to leave the parental homestead and to establish themselves as married adults, usually in houses of their own built on family land designated as the married son's responsibility. The late age at which so many second-generation sons married during this period indicates both the difficulties experienced in acquiring sufficient means to support separate families and also the reluctance of many parents to allow their sons to set up households of their own. The examples of several families suggest the reasons.

The Allens probably were typical of the majority of the families in Andover with estates of more than 100 acres in the town. The negotiations in 1681 for the marriage of Andrew Allen's oldest son, Andrew, Jr., to Elizabeth Richardson, of nearby Chelmsford, indicate the role of parental settlements in

[4] In Gosforth, Williams found that "the heir to the family holding is bound by loyalty to adjust or postpone any decision he may make concerning marriage to suit fluctuations in the family circle." He also discovered that "marriage . . . is closely linked to methods of inheritance, and the cohesive family organization ensures that farmers' sons take the 'long view' of marriage in comparison with the members of those families which are not also economic units" (*Gosforth*, pp. 51, 49). Conrad M. Arensberg and Solon T. Kimball, in *Family and Community in Ireland* (1940; reprint ed., Gloucester, Mass., 1961), pp. 107–144, discuss similar problems involving marriage and the transference of estates.

making marriages of sons possible.[5] Andrew Allen, Sr., then about sixty-five years old, had been among the first settlers of Andover, receiving a five-acre house lot and appropriate accommodation lands from the town. His eldest son was twenty-four years old when he sought to marry, but the negotiations for his marriage were conducted on his behalf by his father. Two of his prospective bride's kinsmen, Major Thomas Hinckman and Captain Josiah Richardson, from Chelmsford, came to Andover to inquire about the marriage settlement which Andrew's father proposed to give the couple. Meeting at William Chandler's inn, they asked the senior Allen "what he would give his son for incouradgement for a Livelyhood," a question which vividly reveals the customary expectations regarding marriage portions and the father's role in determining their sons' ability to support a wife and family. Allen promised that upon the contract of marriage "he would give his son Andrew at present if he married wth Elizabeth Richardson his house & Land laying ab^t 3 miles from ye town & ye meadows belonging to it, & half his orchard at home," thus providing his son not only with a house but also with land to farm for himself out of the original family estate in Andover. In addition, Allen also promised to give his son "all his house & land at Town & ye home meadow that belonged to it" after both he and his wife were dead. The couple married January 1, 1682, and resided in the house promised to them by their paternal family and given as an inheritance after Andrew's father's death.[6]

[5] Essex Deeds, vol. 5, p. 502, quoted in Mary Lovering Holman, *Ancestry of Charles Stimson Pillsbury and John Sargent Pillsbury* (Concord, N.H., 1938), II, p. 1015 n. See also the marriage negotiations between widow Hannah Osgood, of Andover, and Samuel Archard, Sr., of Salem, about 1660, in *Essex Quarterly Court*, VIII 82.

[6] See Andrew Allen, will, October 6, 1690, PR 370.

In the case of sons whose occupation as husbandmen made them totally dependent upon the land for their livelihood, the possession of land by their families clearly was a factor shaping their relationships to their parents and influencing their decisions to marry. In the case of sons whose occupations were not essentially dependent upon the land, parental influence continued to be exerted and felt despite their relative economic independence. Fathers evidently continued to play a significant role in the lives of sons who became craftsmen as well as those who became farmers. A trade did not necessarily indicate independence from family ties or family influence.

That fathers often continued to influence the marriage decisions of sons long after they had come of age and no matter what their occupation was is indicated by the experience of Henry Ingalls, Jr. A carpenter and the second of seven sons, he did not marry until 1688, at the age of thirty-two. Ten years later, his father, a husbandman, gave him a deed of gift to ten acres of upland and swamp and a few other small pieces of land for the love which he felt for his son and "in Consideracon of a Marriage with my allowance approbation & good liking Contracted & Consummated" between his son and Abigail Emery of Newbury.[7] What is significant is not so much the land itself, for the acreage was comparatively small, but the reasonably explicit assumption that this marriage settlement and inheritance was given to this son as a result of his father's approval of his marriage. The fact that a middle-aged craftsman would feel the need to seek and to obtain the consent of his aged father before proceeding in marriage is a suggestive indication of the persistence of paternal authority.

Paternal consent, marriage, settlements, and inheritances were all closely interrelated in the actions of most families in

[7] Essex Deeds, vol. 14, p. 40.

seventeenth-century Andover. It could scarcely be otherwise considering the fact that marriage of sons generally brought about a division of a family's land. Since in most instances it was the father's own estate which was to be settled, in part or in its entirety, upon the couple, the father necessarily had a major role in deciding what was to be done with it. And the actions taken by most first-generation fathers indicates their unwillingness to give up legal control of their property to their children at the time of their marriages. This propensity for maintaining control of family property used for the marriage settlements of children is revealed in usual detail by the surviving accounts of the negotiations between Simon Bradstreet, the wealthy, influential leader of Andover, and Jonathan Wade, an equally wealthy merchant and gentleman from Ipswich, over the proposed match between two of their children in 1672.

In the fall of 1683, Simon Bradstreet stated in a deposition that "When Mr. Jonathan Wade of Ipswitche came first to my house att Andov' in ye yeare 72 to make a motion of marriage Between his sonne Nathanielle & my Daughter mercy, he freely of himself told me what he would give to his sone," which was to consist principally of "one half of the ffarme att mystick & one third part of his Land in England when he dyed."[8] In addition, Wade promised Bradstreet that his son would "have liberty to make use of" part of the "improved & broken up ground upon" the farm "till he could gett some broken up for himself apon his owne part," and that

[8] Deposition of Simon Bradstreet, September 21, 1683, in the Verbatim Transcriptions of the Records of The Quarterly Courts of Essex County Massachusetts, compiled by the W.P.A., vol. 43, p. 60. Also see the MS deposition of his son, Dudley, August 31, 1683, Essex County Court Papers, vol. 41, p. 59. Both collections are located in the Clerk of the County Courts Office, County Court House, Salem, Mass.

he could also live in the house there until "he had one of his own built upon his part of ye ffarme." Bradstreet noted that he "was willing to accept of his offer or at least said nothing against itt; but propounded" that Wade make his son "a deed of guift" for the third part of Wade's land in England, which he had also promised as part of the marriage portion, so that Nathaniel could have it "to Enjoye to him & his heirs after his death." Wade refused to provide such a deed conveying the land to his son, saying that "he was not free to doe" it "butt said itt was as Sure for he had so putt itt into his will" that his three sons should have the land in England to divide equally amongst themselves. Bradstreet "objected he might alter his will when he pleased, & his wife might Dye & he Marrye againe & have other children," which Wade "thought a vaine objection." The objection, however, was cogent, and Wade's own response indicates why. Wade remained adamant in his refusal to give a deed for the land in England "Saying he might live to spend itt" himself, although he assured Bradstreet that he would never alter his will "without great necessitye."

Bradstreet's desire to see the land in England conveyed to his prospective son-in-law by means of a deed of gift, rather than as an inheritance, reflected his awareness that intentions can change, and that only a legal deed could assure the transference of this English (or any other) property from father to son. A deed would make the property the son's, freeing him to use it as he chose.[9] An inheritance, on the other hand,

---

[9] The unusual example of William Chandler, who sold his inheritance and left Andover, is suggestive, too. In 1687, Chandler, the second of five sons, married at the age of twenty-eight and settled upon land provided by his father who waited, however, for another ten years before giving his son a deed of gift for this land. On June 12, 1697, Thomas Chandler gave his son a deed for about sixty acres of land "together with y⁰ house barns orchard fences Meadow

did not belong to the heir legally until after the death of the
father, who might, and undoubtedly often did, change his
mind about a particular inheritance (Bradstreet himself was to
do this later in his own will), giving it to someone else or,
more probably, selling it, leaving nothing for an heir to inherit.[10] Only an outright deed of gift could assure a son that
property promised by his parents would be his without question. Even when sons settled upon land promised at marriage
but not legally conveyed, the possibility always existed that
the father would ultimately decide to dispose of it to someone
else. Bradstreet's wish for a deed, and Wade's wish for a
clause in his will, both assumed that the land promised would
eventually be obtained by Nathaniel Wade. But both fathers
also knew, as this deposition reveals, that the method of con-
veyance was a matter of the utmost importance.

For Jonathan Wade, control over his own property was
important, more important, probably, than the prospect of
financial need. There was little chance that such a man, whose
estate at his death totalled nearly £8,000—an immense for-

---

ground within." Three months later, with his inheritance fully in his
own control, William sold his entire Andover homestead and moved
with his wife and family to Westford, Massachusetts, where they
resettled. See Essex Deeds, vol. 11, p. 253, and Thomas Chandler's
will, September 30, 1700, PR 4974.

[10] See Simon Bradstreet, MS will, February 20, 1689, in Suffolk
County Probate Record 2364 (City Hall, Boston, Mass.). The will is
transcribed in vol. 11, pp. 276–282, of the old series of Suffolk County
Probate Records. In a codicil to his will, dated January 27, 1693,
Bradstreet revoked the gift of a farm in Topsfield to his daughter,
Mercy Wade, since he could sell it for £250, of which £100 was to
be given to his wife. Earlier he had also revoked his gifts of two
farms in Lynn, one of which he then disposed of. So long as he
retained title to the land, he could, and did, feel that he had the right
to do what he wished with it. For another example of the importance of a deed, see John Demos, "Notes on Life in Plymouth
Colony," *WMQ*, XXII (1965), 281–282.

tune for this period—would fail to keep his promise. But his desire to maintain his own control over land which was originally his, rather than to turn it over to his son, lies at the center of patriarchalism in this period.[11] The majority of

[11] Wade's reluctance to hand over the control of his property to his son was evident in other ways as well, since all three of his sons felt the prolonged touch of their father's hand upon their inherited estates. Sometime before his death, Wade journeyed from Charlestown to Lynn in the company of Joseph Goodhue, who later stated that "in our Journey we had a great deale of discourse. Some of which was of his owne concerns," particularly "how he had setled his children." Wade told Goodhue that "my land in England I intend shall be devided to my three sons each a third part." In addition, Wade said that "I have setled two of my sons at mistick yet said he," in very revealing words, "I count that I have Eight or Interest there still but I intind that they shall have it between them." Two days before his death, he reiterated the same intention, indicative of the control over his estate which he retained to the very end of his life. No inheritance was absolutely certain until death sealed the promise. Wade's intentions also included the settlement of his third son, who remained with him in Ipswich. As Goodhue noted, "I also spake to him about his son Thomas that dwells with himself at Ipswich and about his labouring so hard." Wade replied that "it is hard Indeed but I hope it will be better shortly." Goodhue then asked "how thay two carryed on and whether there was any division in the Land or Estate or whether thay carryed on both as one: he said there was no division now but said he we carry on Joyntly together now but," he added, "*I intend he shall have all* at Ipswich" (italics added), (deposition of Joseph Goodhue, February 11, 1683, in Essex County Court Papers, vol. 41, p. 50). Later Thomas Wade himself confirmed Goodhue's testimony, stating: "I have dwelled with my Parents ever since I had a being untill deth Seperated us viz: all wayes at Ipswich unless absent upon ocasions for a month or two sometimes and I was imployed about any and all business according to my capasitie And in the time when my honored ffather was in England last I dwelt with my honored mother and helped to manage affairs." Thomas Wade was a dutiful son, honoring, obeying, and assisting his parents. His reward was to be his inheritance. See Thomas Wade's deposition, March 1684, Essex County Court Papers, vol. 41, pp. 59, 61.

fathers in seventeenth-century Andover, nearly all of whom had far less in land and estate than Wade, shared his reluctance to allow the land to pass out of their hands. They, too, generally refused to convey the lands to their sons by deeds of gift; and their refusal, like Wade's, must have been acceded to by the other parties to the negotiations for marriages. As Bradstreet testified, Wade "told Severall of my ffriends & others as they Informed me, that he had proffered to give his sone Nathaniell better" than £1,000 and "I would not accept of itt." Later, however, "perceivings his resolution as formerly I Consented to accept of wh^t he had formerly Engaged, & Left itt to him to add what he pleased toward ye building of him a house &^{c}" and "so agreed" that the "young persons might proceed in marriage wth both [our] Consents which accordingly they did." Wade had made his bargain, and Bradstreet, in the end, agreed. Nathaniel was to wait until his father's death to inherit the lands which he was to be settled upon in Mystic, as well as those which he was to acquire in England. His experience was common.

The reluctance of most first-generation fathers to hand over the control of their property to their second-generation sons is evident in their actions recorded in deeds and their last testaments. Only two first-generation fathers divided their land among all of their sons before their deaths and gave them deeds of gift for their portions of the paternal estate, although both waited until late in life before giving the sons legal titles to their portions. Seven first-generation fathers settled their sons upon their family estates in Andover but gave a deed of gift for the land to only one of their sons;[12] the rest of their

---

[12] George Abbot, Sr., before his death in 1681 at about sixty-four, "being aged and crasey in body," bequeathed his entire estate to his wife, except for the double portion which he had already given to his eldest son—perhaps, but not certainly, by deed. Since this portion

sons had to await their father's death before inheriting the land which they had been settled upon. Two men gave deeds to more than one son. Fourteen of the settlers retained the title to all of their land until their deaths, handing over control to their sons or daughters only by means of their last wills and testaments. The actions of four are uncertain. For the great majority of the second generation, inheritances constituted the principal means of transferring the ownership of land from one generation to the next.

The general use of partible inheritances in Andover is evident in the division of the estates of the first-generation families. Twenty-two out of twenty-three first-generation families that had two or more sons divided all of their land among their surviving sons. Out of a total of eighty-five sons whose inheritances can be determined, eight-two or 96.5 per cent received land from their father's estates. Often the land bequeathed to them by will was already in their possession, but without legal conveyances having been provided. Thus although the great majority of second-generation sons were settled upon their fathers' lands while their fathers were still alive, only about one-quarter of them actually owned the land

---

of his estate was purposefully excluded from the inventory, taken January 18, 1682, I presume that it had been formally conveyed before his death. The inheritances of his other sons were left to the discretion of his wife, who was directed to treat them equally unless "by their [disobedient] carige to hire there be rasen to cut them short." Abbot justified leaving his estate in the hands of his wife in terms which tell us more than most last testaments about his feelings and her role in his life: "considering the grate love and afacon I beare unto my loveing wife hanah abbute and also considering hire tender love and respect shee hath had to mee: and also considering hir care and diligance in helping to get and save what god hath blessd us with all and also hire prudent [prudence] in management of the same," the "hole astate" was left to her. See George Abbot, will, December 21, 1681, PR 43.

which they lived upon until after their fathers' deaths. With their inheritances came ownership; and with ownership came independence. Many waited a long time, as the experiences of members of several illustrative families reveal.

Like most of the men who wrested their farms from the wilderness, William Ballard was reluctant to surrender control over his land. When Ballard died intestate in 1689, aged about 72, his three sons, Joseph, William, and John, agreed to divide the estate among themselves "as Equally as they could."[13] They also agreed to give their elderly mother a room in their father's house and to care for her as long as she remained a widow, thus adhering voluntarily to a common practice for the provision of widows.[14] The eldest son, Joseph, had married in 1666, almost certainly as a rather young man, whereas his two brothers did not marry until the early 1680's, when their father was in his mid-sixties. William, Jr., must have been well over thirty by then, and John was twenty-eight. Both Joseph and William received as part of their division of the estate the land where their houses already stood, as well as more than seventy-five acres of land apiece. The

[13] Articles of Agreement, October 23, 1689, Essex County Probate Records, vol. 304, pp. 388–389 (photostat copy). The inventory of his estate, October 23, 1689, valued the land at £150 and the personal estate at about £57. He had no money and no debts (pp. 387–388).

[14] Nearly all of the wills provide carefully for the surviving wife. Andrew Allen, for example, "being aged," left his wife "ye Living in ye new end of my house w^e shall be at her dispose wth out controule," to be maintained by his son, Andrew, Jr., who was required to pay his mother "five bushels of good wheat & five bushels of good Indian corn & two bushels & an half of Ry & four score weight of good pork & half her firewood Cut fit for ye fire . . . & ten pounds of good flax" for as long as she lived, in return for the use of her land. Andrew, Jr., inherited the other end of the paternal house, and was to get the entire house at her death. His brother inherited land and was also required to provide for his mother during her lifetime. See Andrew Allen, will, October 6, 1690, PR 370.

youngest son, John, got all the housing, land, and meadow "his father lived upon except the land and meadow his father gave William Blunt upon the marriage with his daughter," which had taken place in 1668. It is unclear whether John lived with his wife and their four children in the same house as his parents, but it is quite likely that he did, because there is no mention of another house, and since he lived there after his father's death. His two brothers had been given land to build upon by their father before his death, but no deeds of gift had been granted to them, thus preventing their full independence so long as he remained alive. Their family remained closely knit both by their establishment of residence near their paternal home on family land and by the prolonged control by William Ballard, Sr., over the land he had received as one of the first settlers of Andover. It was a pattern repeated many times in many families.

The prolonged control of Richard Barker, Sr. (?–1693), over the land which he received from the town and used for the settlements of his sons was also characteristic of the actions of first-generation fathers. Barker was the first settler known to reside in Andover in 1643, and he long remained an active leader in the community. His estate consisted of the division lands for his original seven-acre house lot, and those for an additional three-acre lot subsequently granted to him by the town, bringing his total holdings in Andover to about 310 acres.[15] All six of his sons survived adolescence and eventually settled upon land given to them by their father. All but one remained permanently in Andover, and all married relatively late, between the ages of 25 and 35. With the exception of the eldest son, none received deeds to the land which they had from their father but waited, instead, to inherit it. Much

---

[15] See Barker's grants, Town Roads and Bounds, pp. 27–29.

of Richard Barker's land remained in wilderness for more than twenty years after the final division grants of 1662, since he waited until January 15, 1684, to take up 60 acres of his great division and until December 14, 1686, to take up his final 80 acres of the 200-acre division. All of this land eventually was settled upon his sons. The eldest of the Barker sons, John, married in 1670 at the age of 27 and built a house upon part of his father's third-division land, but he did not receive a deed for this land from his father until March 15, 1683.[16] By the same deed, his father also gave him three parcels of meadow and an additional 40 acres of upland, "not yet laid out," which he finally took possession of in late 1686, when the town laid it out. The land was legally his, but much was still unusable. Although the eldest son, John Barker had waited thirteen years before becoming a fully independent proprietor of his own lands, as a middle-aged man of forty. He was the only son to be given full legal ownership of family land during his father's lifetime; his younger brothers had to wait for their father's death before achieving the same degree of independence.

The experiences of Barker's second and third sons are suggestive of the prolonged dependence of sons upon their father. Both William and Ebenezer bought twenty-acre lots from the town but neither married or attempted to raise families immediately thereafter, as one might have anticipated. On March 22, 1670, the town "sold and granted" William "twenty acres of land by Rowley bounds," but he did not settle upon this town lot.[17] By January 5, 1674, he evidently was living in a house built upon a piece of swampland given to him by his father. Not until February 20, 1677, did he finally marry, at the age of 31. His father did not give him additional

[16] Essex Deeds, vol. 29, pp. 115–116.   [17] Ancient Town Records.

land, though, until December 1686, when he received forty acres of the division land laid out to his father's right.[18] His full inheritance included only three additional pieces of meadow from his father.[19] Life evidently was difficult for Barker's second son, for he testified, as a self-confessed witch in 1692, that

he has been in the snare of the devil three yeares. . . . That the devil demanded of him to give himself soul & Body unto him, which he promised to doe. He said he had a great family, the world went hard with him and was willing to pay every man his own, And the devil told him he would pay all his debts and he should live comfortably.[20]

Perhaps his brother, Ebenezer, a carpenter, also found life difficult; he too waited until 1686 and the age of 35 to marry, despite the twenty-acre lot which he had from the town in 1677. Ebenezer and his wife received sixty acres of his father's great division of upland "upon which he now dwells" in his father's will, written on April 27, 1688—land which had been laid out only in 1684. Both sons thus delayed their marriages, both failed to use their town lots to support families, and both settled upon their father's own land, waiting until his death to become the legal owners.

The three younger Barker sons also depended upon their father for the land which they settled upon after their marriages. In 1682, Richard, Jr., married at the age of twenty-eight and settled upon paternal land, receiving thirty acres of the great division, some meadow, and some land by the Great

[18] Town Roads and Bounds, p. 29. The other half of the fourscore acres went to his brother, John.

[19] See Richard Barker, will, April 27, 1688, PR 1708.

[20] William Barker's examination (Mass. Archives, vol. 135, no. 39) in Verbatim transcriptions of Salem witchcraft papers, vol. I.

Pond as an inheritance. Stephen, the fifth son, also married at twenty-eight in 1687, waiting to inherit the land which he dwelled upon together with thirty acres of upland and some meadow. The youngest son, Benjamin, remained at home with his aging parents. His father promised to give him the homestead land and buildings and half of all the household effects after his death, and this prospect probably encouraged Benjamin to marry in the winter of 1688, the youngest of them all at the age of twenty-five. Since his father continued to live until early 1693, Benjamin and his wife probably resided with the elder Barker until his death, caring for him in return for his inheritance, as other dutiful sons were to do.

The third largest estate in Andover, owned by Nicholas Holt, provided the basis for the settlements of five sons and for the maintenance of paternal control for most of a long lifetime.[21] At some time prior to 1675, Holt removed his family from the village and built a house on his third division of land in the area which was later to become the South Parish. Although a small portion of his land still lay to the north and west of the old village center, the greatest part of his estate lay in a reasonably compact farm south of his new house. Holt owned no land outside of Andover and he acquired very little besides the original division grants from the town. This land eventually provided settlements for all of his sons. In 1662, however, when Holt received the fourth-division grant of 300 acres from the town, his eldest son, Samuel, was twenty-one and three other sons were eighteen, fifteen, and eleven, with the fifth as yet unborn. His sons were still young, but they were old enough to provide the physical labor needed to clear and cultivate the land which had been readied for husbandry.

[21] For Holt's grants, see Town Roads and Bounds, pp. 18–19.

The family must have provided most of the labor, since there is little evidence to indicate that servants or hired laborers were numerous in Andover at the time. With the exception of two daughters who married in the late 1650's, the Holt family remained together on their farm until 1669, when the two oldest sons and the eldest daughter married.

At that time the only possible means of obtaining land from the town to settle upon was to purchase one of the twenty-acre lots which were offered for sale. Since house-lot grants with accommodation land had long since been abandoned by the town, Samuel's marriage probably depended upon his father's willingness to provide him with sufficient land to build upon and to farm for himself. Evidently his father proved unwilling for many years, but when Samuel did at last marry, at the age of twenty-eight, he was allowed to build a house for himself and his wife upon his third division or "Three-score Acres of upland." Soon afterwards the second son, Henry, married and was also given land to build upon in the third division. Neither Samuel nor Henry was given a deed to the land which they settled upon. Their marriages and their establishment of separate households left their three younger brothers still living with their aging father and step-mother, as well as their stepbrothers and sisters. Five years passed before the next son married. James, the fourth of the five sons, married in 1675 at the age of twenty-four, where-upon he, too, was provided with a part of his father's farm to build a house upon. The third son, Nicholas, Jr., continued to live with his father, waiting until 1680 to marry at the late age of thirty-two. His willingness to delay even token independ-ence so long suggests that personal factors must have played an important role in his continued assistance to his father, who was then about seventy-seven years old. The youngest of the sons, John, married at the age of twenty-one, shortly before his father's death.[22]

For Nicholas Holt's four oldest sons, full economic independence was delayed for many years. Although three had withdrawn from their father's house and had established separate residences of their own, they nonetheless were settled upon their father's land not too far from their family homestead, and they had not yet been given a legal title to the land they lived upon. Until Nicholas Holt was willing to give his sons deeds of gift, he retained all legal rights to his estate and could dispose of it in any way he chose. Without his consent, therefore, none of his sons could sell or mortgage the land where they lived. In the Holt family, paternal authority rested upon firm economic foundations, a situation characteristic of the majority of Andover families of this period.

Nicholas Holt eventually decided to relinquish his control over his Andover property by giving his sons legal titles to the lands which they lived upon and farmed. In a deed of gift dated February 14, 1681, he conveyed to his eldest son, Samuel, one-half of his third division, "the Said land on which the said Samuels House now Stands" and which had the land of his brother, Henry, adjoining on the west, as well as an additional 130 acres of upland from the fourth division, several parcels of meadow, and all privileges accompanying these

---

[22] A Salem deposition of 1690 indicates that prolonged assistance by sons was not unusual. Richard Hollinsworth, Sr., was said to have given his younger son, Richard, Jr., his dwelling house and land in Salem "for and in Consederation of his living with his father after said Richard was of Age and for servic said Richard had don for his said father who Caryed on his fathers business soe long as his father lived and in Consederation that sayd Richard should keep and maintain his mother soe long as she would be pleasedd to live with him" (deposition of Richard More, Sr., November 25, 1690, Essex County Court Papers Transcript, vol. 49, p. 76).

lands.[23] In return for this gift, Samuel, then forty years old and married almost twelve years, promised to pay his father for his maintenance so long as "his naturall life Shall Continue," the sum of twenty shillings a year. Ten months later, Nicholas Holt conveyed almost exactly the same amount of land to his second son, Henry, and also obligated him to pay twenty shillings yearly for his maintenance.[24] Nicholas had already given his fourth son, James, his portion, which consisted of one-third part of "my farme" including the "land where his house now stands," some upland, a third of the great meadow, and other smaller parcels.[25] In return, James promised to pay his father £3 a year for life (three times the sum his two elder brothers were to pay), and to pay his stepmother forty shillings a year when she became a widow. The farm which James received was to be shared by his brothers, Nicholas, Jr., and John. In a deed of June 16, 1682, Nicholas, Jr., received "one third part of the farme where he now dwells," some meadow and, most importantly, his father's own dwelling house and homestead; he promised, in return for "this my fathers gift . . . to me his sone," to pay £3 annually for his father's maintenance.[26] Thus Nicholas, Jr., in return for his labors and sacrifices as a son who stayed with his father until the age of thirty-two, received a share in the family farm equal to the shares of his two younger brothers, with an additional gift of the paternal house and homestead.

The only one of the five Holt sons to receive his inheritance from his father by deed prior to marriage was the youngest, John, whose eighty-three-year-old father gave a deed of

[23] Essex Deeds, vol. 32, pp. 130–131.
[24] Essex Deeds, vol. 34, pp. 255–256.
[25] Essex Deeds, vol. 7, pp. 292–296.
[26] Essex Deeds, vol. 6, pp. 814–816.

gift to his "Lovinge" son for a parcel of land on the easterly side of the paternal dwelling house, some meadow, and fifteen acres of upland "as yett unlaid out."[27] One month later, John married, having already built himself a house upon the land his father promised to give him. Unlike his elder brothers, John Holt thus gained his complete independence in 1685 as an exceptionally young man. His brothers, however, still were not completely free from obligations to their father since each had agreed to the yearly payment of money in return for full ownership of their farms. Not until Nicholas Holt's death at the end of January in 1686 could his sons consider themselves fully independent of their aged father.[28] He must have died content in the knowledge that all of his sons had been established on farms fashioned out of his own ample estate in Andover, all enjoying as a result of his patriarchal decisions the rewards of his venture into the wilderness.

Some families were less reluctant than Nicholas Holt to have their sons marry early and to establish separate households, although the control of the land usually still rested in the father's hands. The Lovejoy family permitted the four oldest of seven sons to marry at the ages of twenty-two and twenty-three. John Lovejoy, Sr., who originally emigrated from England as a young indentured servant, acquired a

[27] Essex Deeds, vol. 9, p. 12.

[28] Even among ranchers in the Canadian prairies, prolonged control of the land is still evident. "Aged ranchers typically prolong their control over their enterprise (and their succeeding sons) even when they are physically unable to perform many routine tasks. The father who refused to retire is a common figure in the region: almost a folk figure, judging by the many anecdotes told about such men" (Seena Kohl and John W. Bennett, "Kinship, Succession, and the Migration of Young People in a Canadian Agricultural Community," *International Journal of Comparative Sociology*, VI [March, 1965], 104). See also Williams, *Ashworthy*, pp. 90–91, and *Gosforth*, pp. 49–51.

seven-acre house lot after his settlement in Andover and eventually possessed an estate of over 200 acres in the town.[29] At his death in 1690, at the age of sixty-eight, he left an estate worth a total of £328 with housing and land valued at £260, a substantial sum at the time.[30] Although he himself had waited until he was twenty-nine to marry, his sons married earlier. His eldest son, John, Jr., married in March 1678, built a house, and began to raise crops on land which his father gave him for that purpose. He did not receive a deed of gift for the land, however; his inventory, taken in 1680 after his premature death, showed his major possessions to consist of "one house and a crope of corn" worth only £20. His entire estate, both real and personal, was valued at only £46 and was encumbered with £30 in debts.[31] On April 6, 1683, the land which he had farmed without owning was given by his father to his three-year-old son. In a deed of gift, the elder Lovejoy gave his grandson, as a token of the love and affection which he felt for his deceased son, fifty acres of upland, a piece of meadow, and another small parcel of meadow, all of which lay in Andover.[32]

His grandaughter continued to live with her grandparents after the remarriage of her mother, as indicated by the codicil added to Lovejoy's will, written September 1, 1690: "my Will concerning my Grandchild Frances Lovejoy y^t is now under my Care & Charge . . . is y^t She remain wth her granmother my loving wife & her uncle my son Ebenezer until she be of ye age of eighteen years." Lovejoy also noted in his will that to William, "my Eldest Son now liveing I have

---

[29] For Lovejoy's grants, see Town Roads and Bounds, pp. 96–98.

[30] John Lovejoy, inventory, PR 17068.

[31] For the inventory of John Lovejoy, Jr., see *Essex Quarterly Court*, VIII, 56.

[32] Essex Deeds, vol. 33, pp. 40–41.

given him his portion allready as may appear by deeds confirmed to him of y° Land which he now Lives upon." William was the only son to receive his inheritance by deed during John Lovejoy's lifetime.[33]

The other Lovejoy sons received the control of their lands as an inheritance. Christopher received thirty acres in addition to unstated amounts of land in return for an annual payment of corn and pork to his widowed mother and a payment of £5 in corn or cattle to his sisters within nine years of his father's death. Nathaniel received as his portion the land which his father had originally intended to give his brother, Benjamin, who had been killed in 1689. Benjamin was twenty-five and unmarried at the time of his death, and left an estate worth only £1—his wages as a soldier.[34] Without their father's land, many second-generation sons would have been as impoverished as Benjamin.

The youngest of the Lovejoy sons, Ebenezer, also was provided for by his father, who declared in his last testament that his "Will & desire" was that

my brother Thomas Osgood & my son Willm Lovejoy & my son Joseph Lovejoy, be y° men y^t shal have y° oversight of my son Ebenezer until he come to age also y° oversight of my grandaughter . . . until her marriage, desiring y^m to exercise that parental Care & Authority towards y^m in all things as If y^r were y^r own children & also see y^t y^r do Carry themselves well & dutifully towards their mother . . . y^t they greive her not in her old age, as you expect y° blessing of God upon you & yours.[35]

[33] John Lovejoy, will, PR 17068. The deed to William is not recorded in the Essex Deeds, however.

[34] Benjamin Lovejoy, inventory, 1701, PR 17048.

[35] It is worth noting that his "brother," Thomas Osgood, was actually the brother of his first wife, Mary, which indicates that kinship relations were maintained and recognized even after the death of one spouse, as Edmund Morgan suggests in *The Puritan Family*, pp. 151–152.

His desire to see "that parental Care & Authority" maintained over his son and grandaughter is indicative of his own authority and concern for his family.

Ebenezer, as the youngest son, was to inherit the paternal homestead and house, but only in return for extended services to his widowed mother. These services were spelled out in detail by Lovejoy. His wife was to receive the east end of the house to live in, 12 bushels of "good & marchantable corne" consisting of "six of Indian, 3 bushels of wheat & three of Rye," 120 pounds of pork, 2 barrels of cider, 12 bushels of apples, and 1½ bushels of malt annually during her lifetime. In addition, she was to have one milk cow, £5 in money yearly for expenses "Either at y° marchants, or at home for Clothing," as well as a horse and a man to carry her to the weekly meeting and "Suteable help in Sickness or weakness provided for her & mentained by my son Ebenezer," so long as she remained a widow. Ebenezer obviously was expected to reside in the west side of the house with his own wife and family, dutifully obeying the last wish of his father in return for his inheritance. Undoubtedly he did. With the residence of the widow in one son's house, with all of the surviving sons living upon land provided by their father in Andover, and with only one son, the eldest to survive, receiving a deed for his land during their father's lifetime, the Lovejoys epitomized some of the principal characteristics of family life in seventeenth-century Andover.

Exceptions to the general pattern of prolonged paternal control over the lands given to sons were rare. The unusual swiftness with which Edmund Faulkner established his oldest son independently, while providing for his second son conventionally, is instructive because of its distinctiveness. Edmund Faulkner's oldest son, Francis, was admitted as a townsman of Andover on January 4, 1675, "upon the account of the land he now enjoyeth," which probably was part of his father's own estate.[36] The following October, aged about 24, Francis married the minister's daughter. A year and a half later, in a deed of gift dated February 1, 1677, Edmund Faulkner freely gave his eldest son "one halfe of my Living here at home" to be "Equally Divided between us both." Francis was to pay the town rates on his half, and was to have half the barn, half the orchard, and half the land about his father's house, and both he and his father were to divide the meadows. Significantly, Edmund added that "all my Sixscore acres over Shawshinne river I wholly give unto him," thus handing over, at the relatively young age of 52, most of his upland and half of the remainder of his estate to his eldest son.[37] The control of most of his estate was thereby transferred legally and completely from the first to the second generation, leaving the second of the two sons still unprovided with a settlement.

John Faulkner was unmarried at the time his brother received most of the land which had been granted to their father's six-acre house lot. With relatively little left to give, Edmund chose to use the twenty-acre lot which he had purchased from the town on March 22, 1670, as part of his younger son's settlement. The town had voted that "in case the said Edmond shall at any time put such to live upon it as the town shall approve, or have no just matter against them, he is to be admitted to be a townsman." On March 4, 1678, John Faulkner was "allowed a townsman" by the town, "his father confirming . . . him upon his twenty acres he had

[36] Town meeting, January 4, 1675, Ancient Town Records.

[37] Essex Deeds, vol. 39, p. 250. Only one other specific reference to the copartnership of father and son appears in the wills for seventeenth-century Andover, although not among the first generation of settlers; see the will of Andrew Peters, a distiller who came late in the century, PR 21550.

granted him."[38] John did not marry for another four years, when he was twenty-eight. Eventually, he received a small amount of upland and meadow as an inheritance from his father's estate, but it was clear that his elder brother had been favored.[39]

Edmund Faulkner's eagerness—notable for its rarity among the settlers of this town during this period—to hand over the control of his estate to his eldest son reflected a desire to keep most of his estate intact, a modified form of primogeniture.[40] The fact that Faulkner himself had been a younger son of an English gentry family might have influenced his decision. If so, it would only serve to emphasize his distinctiveness from his neighbors, for whom partible inheritances and delayed control by the first generation over the land were the rule.

From the complex details of particular family histories emerge unexpected patterns of family relationships and forms of family structure.[41] The majority of households established

[38] Town meeting, March 4, 1678, Ancient Town Records.

[39] See Edmund Faulkner, will, September 16, 1684, PR 9305. His estate was inventoried and consisted of land and buildings worth £330 and a personal estate worth about £55 in January 1687. Faulkner also left his son-in-law, Joseph Robinson, a pillow, "being willing, would my Estate have reacht it, to have manifested my love towards him in a larger manner."

[40] The only instance of impartible inheritance, or primogeniture, to be found in the first generation of Andover's settlers occurred within the first decade of its settlement, before the extensive land grants of 1662 had been voted by the town. John Osgood, one of the leaders of the town, left his entire estate to the eldest of his two sons. See his will, April 12, 1650, in *Essex Quarterly Court*, I, 239.

[41] Bernard Bailyn, for instance, assumed that the basic structure of seventeenth-century English families could be described as a "patrilineal group of extended kinship gathered into a single household" (*Education in the Forming of American Society: Needs and Opportunities for Study* [Chapel Hill, 1960], pp. 15–16). Peter Laslett and John Harrison, on the other hand, demonstrated that the basic

by second-generation sons after their marriages were nuclear
in the sense that such families resided apart from the paternal
house; occasionally, however, in those instances in which one
son inherited the paternal homestead, three generations did
reside together in a single house. Because of the proximity of
their residences to those of their parents and siblings, the
majority of the first- and second-generation families were
extended in structure. The basis was laid for the creation of
elaborate kinship networks which continued to expand, in
greater and lesser degrees, for generations to come.

Equally important, and a fundamental characteristic of
most first-generation families, was the prolonged exercise of
paternal authority and influence over sons. Long after the
ostensible achievement of maturity, indicated by marriages
which often were delayed until men were in their late
twenties, sons remained economically dependent upon their
fathers, who usually continued to own and to control the land
upon which their sons had settled.[42] This, above all, was of the

-----

structure found in seventeenth-century Clayworth and Cogenhoe was
that of a "nuclear independent family, that is man, wife, and children living apart from relatives" ("Clayworth and Cogenhoe," in
H. E. Bell and R. L. Ollard, eds., *Historical Essays, 1660–1750, Presented to David Ogg* [London, 1963], p. 168). John Demos, in his
study of Plymouth families, also emphasized the nuclearity of family
structure, both in terms of the household and in terms of kinship networks ("Life in Plymouth," esp. pp. 279–285). For a discussion of
terminology and a definition of my terms, see Chapter 1, pp. 14–16;
and for a general discussion of the nature of family structure in the
seventeenth, eighteenth, and twentieth centuries in England and
America, see Chapter 9, pp. 263–268, 283–288.

[42] Unfortunately, one of the most important and fascinating aspects
of this prolonged dependence of sons upon their fathers—the psychological and emotional effects—simply cannot be determined from
the evidence which has survived. My own intuitive conviction is
that there probably was remarkably little open conflict between the
first two generations of men in Andover, a conviction which is

utmost importance in creating, and in maintaining, the extended, partriarchal families characteristic of the first and second generations in Andover. In this seventeenth-century American community, at least, patriarchalism was a reality, based firmly upon the possession and control of the land.[43]

---

suggested, in part, by the absence of evidence of internal family conflict in the extant court records. In addition, it seems to me that late marriages, and perhaps prolonged dependence of sons upon fathers, had been customary, and may not have been productive of much intergenerational discord. In fact, the evident prolongation of paternal control over the land may have fostered the sustained deference of sons to the authority of their fathers in other areas of life as well. Sons who were dutiful, obedient, and in some measure dependent were probably the rule among the extended, patriarchal families of seventeenth-century Andover. Their actions, and the language of wills and deeds, suggest this strongly, but we cannot be entirely certain.

[43] Patriarchalism in families living in rural communities in seventeenth-century England may have been as pervasive as Peter Laslett assumes in *The World We Have Lost* (New York, 1965), but it has yet to be demonstrated by specific studies of actual families. Undoubtedly some English families, and particularly some yeoman or husbandmen families, were patriarchal in character in *some* communities during *some* period of their history, but it is doubtful that circumstances were conducive to effective patriarchalism in *all* families at this time. In particular, I doubt very much if families which were nuclear in structure and highly mobile geographically would, or could, have been patriarchal in character. Certainly the experience recounted by John Dane, recollecting his own youth in Bishops-Stortford, Herts., during the early decades of the seventeenth century, belies the assumption that all families were patriarchal. However much men might have wished to behave in the manner of patriarchs, their ability to do so depended in large measure upon circumstances; see John Dane's "A Declaration of Remarkabell Provedenses in the Corse of My Lyfe," *NEHGR*, VIII (1854), 147–156. For a discussion of patriarchalism in nineteenth-century America, see Paul Connor, "Patriarchy: Old World and New," *AQ*, XVII (1965), 48–62.

PART II

❧⚜❧

THE SECOND AND THIRD
GENERATIONS

5

The Expanding Population
in a Farming Community

The last two decades of the seventeenth century and the first decade of the eighteenth century constituted a period of unparalleled growth in the population of Andover. Yet, as so frequently happens in demographic history, this phase of rapid growth was not to be repeated for at least another century in this community. Accordingly, the demographic history of these decades and of the second-generation families which produced most of their children during this time is of the utmost importance as a factor shaping the lives and actions of individuals and families during the early decades of the eighteenth century. Indeed, without an awareness and an understanding of the demographic history of this period, much of the underlying basis of family life in eighteenth-century Andover would remain mysterious.

The combination of circumstances found in Andover during this time—a relatively small local population, much of which was dispersed by then throughout the town on isolated farms; relatively few deaths from epidemical diseases, suggesting healthful conditions of life; and relatively youthful ages at first marriage for women—fostered the rapid growth of the population. The total population of the town in 1680 was approximately 435 people (based upon a conversion factor of

5 for male polls on the rate lists);[1] the population grew to approximately 945 people by 1705, more than doubling the total population twenty-five years earlier. The full impact of this growth was to be felt with the maturing of the third generation, many of whom began to marry and begin families of their own after 1705. The effects of this growth reshaped families, fostered mobility, and changed the lives of many individuals. Growth is the key to an understanding of this period in Andover's history.

The most striking measurements of growth during this period are the index which can be calculated for fertility and the approximate rates which can be calculated for births. The average number of births per marriage in the three decades from 1650 to 1679 was 5.8, 5.3, and 5.7 (see Table 1, p. 23). During the 1680's this figure rose to 6.0 and then increased to the astonishing figure of 7.6 during the 1690's and 7.5 during the first decade of the eighteenth century (see Table 6). This index of fertility suggests that the last two decades of the seventeenth century and the first decade of the next century were periods of extraordinarily high birth rates. In England, even during the late eighteenth century—a period of exceptionally rapid population growth—the baptisms per marriage

[1] In the absence of reliable figures for the population of Andover prior to the census of 1764, (a manuscript version of which is to be found in the Tucker Family Manuscripts, vol. I, [Essex County Innholders and Miscellany, 1680–1812], Essex Institute, Salem, Mass.), one must rely upon approximations based upon the extant tax lists. The census of 1764 indicates that Andover had 533 polls—white males above the age of 16—and a total white population of 2,356, which provides a multiplier of 4.4 to convert polls to the total population, but a conversion factor of 5 seems more likely during the earlier period, and perhaps even a factor of 6 might be possible (using family size as an index). Any conversion figure is quite arbitrary, yet it is too useful a tool to be given up.

Table 6. Births per marriage, 1680–1724

| Marriages | | Births | | |
Years	Number	Years	Number	B/M
1680–1689	55	1685–1694	331	6.0
1690–1699	44	1695–1704	335	7.6
1700–1709	58	1705–1714	435*	7.5
1710–1719	94	1715–1724	534	5.7

* Estimate. For explanation, see note 6 in Chapter 1.

in industrial villages of Nottinghamshire never exceeded 4.8.[2]
The calculation of birth rates for Andover during this period is based upon an approximation of the total population in a given year (male polls multiplied by 5) and an averaging of births recorded during a five-year period (including the two years before and after a particular year). This method provides some suggestive but very crude rates: 51 per thousand in 1680; 52 per thousand in 1685; 59 per thousand in 1690; 46 per thousand in 1695; 50 per thousand in 1700; 39 per thousand in 1705; and 45 per thousand in 1710. If the total population is calculated by a multiplier of 6 rather than 5, the following rates are found: 42 per thousand in 1680; 43 per thousand in 1685; 49 per thousand in 1690; 39 per thousand in 1695; 42 per thousand in 1700; 33 per thousand in 1705; and 38 per thousand in 1710. The significance of such birth rates can be seen by comparison with some rates in English towns and villages, where a birth rate of 37.7 per thousand has been considered "abnormally high" for the eighteenth century,[3]

[2] J. D. Chambers, "The Course of Population Change," in D. V. Glass and D. E. C. Eversley, eds., *Population in History: Essays in Historical Demography* (Chicago, 1965), p. 333.

[3] T. H. Marshall, "The Population Problem During the Industrial Revolution: A Note on the Present State of the Controversy," in Glass and Eversley, *Population in History*, p. 256.

and where a birth rate of 37.2 per thousand for the period from 1676 to 1688 in Clayworth also was considered to be "very high indeed."[4] In the town of Nottingham, the birth rate after 1770 was "explosive," with rates varying between 40.32 per thousand and 46.29 per thousand between 1770 and 1801.[5] By such standards, the rough calculations for Andover suggest that the birth rate in this colonial town during this period was at least as high as rates in England during periods of maximum height, and perhaps considerably higher at times.

This is confirmed in the town records. The population increase during the period from 1675 to 1699 was nearly three times greater than that between 1650 and 1674; 702 births and only 155 deaths were recorded, giving a net increase of 547 people, compared to an increase of 187 during the previous quarter-century. The increase during the next quarter-century, 1700–1724, was 859, only 1.6 times the increase in the last quarter of the seventeenth century. Judging by these various indications, none of which can be considered totally reliable yet all of which seem to point clearly to the same conclusion, the period in which the second generation was producing children was one of remarkable demographic growth.

Apparently, relatively few deaths were recorded during the period from 1670 to 1699, and a large proportion of children born in the community survived infancy and adolescence during these years. Data drawn from the family reconstitution forms indicate that 855 children out of every 1,000 born survived to the age of ten, and 830 lived to the age of twenty

[4] Peter Laslett and John Harrison, "Clayworth and Cogenhoe," in H. E. Bell and R. L. Ollard, eds., *Historical Essays, 1600–1750 Presented to David Ogg*, (London, 1963), pp. 173, 182, Table 2.

[5] J. D. Chambers, "Population Change in a Provincial Town: Nottingham, 1700–1800," in Glass and Eversley, *Population in History*, p. 349.

this was a very high rate of survival indeed. The proportion of deaths recorded in the town records to the births recorded was 20.8 per cent during the 1670's, 22.5 per cent during the 1680's, 21.0 per cent during the 1690's, and approximately 23.6 per cent during the 1700's, and these percentages are very similar to those for the first decades following the settlement of Andover.

The town records give no indication of the presence of any serious disease until November 1690, when the first death from smallpox was recorded; this was followed by eight more smallpox deaths during November and December and one in January 1691. We now know that smallpox was brought into Andover in the autumn of 1690 by the married daughter of an Andover family, so it appears almost certain that Andover had been spared the ravages of smallpox prior to that year.[6] Since Boston, only twenty miles away, had had periodic epidemics of smallpox during the course of the seventeenth century, Andover's isolation from the disease is most significant.[7] Whatever other diseases might have caused sickness and deaths among Andover's population prior to 1690, smallpox had not. The community appears to have been generally healthy and never suffered from an epidemic sufficient to kill a major portion of the population of children or adults. On balance, then, it seems that the rate of mortality probably continued to be quite low during the latter part of the seventeenth century.

[6] See the transcriptions of town records in Sarah Loring Bailey, *Historical Sketches of Andover* . . . (Boston, 1880), pp. 202–203. The selectmen were aware of the contagiousness of smallpox and sought to contain the infection by quarantining the Allen family, whose daughter, Martha Carrier (later to be put to death as a witch) had brought the disease to Andover.

[7] See John B. Blake's excellent study, *Public Health in the Town of Boston, 1630–1822* (Cambridge, Mass., 1959), esp. chs. 1, 4, and 5.

Evidence about the ages of men and women at the time of their deaths is derived from data from the family reconstitution forms for persons born between 1670 and 1699—when the majority of the third generation were born. Again, it must be emphasized that the data are imperfect and that they provide only a partial insight into the lifespans of the individuals. We have data for 246 men out of a total of 292 known to have been born during this period (data are unavailable for 15.8 per cent), and for 141 women out of a total of 220 known to have been born between 1670 and 1699 (data are not available for 36 per cent). By assuming that all those who are known to have died young, but whose age at death is uncertain, died between birth and one year of age, the percentages of men and women dying at various ages can be determined, thus providing a useful picture of their lifespans and the proportions surviving to advanced ages (see Table 7). What emerges is strong confirmation of the fact that rela-

Table 7. Age at death of persons
born between 1670 and 1699

Age	Male		Female	
	No.	%	No.	%
0–1	37	15.0	22	15.6
2–9	12	4.9	3	2.1
10–19	5	2.0	8	5.7
20–29	17	6.9	10	7.1
30–39	13	5.3	9	6.4
40–49	12	4.9	11	7.8
50–59	13	5.3	13	9.2
60–69	45	18.3	23	16.3
70–79	51	20.7	22	15.6
80–89	34	13.8	12	8.5
90–99	7	2.8	7	5.0
100 and over	0	0.0	1	0.7
Total	246	99.9	141	100.0

tively few died in childhood and adolescence and that a remarkable number survived to live to advanced ages. Of the
246 males whose ages at death can be determined at least approximately, 21.9 per cent died before reaching their twentieth year; for females this figure is 23.4 per cent. Of the
same 246 men, 60.9 per cent lived to be at least fifty years
old, and an astonishing 37.3 per cent lived to be at least
seventy. Of the 141 women, 55.3 per cent lived to be at least
fifty, and 29.8 per cent lived to be at least seventy. Men
evidently tended to outlive women, undoubtedly owing to
the hazards of childbirth and motherhood; but women were
stronger and survived longer than one might assume.

Since adult deaths were almost always recorded in Andover, and since many people lived their entire lives in the
community, the data on adult males and females are reliable
on the whole. This means that the percentages dying at particular ages provide a reasonably accurate guide to the longevity of people born during this period. Of the 192 men
known to have survived at least to the age of 20, only 15.7 per
cent died between the ages of 20 and 39; 13.1 per cent died
between the ages of 40 and 59; 50.0 per cent died between the
ages of 60 and 79; and a remarkable 21.3 per cent lived to be
older than 80 (see Table 8). In other words, of those men
who survived to adulthood and whose ages at death are
known, more than 70 per cent reached the age of 60, and
nearly half reached the age of 70. Of the 108 women who
survived at least to the age of 20, only 17.6 per cent died
during the critical childbearing years between 20 and 39.
Between the ages of 40 and 59, however, a larger percentage
of women died than men, (22.2 per cent versus 13.1 per
cent). More than 70 per cent of these women reached the age
of 50, and 60.2 per cent reached the age of 60; this was about
11 per cent fewer than for men but remarkably high never-

Table 8. Age at death of persons born
between 1670 and 1699 and surviving to age 20

Age	Male		Female	
	No.	%	No.	%
20–29	17	8.9	10	9.3
30–39	13	6.8	9	8.3
40–49	12	6.3	11	10.2
50–59	13	6.8	13	12.0
60–69	45	23.4	23	21.3
70–79	51	26.6	22	20.4
80–89	34	17.7	12	11.1
90–99	7	3.6	7	6.5
100 and over	0	0.0	1	0.9
Total	192	100.1	108	100.0

theless. Nearly 40 per cent of the women reached the age of 70, and twelve died in their eighties, seven in their nineties, and one reached 100 years.

It seems justified, then, to say that both men and women born during this period lived relatively long lives, with a large percentage living to advanced ages. For women, especially, this is impressive; it implies that the conditions of life in Andover during the latter part of the seventeenth century and the first decades of the eighteenth century permitted a large proportion of mothers to produce their children and to survive to care for them. Even allowing for the intrusion of smallpox by the end of the seventeenth century and its recurrence thereafter, and for the effects of other unknown diseases, Andover continued to be a surprisingly healthy place in which to live and to raise families.

Remarriage for the third generation depended in large measure upon the longevity of the marriage partners, since no record of divorce among Andover couples in this period has come to light. An examination of the marriages of third-gen-

eration males remaining for all or most of their lives in Andover indicates that out of a total of 152 men who married at
least once, 98 (64.5 per cent) married only once, with 34
(22.4 per cent) know to marry twice, with only 4 (2.6 per
cent) known to marry three times, and with the possible remarriages of 16 being uncertain. None are known to have married
more than three times. If we exclude from the calculations the
16 men whose possible remarriages are uncertain, then 72.1
per cent of the men married only once, 25.0 per cent married
only twice, and 2.9 per cent married three times. Significantly, only 5.5 per cent fewer married only once in the third
generation than had done so in the second generation, additional confirmation of the frequency with which husbands
and wives successfully lived out their lives together. In a
number of instances, of course, both partners died relatively
young, or one died young and the other would fail to remarry. But in the majority of cases, both partners lived together into old age, surviving to care for and to raise large
numbers of children to adulthood.

In the light of the high birth rate and the relatively low
percentages of persons dying in childhood and adolescence,
the large size of second-generation families is not surprising.
The average number of children born to the families of
eighty-four second-generation fathers (including the children
of all wives) was 8.1, with an average of 6.6 children surviving
to the age of 21. Even larger, of course, was the size of the
average completed family, with 8.7 children known to have
been born and an average of 7.2 children known to survive to
the age of 21; these figures are very similar to those for
first-generation families. If we view this matter from a slightly
different perspective and calculate the offspring of all completed marriages occurring between 1685 and 1704 without
reference to generation, the averages are identical to those of

second-generation marriages: 8.7 and 7.2, respectively
Forty-four of the fifty-seven completed second-generation
families (77.2 per cent) had seven or more children born, and
thirty-five of these families (61.4 per cent) had seven or more
children surviving to the age of 21. Only 14 per cent of the
completed families had fewer than five children born (see
Table 9), nearly half (47.4 per cent) had between eight and
eleven children born, and 21.1 per cent had twelve or more
children. The largest families were one with fourteen births
and another with eighteen births—indicative of the upper

Table 9. Family size of completed second-generation families

No. of children	Children born		Children living to 21	
	No. of families	% of families	No. of families	% of families
0–4	8	14.0	10	17.5
5–7	10	17.5	22	38.6
8–11	27	47.4	22	38.6
12 or more	12	21.1	3	5.3
Total	57	100.0	57	100.0

limits of size which prevailed in Andover during this period.
Since the average interval between births in a completed family begun between 1685 and 1704 was 24.1 months (or 23.5
months if all intervals over 59 months are excluded), the
average maximum number of births to be expected during this
period would be thirteen. The average intervals between
births during this period were lower than at any time before
or afterward, another strong indication of the relatively high
birth rate prevalent during this period.

Birth intervals are significant not only for the ultimate sizes
of families, but also for the information which they provide
about the practice of premarital sex between men and women

who later married and produced children.[8] With an average interval between marriage and first births of 15.1 months for the period 1685–1704, the presumption probably is justified that premarital sex was neither customary nor frequently practiced among second-generation Andover couples. Between 1655 and 1674, not one of the twenty-one first births whose interval can be determined was less than nine months after marriage, although after 1675 occasional instances did occur, with five between 1675 and 1679, and three between 1685 and 1699. Out of a total of eighty-five first births between 1655 and 1699, including all generations, only six occurred less than eight months after marriage (7.0 per cent) and only eight occurred less than nine months after marriage (9.4 per cent). During the first three decades of the eighteenth century, the percentage of births occurring less than nine months after marriage rose slightly, to 11.3 per cent, or 13 births out of a total of 115. Judging by this data, some premarital sexual intercourse took place, but compared to that of other times and places its frequency was very low.

[8] The evidence for premarital sexual behavior in Bristol, R.I., provides a suggestive comparison. John Demos found that no couples married between 1680 and 1720 had their first child within eight months of marriage, whereas between 1720 and 1740, 10 per cent had a child within eight months; the figure was a startling 49 per cent between 1740 and 1760, and 44 per cent between 1760 and 1780. ("Families in Colonial Bristol, Rhode Island: An Exercise in Historical Demography," *WMQ*, XXV, [1968], p. 56, Table 10). In England during the seventeenth century, premarital intercourse evidently was quite common: 10.2 per cent of first baptisms occurred eight months after marriage in Clayworth, Notts., between 1650 and 1750, 13.2 per cent in Cartmel, Lancs., between 1660 and 1675, and 46.2 per cent in Colyton, Devon, between 1538 and 1799. In Crulai, France, 9.5 per cent of first baptisms occurred eight months after marriage between 1674 and 1742 (Peter Laslett, *The World We Have Lost* [New York, 1965], pp. 139–146, especially the table, "Pre-nuptial pregnancy [England and France]," p. 139).

The inferences from the data on birth intervals can be supplemented and amplified, fortunately, by the surviving evidence in the Essex County court records for the seventeenth and early eighteenth centuries. The manuscript records of the County Court and the Court of General Sessions contain information on individuals presented for the crime of fornication, and occasionally testimony and depositions taken at the time also survive, providing an exceptional glimpse into the lives and behavior of second- and third-generation men and women in Andover. Between 1675 and 1699, at least nine people were convicted in separate instances of fornication by the County Court, five of them between 1680 and 1684. Between 1700 and 1729, twenty-one cases were considered by the Court of General Sessions, five of them between 1700 and 1709, eight between 1710 and 1719, and eight between 1720 and 1729. These undoubtedly represent only a portion of the cases, since the records are incomplete, but there were probably relatively few additional cases during this period. For the most part, the records simply noted that a person was presented to a court for fornication, usually prior to marriage. In 1683, for instance, Hannah Tiler acknowledged guilt of fornication before marriage, and at the same session Naomy Lovejoy, the widow of John Lovejoy, "came in voluntaryly of her selfe" to acknowledge her sexual relationship with Benjamin Abbot, then a young man of twenty-two.[9] In 1706, Mary Grainger confessed her guilt, accusing Samuel Blanchard, an unmarried man of twenty-six, of fathering her child, an accusation which the Sessions Court accepted despite his denials. Blanchard waited until he was twenty-nine to marry, and then married another woman. Similarly, Daniel

[9] County Court Papers, Salem, 1679–1692, pp. 37–38, (in Essex County Registry of Deeds and Probate Court Building, Salem, Mass.).

Faulkner was accused of fathering a child in 1711, when he was about twenty-five, yet waited until 1724 to marry. Others, like Edmund Faulkner, a cousin of Daniel, and Benjamin Lovejoy, both men being twenty-seven at the times of their marriages in 1715 and 1718, came into court to confess premarital intercourse with their wives; this was a common confession, and at least thirteen of the cases between 1700 and 1729 involved husbands and wives.[10]

The brevity of most of the entries in the court records adds to the interest of the vivid testimony recorded in the bastardy case involving Elizabeth Sessions, a single woman of Andover, who confessed, October 9, 1690, that

she being unmarried is with child; y^t about five months since she was by violence abused by Joseph Chandler Son of Capt Tho: Chandler of Andover; in the high way neer his Bro: John Chandlers; wch she did not make known because of his relations being great men & y^t no other person in that kind ever had to do wth, or knew her.

Two days later she said that Joseph Chandler had slept with her only once and that no one else had done so at any time, and that Chandler had "never profered marriage to her" although "She had had love for him along while." Despite her declaration of love for the man she accused of fathering her child, other evidence suggested that he was actually innocent and that John Russ, a young man of nineteen, was the more likely culprit. Daniel Bixby and his wife testified that Elizabeth Sessions had lived with them for "about a querter of a yeare" during which time John Russ, Jr., kept her company "two or three nights in a weeke and some times they wad be gone out of our house a great part of the night," which they

---

[10] Court of General Sessions, 1696–1718, pp. 166, 240, 303, 356. For later cases, see Court of General Sessions, 1719 to 1727.

continued despite Bixby's opposition, offering the excuse "that they intended marige with [one] a nother." Two of Russ' friends, one nineteen and the other eighteen, deposed in March 1691:

> That being in company with John Russ junior last planting time he asked us whether we ever had anything to doe with Elizabeth Sissions we told him no: then we asked him if he had ever had any thing to doe with hir he told us yes a Hundered times for ought he did know: and further he sayd any body might have to doe with her that had a mind to it and by this having to doe with hir we under stud lying with hir.

The decision of the Court is unrecorded. But John Russ' reply to Thomas and Hannah Astin speaks for itself. They told him that "it was brase that he should gat a Basterd and another man maintayne [it] he s^a so it was an he wad gat another if Joseph Chandler would keep it."[11]

Colorful though such testimony is, it still serves only to illustrate the exceptional rather than to document the general patterns of premarital sexual behavior among Andover men and women during the seventeenth century. Evidently the normal behavior reflected continence—a period of sexual abstinence which was unduly prolonged, in fact, by the frequent postponements of marriage.

The number of marriages recorded in the town records did not increase steadily throughout the last decade of the seventeenth century and the early part of the eighteenth century; rather, they declined somewhat. A total of 29 marriages were recorded between 1685 and 1689, and then the numbers fell to 24 between 1690 and 1694, and to only 20 between 1695 and 1699. After 1700, however, the numbers rose again, to 24

[11] MSS depositions of Elizabeth Sessions (October 9 and 11, 1690), Daniel and Hannah Bixbe (March 26, 1691), John Farnum and James Johnson (March 26, 1691), and Thomas Astin and Hannah Astin (March 26, 1691), in Essex County Court Papers, vol. 50, pp. 62–63.

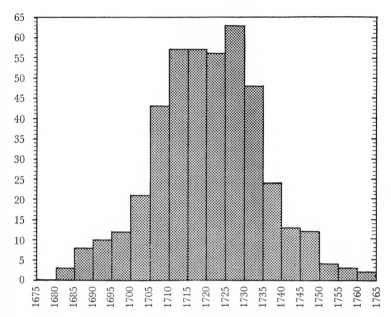

Graph 2. Third-generation marriages in consecutive five-year intervals

between 1700 and 1704, to 34 between 1705 and 1709, then to a high of 54 between 1710 and 1714, dropping to 40 over the next five years, and then rising again. In part, at least, these figures reflect the maturing of the third generation, which married in the greatest numbers between 1710 and 1729 (see Graph 2). The third generation in Andover thus reached maturity for the most part during the first third of the eighteenth century, which was a period of growth and expansion throughout New England.

During the first three decades of the eighteenth century, as throughout most of the previous four decades of the seventeenth century, the age at marriage of men remained high. The average ages for men marrying for the first time in successive five-year intervals between 1685 and 1729 were as follows: 26.4, 23.5, 27.0, 26.4, 26.9, 27.2, 26.4, 27.1, 26.9.

With only one exception, between 1690 and 1694, the average age always was over 26.0 years, which indicates a remarkable stability in the average age at marriage for men throughout this period. Generationally, the age at marriage rose slightly for men, from an average of 26.7 years for second-generation men to an average of 27.1 years for third-generation men.[12] This slight rise reflects the fact that only 34.8 per cent of the third generation married before the age of 25, compared to 39.4 per cent of the second generation; 26.4 per cent of the third-generation men married at the age of 30 or older, compared with 23.0 per cent of the second generation (see Table 10). Fewer were marrying at very young ages and more were marrying at late ages than had been the case with the previous generation. Only 6 of the 224 third-generation men who married, married at less than 21 years of age, a proportion which demonstrates clearly that the commonplace assumptions about the tendency to very early marriages for young men during this period are misleading. The high average ages evidently affected third-generation sons regardless of their birth order, since 72 eldest sons married at an average age of 27.3 years, 56 second sons married at an average of 27.8 years, and 52 youngest sons married at an average of 27.4 years. Similarly, 54 sons who are known to have followed a trade and whose age at marriage is known married on the average at

[12] This average age for the third-generation grandsons of the original settlers corresponds closely with that of sons of later-comers who settled in Andover after 1662, many of them with considerably less land and therefore less in the way of resources to transmit to their sons marrying between 1700 and 1729. During this period, the average age of marriage for forty-three sons or grandsons of late-comer families was 27.6 years, and the average age for twenty-six men marrying between 1700 and 1719 was 26.2 years. In terms of their ages at marriage, these families, who constituted most of the additional population of Andover, did not differ significantly from the third generation of settler families.

Table 10. Age at marriage of second- and third-generation males

Age	Second generation No.	Second generation %	Third generation No.	Third generation %
Under 21	5	4.8	6	2.7
21–24	36	34.6	72	32.1
25–29	39	37.5	87	38.8
30–34	17	16.3	39	17.4
35–39	4	3.8	12	5.4
40 and over	3	2.9	8	3.6
Total	104	99.9	224	100.0
24 and under		39.4		34.8
25 and over		60.5		65.2
Total, all ages		99.9		100.0
29 and under		76.9		73.6
30 and over		23.0		26.4
Total, all ages		99.9		100.0

27.4 years. During this period, being an eldest or a youngest son, a farmer or an artisan, evidently made very little difference: marriage usually came late. The great majority of the third generation eventually married, of course; only 15 were definitely known to be bachelors after the age of 25, and only 9 died unmarried between the ages of 21 and 25. Out of a total of 281 third-generation men, therefore, only 33 remain unaccounted for in terms of marriage, leaving a minimum of nearly 80 per cent known to have been married during their lifetimes.

This generation of men, like their fathers before them, found it necessary to postpone marriage much longer than most historians hitherto would have assumed likely. But it must be borne in mind that this pattern of late marriage ages, and the generational average of 27.1 years, were also characteristic of European and English marriage ages throughout this entire era. Significant though the specific features of the local economy and the patterns of inheritance were in shaping the lives and decisions of this generation, the force of custom, of tradition, must also have continued to exercise some influence. This is worth emphasizing, since so much of the evidence which remains for this generation reflects their economic resources and familial circumstances.

In contrast to the notable steadiness of the average age at marriage of third-generation Andover men, the age of marriage for women increased perceptibly after the beginning of the eighteenth century. The average age at marriage for second-generation women had been 22.3 years; the average for the third generation rose to 24.5 years. This increase of slightly more than two years is significant with respect to the potential sizes of families and probably affected the emotional life of the women whose marriages were thus delayed. The possible emotional effects, and the effects upon the families and husbands, cannot be assessed since no direct evidence whatsoever survives, but the effects upon fertility and reproduction are measurable, as will be evident in the discussion of sizes of the families of the third generation in Chapter 7.

What is striking, however, is the sudden increase in the average age at which women in Andover married, an increase which is apparent in the average ages at which women of all generations married in successive five-year intervals. For the period from 1680 to 1704, the averages were as follows: 21.6, 22.5, 21.6, 22.0, 21.1 years. After 1705, however, a sudden increase began and was maintained continually for at least the next fifty years without returning to the low averages characteristic of female marriage ages throughout the seventeenth century. The average age during the second half of the first decade of the eighteenth century was 3.6 years higher than the average of the first half of the decade, rising from 21.1

years to 24.7 years during the period from 1705 to 1709. Thereafter, the averages in successive five-year intervals from 1710 to 1729 were 24.0, 23.6, 23.9, and 23.5 years. The percentage of women marrying at less than 21 years decreased from 35.8 for the second generation to 27.6 for the third generation (see Table 11). The youngest age at marriage was 16 years, but 17 was more common. None married between

Table 11. Age at marriage of second- and third-generation females

Age	Second generation		Third generation	
	No.	%	No.	%
Under 21	29	35.8	58	27.6
21–24	32	39.5	74	35.2
25–29	14	17.3	48	22.9
30–34	3	3.7	12	5.7
35–39	2	2.5	10	4.8
40 and over	1	1.2	8	3.8
Total	81	100.0	210	100.0
24 and under		75.3		62.8
25 and over		24.7		37.2
Total, all ages		100.0		100.0
29 and under		92.6		85.7
30 and over		7.4		14.3
Total, all ages		100.0		100.0

the ages of 12 and 15 years. Of the 210 third-generation women who married, 30 (14.3 per cent) married after reaching the age of 30, and 8 were at least 40 before marrying for the first time. Only 20 third-generation women out of a total of 256 (7.4 per cent) are known to have remained spinsters throughout their lifetimes, having lived at least to the age of 26. However long they might wait, the overwhelming majority of women in this generation ultimately married, and compared with many of their English counterparts during this same period, they still were marrying at comparatively young ages. Nevertheless, the average age at marriage for the third-generation females proved to be the highest average reached by the first four generations of women in Andover.

Unfortunately, it is simpler to demonstrate the increased age at marriage for women than to explain it. It is worth noting, however, that the increase occurred during the decade *before* appreciable numbers of Andover men began to depart from the community, thereby creating a potential shortage of husbands for the marriageable women of the town. The general ratio of men to women in the community, measured by births and by surviving children among these particular Andover families, was sufficiently close to have provided a husband for most of the women choosing to marry. Of the third-generation children born to second-generation families, 51.6 per cent were male and 48.4 per cent were female, but of those children surviving to the age of twenty-one, 50.6 per cent were male and 49.4 per cent were female; this is indicative of an even sexual balance at the start of adulthood for the third generation.

One clue might be the proportion of Andover women marrying within the community during this period compared to earlier and later periods. An analysis of the marriages recorded in the town records, although at best only an approximation of the origins of the partners owing to the difficulties of ascertaining the towns from which some came, nevertheless suggests that relatively fewer women in Andover were marrying men from outside the town during the period 1700–1719 than had done so between 1650 and 1699, and far fewer than were to marry outside the town between 1720 and 1749. Between 1700 and 1719, only 6 per cent of the marriages involved husbands from outside Andover, in contrast to 18.5 per cent from 1650 to 1699, and 29.6 per cent from 1720 to 1749. Proportionately more marriages during the first two decades of the eighteenth century involved husbands and wives who were both residents of Andover than had been the case earlier: in 66.5 per cent of the marriages between 1700 and 1719 both partners came from Andover, compared with 48.1 per cent between 1650 and 1699, and 58.4 per cent between 1720 and 1749. Perhaps the higher proportion of men who married outside the town (27.5 per cent) than women who did so (6.0 per cent) during the period between 1700 and 1719 accounts for the increased delays in the marriages for many women during this period, but it is almost impossible to be sure. All that is certain is the fact of the increased average age. Beyond that, the dearth of evidence forces the researcher to speculate.

One of the most important consequences of the demographic developments of this period was the marked increase in the geographical mobility of the third generation. Nearly two-fifths of the third-generation sons who reached maturity eventually left Andover. Out of a total of 287 third-generation sons who are known to have lived to at least twenty-one years of age, 112 (39 per cent) either are definitely known to have moved away or can be reasonably assumed to have moved, leaving 61 per cent as permanent residents of the town. The proportion of second-generation sons who left Andover had been about 22 per cent.

Proportionately more sons moved away from families in the South Parish than from the North Parish in the third generation, in contrast to the movement of sons in the previous generation. Of the 112 third-generation sons leaving Andover, 32 per cent were from the North Parish (and 68 per cent from the South Parish), compared to 64 per cent from the North Parish in the second generation. In part, the higher percentage of sons departing from South Parish families reflected the higher proportion of sons in this parish. Of the 287 sons born to second-generation families in Andover, 39 per cent were born in the North Parish, and 61 per cent were born in the South Parish. This indicates that the actual proportions of emigrants from families in the two parishes were fairly close, with slightly more leaving the South Parish than leaving the North Parish.

In summary, Andover felt the effects of a remarkable population "explosion" during the latter part of the seventeenth century and the early part of the eighteenth century, a consequence of the extraordinarily high birth rate and the unusually low mortality rate among both children and adults of the second and third generations. The full impact of this demographic experience is revealed in the problems faced by these families in providing land and livelihoods for their numerous offspring, and it underlies many of the changes in patterns of relationships and of action which had characterized family life in seventeenth-century Andover. The maturing of the third generation marked a new stage in the history of this rural community.

6

Control and Autonomy: Families and the Transmission of Land

The three decades between 1705 and 1735 witnessed many changes in the shapes and characteristics of families as the third generation grew to maturity and established themselves in Andover and elsewhere. When families sought to provide livelihoods and settlements for their sons, as their parents had done for them, they often felt the pressures which the demographic growth of the last part of the seventeenth century put upon the land and the economic resources that they had inherited.[1] The parceling of the original estates of the first-

---

[1] The experience of land pressure in the third generation in Andover undoubtedly was characteristic of other New England towns as well. In Kent, Conn., for example, Charles Grant found that "there was insufficient land for the third generation. Some stayed and remained in a poorer status than that of their fathers and much poorer than that of their grandfathers. Others left at the rate of about fifty a year." He also noted that "increased poverty" in Kent during the 1780's (Kent had been founded in 1738) "stemmed from the pressure of a population swollen by a fantastic birth-rate against a limited amount of land. The land may have seemed inexhaustible to the first generation in 1740, ample to the second generation in the 1750s and 1760s, but it appeared quite limited to the third generation after 1780." This generational pattern appears to be very similar to Andover's. In retrospect it is regretable that the Grant study did not focus upon either the demographic history of the town or the

generation settlers created problems for the second generation when the time came for them to consider the divisions of their estates and the establishment of their sons upon the land. As earlier, though, the nature of the families in this community depended largely upon the decisions about the distribution of estates and the consequent actions of the third generation in either settling in Andover or moving away to other towns. Families were affected in various ways, of course, depending upon the number of sons to provide for and upon the amount of land at their disposal.

Families were also affected by the attitudes of fathers toward their sons and toward their land. Although they often had less land at their disposal than their own fathers had had, they nevertheless continued to use their land as a means of maintaining their positions of influence and authority within their families. The sustained control of the land by the older generation and the delayed maturity of many third-generation sons who waited not only to marry but also to gain their full economic independence continued to be prominent characteristics of family life in Andover. Yet in contrast to the earlier period, some third-generation sons managed to gain their autonomy relatively early, often with the encouragement and the assistance of their fathers, who either settled them in trades for their livelihoods, gave them deeds for their land, or helped them to emigrate to other places, often at considerable distances from Andover, to live and raise their families. As a

---

changing patterns of inheritance used by families there (Charles Grant, *Democracy in the Connecticut Frontier Town of Kent* [New York, 1961], pp. 98–100). For a more general, and very suggestive, treatment of the pressures of population upon the land in New England, see Kenneth Lockridge, "Land, Population and the Evolution of New England Society, 1630–1790," *Past and Present*, April 1968, pp. 62–80.

result, the pattern of family life and family structure became far more complex than it had been earlier.

Underlying the decisions made by parents concerning the future livelihoods of their sons were the economic resources that they had at their disposal. For the most part, their estates were of moderate size and value. One-quarter of the thirty-five second-generation estates for which complete inventories are extant were valued at less than £200, and nearly three-quarters of them were valued at less than £600, including both real and personal estate. Only five men had estates valued at more than £1,000. The majority of estates consisted of less than 100 acres: of thirty-three estates for which the acreage is either known or can be estimated, twenty had less than 109 acres, nine contained between 110 and 299 acres, and four were over 300 acres in extent. In value, about 44 per cent of the real estates were worth less than £200, and nearly 80 per cent were worth less than £600. Most of these estates could be divided once more to provide inheritances for third-generation sons, although relatively few were large enough to be divided among more than a few sons in families with a considerable number of sons. The third generation as a whole thus faced a relative scarcity of land as they began to mature and to marry.

Within Andover itself, one of the few means available for augmenting the land which families had to provide for the settlements of the third generation, apart from purchases, was the division of the remaining undivided common land possessed by the town.[2] Not since the fourth division of land in 1662 had anything been done with the large tracts of com-

---

[2] For details pertaining to the decisions of the proprietors and the individual grants distributed to them, see the Proprietors' First Book of Records: Meetings, 1714–1798, Land Grants, 1717–1760, in the Town Clerk's Office, Andover.

mon land in the town save for the selling or trading of small
pieces to individuals who wished to consolidate or to add bits
and pieces to their holdings. By the beginning of the eighteenth century, however, the maturing of the third generation
made another major division of common land imperative. In
1702, the town declared 102 men, heirs of the first generation
for the most part, to be the proprietors of the common lands
of Andover. In 1714, an additional 120 men were added to the
proprietors, including many who had been later-comers to
Andover and who had purchased twenty-acre lots from the
town or other lands from earlier settlers. In all, the proprietors
represented fifty-four families living within the town. Between 1714 and 1720, these proprietors voted three successive
divisions of the remaining common land, yet none of these
divisions proved to be as large as the third and fourth divisions
in the seventeenth century. The average increment to private
holdings among the proprietors was rarely more than about
thirty acres, so that even with these additional sources, the
problems of land for the younger generation remained intense
for many families.

Equally significant was the trend toward increasing land
values in Andover after the turn of the century. With the
maturing of the third generation a marked rise in land values
became evident, increasing every decade from 1710 to 1750.
Throughout the second half of the seventeenth century, the
values of land in Andover had remained remarkably steady
and generally very low. With so much land still wilderness,
this is not surprising, although the value even of upland and
arable land remained quite low as well throughout this period.
The average value of real estate from 1660 to 1710 was
generally less than £2 per acre, and never as much as £3 per
acre. Wilderness land and unbroken land throughout this
period usually ranged in value from ten shillings to £1.

Upland and arable land, though, ranged in value from ten shillings to £3, averaging about £2 during the last three decades of the seventeenth century and the first decade of the eighteenth century. Thereafter, however, the average value rose sharply to £4 during the 1710's and £8 during the 1720's; it reached a high of £14 during the 1730's before dropping to £10 during the 1740's. The maximum value of inventoried upland and arable land never exceeded £3 between 1670 and 1710, but the maximum rose to £9 during the second decade of the eighteenth century, to £12 during the 1720's, and to £20 during the 1730's. Similarly, the value of meadowland also increased greatly after 1710; it had been relatively expensive during the seventeenth century, ranging in value from £2 to £5 per acre between 1660 and 1710, and reached its maximum values of £9 during the 1710's, £12 during the 1720's, and £20 during the 1730's. The average value per acre of mixed land inventoried between 1660 and 1710 was less than £2, and the value rose steadily until it reached £11 during the 1740's (see Graph 3).[3]

Undoubtedly some of this increase reflected the inflation of the 1730's and 1740's, but the rise in land values also accurately reflected the increased demands and the decreased availability of land in the community during the period. The constantly increasing value of land in Andover thus made it more expensive to purchase, adding to the economic difficulties encountered by many third-generation men as they reached maturity and sought to establish themselves on the land. Most of the

---

[3] These figures are based upon real estate valuations in the inventories of Andover estates and upon the prices paid for land in various deeds. They are only suggestive indications of the trend rather than a definitive statement of land values in the town. The question of the changing value of land warrants further study for Massachusetts and other colonies as well.

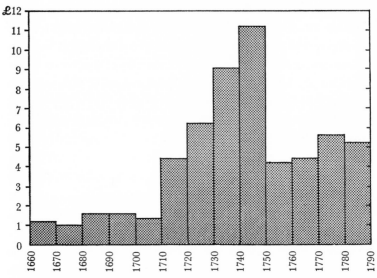

Graph 3. Average value of mixed land per decade, 1660–1789

land, though, was owned by the older generation, and inheritance usually proved as essential in the acquisition of land for
the third generation as it had for the second generation.

The growing complexity of family life and of family structure was reflected clearly in the increasingly complex methods
of transference of estates from the second to the third generations. The second generation, like the first, usually preferred
to divide their land and to give it to more than one of their
sons, thus maintaining the earlier pattern of partible inheritances (three-quarters of them did so); but they transferred
the control of the land to their sons prior to their deaths more
frequently than the first generation did. This is revealed by
the fact that out of 58 second-generation fathers whose actions concerning their estates can be determined by surviving
records, only 11 used their wills exclusively as their method of
distributing their entire landed estate among their sons, and an

additional 18 left at least some of their land to some of their sons by means of their will alone. Out of a total of 160 third-generation sons whose inheritances are known, only 30 (about 19 per cent) got land from their fathers by will alone, although an additional 17 sons got land from the intestate estates of their fathers, distributed to them by order of the probate courts. This meant that a total of 47 sons, or approximately 30 per cent, inherited land *after* the deaths of their fathers.

Significantly, 47 of these 58 estates had been transferred at least in part by deeds given to sons *before* their fathers' deaths. At least 57 third-generation sons were given their portions of paternal estates by deeds of gift from their fathers, and at least 35 sons purchased their portions of the paternal estate and received their land by deeds of sale. More than half of the sons whose portions are known thus received their land by deeds.

In the case of one-quarter of the families with more than two sons (13 out of 52), only one son was given the paternal land, indicative of an increased use of impartible inheritance as well. Out of a total of 214 third-generation sons, 139 are known to have received land from their fathers' estates (65 per cent) and 75 apparently did not (35 per cent). Those sons who did not receive land from their fathers usually received money, trades, or a liberal education, or a combination of these. The distribution of the estates of the second generation thus indicates that about three out of every four fathers still preferred to divide their land among as many of their sons as they could without doing harm to the productivity and value of their estates. Even so, only about two-thirds of their sons were able to inherit any land at all.

Unlike the first generation of settlers, the second generation generally lacked sufficient quantities of land to provide portions for all of their sons. This, undoubtedly, was to be a

factor of the utmost importance in reshaping the characteristics of the family and modifying the attitudes of fathers toward their land and toward at least some of their sons. The
control of the land by the older generation could have little
meaning for sons who were destined to be landless. But it did
have meaning to the majority who eventually inherited it.

The transference of paternal property to sons by means of
deeds rather than as inheritances after death indicates a certain
willingness to enable sons to establish their independence and
to obtain some control over their inherited property prior to
the deaths of the older generation. Prolonged control of the
land, which the first generation had sustained, was often relin-
quished sooner by the second, judging by the increased use of
deeds of gift conveying land from fathers to sons. Yet nearly
60 per cent of the third-generation sons were at least 30 years
old when they received deeds of gift for their portions of the
paternal estate from their fathers: the average age of fifty-
four sons at the time of the deeds of gift was about thirty-one
years.[4] Twenty-eight per cent of the sons received deeds
either before or within one year after their marriages; 54 per

---

[4] In modern Ashworthy, a similar period of delay is evident from
the fact that out of sixty men succeeding their fathers, "only
twenty-three" were "clear-cut examples of direct and full transference of control: the average age at which they took over is 31.3,
nearly four years later than the average age of marriage" (W. M.
Williams, *A West Country Village, Ashworthy: Family, Kinship
and Land* [London, 1963], p. 90). Williams noted: "It seems as if the
sons who remain at home can expect to wait for a few years longer
than their brothers before achieving full status as a farmer." He also
noted that "on the majority of farms, the transition appears to be a
protracted process, which may take as long as ten years or more.
This applies particularly to farm families where the parents remain
on the farm until they die, even when the holding is legally conveyed to a son long before the father's death, and on farms where
father and son are partners."

cent received deeds from their fathers between two and nine years following their marriages; and 18 per cent waited more than nine years for deeds to their land. For 72 per cent of the third-generation sons, then, there was some delay between marriage and full control of their portions of the paternal land.

Since deeds of gift often contained restrictive clauses or specific conditions which had to be fulfilled before the deeds became valid, the transference of part of an estate in this manner did not necessarily assure a son his full independence when he received his portion. Some fathers continued to exert some control over their property even after formally transferring it. The continuation of paternal control over the land remained a factor of the utmost importance in shaping the relationships within many Andover families during the lifetimes of the second and third generations. Patriarchalism was still the rule, however difficult it might be to maintain in practice. Whenever they could, fathers continued to exercise their influence over their sons by means of their control of the land which their sons needed. The delayed marriages and the delayed transferences of land from fathers to sons combined to demonstrate the continued power which many fathers could exert over the lives of at least some of their sons.

It is clear, however, that such control over sons was often either altogether impossible (particularly when sons took up a trade, followed a profession, or moved away) or very difficult. Also, even for those sons who settled in Andover upon paternal land, usually following the livelihood of husbandry, an increasing desire for, and an ability to achieve, complete economic autonomy during the lifetimes of the second generation was evident.

The most pointed indication of the desire for autonomy was the significant innovation of purchasing inheritances.

This involved the payment of substantial sums of money to fathers by sons in return for their portions of the paternal estate.[5] Although this had been done occasionally prior to 1720, the practice of transferring land from one generation to the next by means of deeds of sale increased appreciably thereafter, since 82 per cent of the deeds of sale to the third generation were written after 1720. Nearly three-quarters of the third-generation sons who purchased their portions from their fathers were either eldest or second sons. The average

[5] The practice of buying portions of parental estates is still characteristic of ranching families on the prairies of Canada and probably is still to be found among farmers elsewhere as well. A recent study of a Canadian agricultural community notes: "The reciprocal of this continuity of parental control was the aid given the new family of procreation. The most common form of succession is the purchase of the ranch in installments by the son, and terms are usually arranged so as to make it relatively easy for him to do so. In light of the steadily increasing value of land, acquisition of a ranch is usually impossible or very difficult without this type of arrangement. The 'bound-dependent' features associated with the takeover . . . are viewed locally as the price one must pay in order to obtain a ranch, and the young couple are expected to cope with it and not complain too much. As one young wife put it, 'Sure, I get mad at my father-and mother-in-law, but what can I do? . . . After all, without their help, we would never be where we are'" (Seena Kohl and John W. Bennett, "Kinship, Succession, and the Migration of Young People in A Canadian Agricultural Community," *International Journal of Comparative Sociology*, VI [1965], 104–105). Undoubtedly many of these same considerations underlay the willingness of Andover sons to purchase their shares of their fathers' estates, particularly in view of the rising value of land and its general scarcity in Andover. But as these Canadian families illustrate, sons were not freed of their parents' authority until their debts had been fully paid off. The same must have been true in Andover, although there is no direct evidence to confirm this supposition.

In Ireland, too, some farmers insist upon being paid by their sons for the land. See Conrad M. Arensberg and Solon T. Kimball, *Family and Community in Ireland* (1940; reprint ed., Gloucester, Mass., 1961), pp. 142–143.

age at marriage of twenty-nine sons who purchased their portions was 28.4 years, and the average age of thirty-nine sons at the time of the purchase of their lands from their fathers was 33 years, with their fathers being, on the average, about 67 years old. Forty-two per cent of the sons purchased their portions either before their marriages or within only one year after their marriages; four purchased their portions between two and four years after marriage, seven between five and nine years afterwards, and eight after ten or more years of marriage.

More often than not, the sons who purchased their shares of the paternal estate were mature men rather than youths just out of adolescence or in their early twenties. This is scarcely surprising since the prices they paid were often substantial, and many sons thus undoubtedly had to wait a considerable period of time before either acquiring cash of their own or being in a position to obtain a bond or mortgage to cover their debts to their fathers.[6] What is impressive, though, is the

[6] It is very difficult to determine how sons actually raised cash to pay their fathers, but a few indications are suggestive. Some, of course, signed a bond indebting them to their fathers or to someone else, thereby either making cash unnecessary or raising it from outside the family. James Ingals, Jr., for instance, signed a bond to his father for £1000 in return for his inheritance, although his father continued to reserve the right to use and improve the land during his own lifetime (Essex Deeds, vol. 51, p. 43). Joseph Chandler bought his inheritance of forty acres from his father for £100 in bills of credit on April 7, 1743 (Essex Deeds, vol. 88, p. 72), but died without having repaid his father. In 1745, at the time of his premature death at twenty-five, his estate was in debt "to Tho⁸ Chandler by bond due Principal & Interest," for £117, obviously money lent to him by his father (Administration of estate of Joseph Chandler, March 17, 1746, Essex County Probate Records, vol. 326, p. 243). During this period, others undoubtedly were turning to wealthy men like John Aslebee, James Frye, or Benjamin Stevens, all of them gentlemen in status, whose estates included substantial sums outstanding in bonds and notes from Andover men as well as people

willingness on the part of so many third-generation sons to pay for their own inheritances, thereby acquiring lands which otherwise undoubtedly would be theirs to inherit without cost eventually.

The acquisition of paternal land by deeds of sale reflects a fundamentally different attitude toward inheritances and toward father-son relationships than inheritances either by deeds of gift or by last testaments. More than anything else, it reflects the assumption that sons ought to become fully independent of their fathers while their fathers remained alive, even if this took a long time. What it does not usually reflect, however, is the willingness of fathers to see their sons fully independent upon land which they themselves once inherited and owned, often after considerable delays. It was still unusual to find fathers eager to establish their husbandmen sons independently as youths. But whatever the wishes of fathers in this matter, many sons discovered a way, however expensive it might prove to be, to establish their complete economic independence from their fathers. Even for some farmers, life was no longer the same as it had been before.

From another point of view, though, deeds of sale not only established sons who were independent of fathers, but also ensured that fathers, in their old age, would be independent of their sons. Hitherto, the prolongation of paternal control of the land and the restrictive clauses written into so many deeds

---

from many other towns. They obviously were underwriting the debts of many of their townsmen, including, no doubt, many of the sons who wished to buy their shares in their fathers' estates. See the following inventories: John Aslebee, 1728, with £1,504 in bonds and notes, PR 935; James Frye, 1734, who left £1339 in bonds and notes, PR 10296; and Benjamin Stevens, with £2327 in bonds and notes at interest in 1730, PR 26293. Husbandry must have been sufficiently profitable during this period to have enabled most men to pay off most of their debts, but it is extremely difficult to find this out.

of gift reflected, at least in part, the fears of the older generation that they might not be taken care of in their later years.
In view of the longevity of men and women during these
years, such worries were fully justifiable—quite apart from
any attitudes toward the proper authority of fathers and parents over their children. Since the problem of the aged continued to be largely in the hands of the family, the control
over the land often was one of the most potent means available to parents to sustain their authority over their sons. It
would be a mistake, however, to overemphasize the coercive
element in paternal control of the land, since the language of
the wills and deeds of the period convey affection and love
and remarkably little overt worry about undutiful, disrespect-
ful, or callous children. Yet, one way or another, the problem
of maintenance and care in old age presented itself to more
families than not. Most families still assured the care of the
older generation by means of wills and deeds of gift, and most
sons accepted their responsibilities as mature sons to care for,
and often to live with, their aged parents. But some, at least,
preferred not to do this; their purchasing of their portions
guaranteed that their filial obligations to their parents were
fulfilled by the payment of a sum of money instead of years of
service and care.

Often, though, sons who received the parental homestead as
their portion of their fathers' estates also received part of their
parents' houses and lived in them while their parents were still
alive, thus forming households which effectively consisted of
three generations under a single roof. A widow nearly always
was specifically bequeathed a room or rooms in her husband's
house and provisions to be given to her annually by one or
more of her sons. Sometimes both parents lived in the house
with their sons, as in the case of John Farnum, a husbandman
who died at eighty-three in 1723, having left his wife "y° use

of that Part of my House that I now Dwell in."[7] Generally, of course, married sons lived separately in houses of their own, but aged parents usually expected to share a house with one of their children. Extended households, for the most part, were the product of old age and the necessities for care and attention which elderly men and women obviously required. This was a duty which most third-generation sons, especially those who inherited their parents' own homesteads, accepted and fulfilled.

The permanent settlement of two-thirds of the third-generation sons in Andover augmented and solidified the kinship networks which had been established during the seventeenth century. The extended families established by the first generation were thus continued into the eighteenth century by the marriages and the residences of the majority of sons of most early families. For many, settlement upon paternal land in Andover sustained their close relationships with their parents, both in terms of the control and the use of the land, and in terms of the proximity of their residences to their parents and often to other siblings. Even sons who became fully independent of their parents economically—whether by virtue of trades or by their acquisition of complete control over their land—still continued to live in a community in which their parents, siblings, grandparents, uncles and aunts, and cousins also lived, thereby involving them constantly with people who were related to them by birth and marriage.[8] As the

[7] John Farnum, will, PR 9244. Nathaniel Dane, aged 80, also gave his wife the "Use of that End of my House wherein I now Dwell," in 1725 (will, PR 7120).

[8] The actual functioning of kinship networks is exceedingly difficult to reconstruct from the evidence which survives. Occasionally however, wills and deeds reveal some of the interconnections between members of extended families. Several of the sons of John Stevens (killed prematurely in 1689) would have led lives of poverty

second and third generations acquired their inheritances through the successive divisions of family land, members of families often lived upon adjacent parcels, their boundaries cutting across land which their fathers or grandfathers once had held undivided. Farming land often was bounded on one or more sides by the lands owned by brothers, cousins, or other kindred.[9]

Many members of families lived within reasonably short distances of each other, with family groups often concentrated together in particular areas of the town. The Abbots, Ballards, Blanchards, Chandlers, Holts, and Lovejoys, for instance, were largely concentrated in the South Parish, whereas

---

had two bachelor uncles not given them economic aid. One uncle gave twenty acres to one nephew and bequeathed his homestead land and buildings to another (see Nathan Stevens' will, February 17, 1718, PR 26407; Essex Deeds, vol. 31, p. 79; Samuel Stevens, inventory, May 15, 1718, Essex County Probate Records, vol. 312, p. 351 [photostat]). Another uncle left most of a substantial estate to be divided between two nephews (who were first cousins) rather to the wife whom he had married at the late age of fifty-nine; he also gave land in Haverhill to another nephew (see Benjamin Stevens, will, March 8, 1723, PR 26293; Essex Deeds, vol. 31, p. 19).

[9] Sometimes brothers and cousins acted in partnership in purchasing land, and perhaps even in farming it. Thomas and Benjamin Abbot, first cousins, were "Equal Copartners in the Severall parcells of Upland & Meadow" which they agreed to divide equally in 1724, eight years after Benjamin's marriage at the age of thirty (Essex Deeds, vol. 94, p. 134). In 1728, Thomas Abbot sold a tract of about twenty-five acres to two of his cousins, Benjamin and Samuel Abbot, "they being equal partners in the buying of the same" (Essex Deeds, vol. 94, p. 133; see vol. 93, p. 175 for another joint deed). Sons of John Abbot owned land jointly for periods of time, since one brother sold his share of a tract given to three brothers jointly, who had been "equal partners together" with their land remaining undivided seven years after their father's death (Essex Deeds, vol. 56, pp. 44–45). Generally, of course, brothers and cousins owned and farmed their land separately.

Table 12. Males on tax lists, by families,
1705–1730

Family	1705	1715	1720	1730
Abbot	16	19	23	23
Allen	2	1	1	1
Aslet	1	1	1	0
Ballard	6	5	5	6
Barker	9	13	14	15
Barnard	3	4	4	4
Blanchard	4	3	4	9
Bradstreet	1	0	0	0
Chandler	9	10	10	8
Dane	3	4	5	3
Farnum	6	7	10	12
Faulkner	2	7	5	4
Foster	4	8	10	10
Frye	5	7	7	9
Holt	9	15	13	15
Ingalls	6	6	7	7
Johnson	9	10	11	12
Lovejoy	6	7	11	14
Martin	1	0	3	3
Osgood	9	9	10	13
Parker	3	4	5	6
Poor	1	3	4	5
Russ	2	1	0	1
Russell	3	2	3	3
Stevens	9	11	13	15
Tyler	2	1	1	1
Total	131	158	180	199

the Barker, Farnum, Foster, Frye, Ingalls, Osgood, and Stevens families were concentrated in the North Parish. Some families obviously had been more prolific than others, with the result that more of them lived together in Andover (see Table 12). In 1705, for example, there were sixteen Abbot men taxed in Andover, mostly in the South Parish, and there were nineteen in 1715 and twenty-three in 1720 and in 1730. There were large groups of Chandlers, Farnums, Fosters, Holts, Johnsons, Osgoods, and Stevenses. Other families usually had between four and ten men residing in the town and paying taxes, and often they were connected by marriage and kinship to many other families in the town as well. A few families failed to flourish and died out, including the Bradstreets and Aslebees (or Aslets), or barely maintained the family name in the town, like the Russes, Allens, and Tylers.

With the maturing of the third generation, it was evident that Andover had come to resemble many Old World communities in which families had lived for several generations and formed complex extended family networks. These networks were based upon the continued residence of a family in the town in which they had been born, their marriages among other families within the town, and the extensive kinship ties which they had with many of the people and families living in their community. In large measure, the stability of Andover throughout the eighteenth century rested upon the intricate pattern of family ties and kinship connections, which wove the old established settler families into a complex and familiar social world and often served as the means of integrating outsiders who married into these families.

These generalizations, about both the families which were formed and the kinship networks which were sustained in early eighteenth-century Andover emerge from the discrete details of the actions and decisions of individual men responding to the needs and interests of their own particular families. As earlier with the first generation, it is by seeing precisely how fathers transferred their estates to their sons and how they managed to provide them with livelihoods and inheritances that the essential characteristics of family structure and of father-son relationships can be determined. The following reconstructions of actions preserved in the wills and deeds transferring property from the second to the third generation illustrate the complex variety of methods used and attitudes revealed in the establishment of the different forms of families in Andover during the early part of the eighteenth century.

For Deacon John Abbot's sons, independence came late. Although Deacon Abbot (1648–1721) sold some of his land to four of his sons during his lifetime, much of his estate was bequeathed to his sons by his last will and testament, signed May 16, 1716, five years before his death at the age of 73.[10] In February 1708, Deacon Abbot sold some upland and meadow to his three oldest sons jointly for the sum of £30 in ready money.[11] Ten years later, he sold some more upland and meadow to his oldest and his youngest sons.[12] The remainder of his land was transferred to his sons by will. The oldest of his six sons, John, Jr., who had married in 1703 at the age of 28, divided Deacon Abbot's homestead with the second son, Joseph, who was a bachelor of 44 at the time his father died. Joseph had probably continued to live with his father, farming the land with him in the expectation that half of it would be his to inherit eventually. The fact that he married the year after his father's death, at the advanced age of 45, suggests his prolonged dependence upon his father and continued residence with his parents. Because Deacon Abbot's estate did not suffice to provide land for all of his six sons, he purchased land for two sons' settlements and provided two others with inheritances in the form of money rather than land. The third son, Stephen, who married in 1708 at the age of 29, and Ebenezer, the youngest, who married in 1720 at the age of 30, both built houses and settled upon land in Andover which their father bought from the heirs of Hugh Stone, who had been hanged in 1690 for murdering his wife. Neither son received a deed for his land, however; both waited to inherit it, Stephen for thirteen years and Ebenezer for one. The old pattern continued with the significant difference that the land which they

[10] John Abbot, will, PR 66.
[11] Essex Deeds, vol. 23, pp. 10–11.
[12] Essex Deeds, vol. 74, pp. 247–248.

had been settled upon had been purchased for them by their father. The inheritances of the fourth and fifth sons also reflected the lack of land available to Deacon Abbot's family, since both received their portion of their father's estate in money. Ephriam, who married in 1715 at the age of 32, inherited the "forty pounds which he had Received allredy from me," his father noted, and Joshua, who moved to neighboring Billerica, where he married, inherited £45 from his father, all but £10 of which he had received before 1716. Deacon Abbot also made provisions for the care of his widow, obligating his two eldest sons to give their mother her choice of a room in the paternal house, suitable clothing, provisions, and "phisick and Tendance in case of sickness" for as long as she remained his widow. Not only was the inheritance of the land delayed but it also brought with it an obligation to care for the surviving parent.

In 1717, at the age of 73, Henry Holt transferred his land to his sons, as his father had done before, by deeds of gift. But he had maintained his control of the land for considerable periods after the marriages of seven of his eight sons, who married at the following ages: 27, 27, 30, 21, 31, 28, 23.[13] Four of the sons waited between seven and seventeen years after their marriages before receiving deeds of gift for their land. William, the seventh of the eight sons, was 30 years old and unmarried at the time he received a deed from his father, who, "Shewing a Fatherly Care towards him," gave William thirty acres of upland and meadow together with the house in which his two aged parents lived and the orchard.[14] In return for this deed of gift to the paternal house and homestead land, William was directed explicitly by the deed to "take y° Sole Care

[13] See the following Essex Deeds: vol. 35, pp. 135, 131–132, 130–131; vol. 34, pp. 253, 254–255; vol. 100, pp. 213–214.
[14] Essex Deeds, vol. 35, pp. 130–131.

of his Father Henry Holt and of his Naturall Mother Sarah Holt" for as long as both should live, and to provide them with a convenient room in the house, full provisions, and all other necessities for their complete care during their remaining years. If by any chance William were to fail in the "performance of any one Article aforementioned," his father ordered that the "whole premises" were to return to him. The deed of gift was hedged with onerous restrictions and obligations designed to provide for the maintenance of the couple in their old age; these served to prolong their control over their son, who lived with them, unmarried, throughout his lifetime.

Fathers sometimes retained the right to improve some of their land after transferring its ownership to their sons, thus limiting the independence of their sons and providing for their own maintenance in old age. Thomas Abbot, for instance, sold his homestead land and buildings to the oldest of his three sons for £120 in 1723 but reserved for himself the right to improve half of the land and to use half of the buildings during his lifetime.[15] Similarly, Ebenezer Barker, a carpenter, sold all of "my home liveing that I now live upon" and all of his other divisions of land in Andover to his second and youngest son, Philemon, a husbandman, but reserved "the power of the Improvement of every perticular dureing the time of my life." His son, 27 years old and unmarried when he bought this property in 1722, waited for two more years before marrying.[16] Nathaniel Dane gave his only son, who was unmarried at the age of 34 when given part of his portion

---

[15] Essex Deeds, vol. 57, pp. 142–143. His son was 24 at the time of the deed, marrying two years later. Three of his brothers later moved to Concord, N.H., and three died unmarried.

[16] Essex Deeds, vol. 39, pp. 209–210. His eldest son, also a carpenter, had married in 1711 at 23, buying four tracts of land in Andover from his father in 1722 (Essex Deeds, vol. 39, p. 159).

y deed in 1718, "y⁰ one half of my Homestead in Andover, y⁰ new house yᵗ stands upon said homestead," together ⱱith other lands.¹⁷ Two years after his son's marriage at the ge of 37, he gave him a second deed for the remainder of his ₁nds and meadows, reserving the right to improve it during ₁s lifetime.¹⁸ Since Nathaniel Dane was 73 in 1718, and 78 in '723, his reluctance to turn over the control of his property to ₁s only son is evident.

William Barker conveyed his own house and homestead ₁nd to the second of his six sons by a deed of gift, laden with ₂strictive clauses and conditions.¹⁹ Stephen, a shoemaker, was bachelor of 31 at the time he received a deed for his portion f his father's estate on February 24, 1714. Stephen's father ⱱrote that he was to receive "all my homestead housing and ₁ands that I now possess in Andover" and all stock and ₁usbandry tackling, half immediately and half after the death f his father and mother, provided that "he Shall cearfully & ₁ithfully manure & carry on my Whole Liveing yearly" ₁uring his parents' lifetimes and pay his father "one half of all ° graine of Every Sort that Shall Be produced . . . from y⁰ ₁ands yearly." In addition, his father retained the right to sell ₁ny part of his half of the land "for my Comfortable mainte-

¹⁷ Essex Deeds, vol. 40, p. 232.
¹⁸ Essex Deeds, vol. 45, p. 26.
¹⁹ Essex Deeds, vol. 33, pp. 124-125. Barker gave his third and fifth ₁ns a tract of land in neighboring Boxford as part of their portions. he third son never married, and the fifth son married in 1725 at the ge of 33 (Essex Deeds, vol. 40, p. 175). The fourth son also got a ₂ed of gift for land in Boxford in 1714; he married in 1721 at age 31 ₂Essex Deeds, vol. 45, pp. 144-145). In 1718, Barker's sons, "knowing ⱱhat parcells of Land our Honʳᵈ father had alloted to our youngest ₂rother Abiel Barker for his portion of his Estate" conveyed by ₂ed eighteen acres in Boxford bought by their father and twenty ₂res in Andover in four parcels, with half a common right not yet ₁id out (Essex Deeds, vol. 40, pp. 175-176).

nance if my Son Shall neglect or Refuse to performe ye Articles aforesaid," and included the provision that Stephen was to care for his mother during her widowhood. Stephen died a bachelor at the age of 38, still bound by the obligations incurred by this deed of gift.

Joseph Ballard gave deeds of gift to at least five of his seven sons in 1719 and 1720. The eldest son, Joseph, Jr., received a deed of gift for "That part of my homestead which he is now setled upon" and a six-acre common right as his full portion out of the paternal estate.[20] But this portion was not yet his own, since his father gave him only the use and improvement of the lands until his own son, Timothy, reached the age of 21, when he was to inherit them. Joseph had married in 1698 at the age of 31, and was 52 at the time of the deed. His brother, Hezekiah, a blacksmith, also married at the age of 31 and was 37 years old when he received a deed of gift for "That part of my Ancient Homestead which he is now Settled upon."[21] Uriah, the fifth son, married in 1712 at the age of 28 and waited until the age of 35 to receive a deed for the part of the great division land "which he is now Settled upon."[22] The two youngest Ballard sons, however, were given their portions of the paternal estate as young men before their marriages, and their land was mostly outside of Andover, in Windham, Connecticut.[23] They divided a hundred-acre lot owned by their father in Windham, and both married in 1721, the year after receiving their deeds of gift, at the ages of 24 and 22 years. Since their father was probably in his eighties, it is not surprising that they should have obtained their inheritances at relatively young ages. Their older broth-

[20] Essex Deeds, vol. 47, pp. 241–242.
[21] Essex Deeds, vol. 40, p. 173.
[22] Essex Deeds, vol. 39, p. 25.
[23] Essex Deeds, vol. 40, pp. 159–160.

ers had had to wait longer, and they married later. Settling on paternal land, with delayed control over their inheritances, most of these third-generation Ballards experienced life in much the same way as the previous generation had done.

Christopher Lovejoy, a 62-year-old husbandman, gave deeds of gift dividing his estate among two of his three sons in June 1724. His eldest son, Christopher, Jr., had married in 1718 at the age of 30 and waited six years before taking legal possession of the land which he had been settled upon by his father.[24] His brother, Jonathan, five years younger and also a husbandman, had married the year before but he, too, waited to receive a deed to his portion of the paternal estate.[25] Jonathan received all of the land and meadow which had not been conveyed to his brother by his father, with one important reservation. For the present, his father noted in the deed, Jonathan was to receive only half of the land promised, with the other half to become his after his father's death, "unless," he added, "through necessity I shall be forc'd to sell some part of the last half for my comfortable maintenance before I decease, and all the rest which I shall not so dispose of I give to my said son Jonathan." And, he added, "I promise to sell none unless necessity drives me to it."

By no means did all of the deeds of gift contain restrictions or delay the transference of property to the third generation. Some fathers gave sons deeds of gift either before or shortly

---

[24] Essex Deeds, vol. 51, pp. 219–220. At his death in 1732, Christopher, Jr., left a very small personal estate, valued about £45, of which only £5 was in cash in the form of bills of credit. No land was inventoried, however, despite the deed of gift from his father, and his house and barn were valued together at only £8. The principal value of his estate was in the form of notes and bonds worth £192, owed to him by various people. His own estate was indebted for only £3. See the inventory, April 3, 1732, PR 17051.

[25] Essex Deeds, vol. 84, pp. 124–125.

after their marriages, thus establishing them independently at relatively early ages. Ensign Samuel Frie, a gentleman, for instance, for "that Naturall Love and Parentall Affection which he hath" for his son, Samuel, a husbandman, gave him a dwelling house, barn, and other housing with about forty acres of land in Andover shortly before his marriage in 1719 at the age of 25.[26] Ebenezer Lovejoy, a husbandman, gave the second of his three sons, a joiner, a deed to the land which he dwelled upon and the buildings, with an additional fifteen acres, in 1723, nine months after his marriage at the age of 24.[27] The majority of sons, however, experienced more appreciable delays before receiving deeds of gift to their portions of paternal estates. Their independence often was thus postponed not only by their relatively late ages of marriage, but also by the additional delays in the transference of land from fathers to sons. Undoubtedly, such delays, and such frequent prolongation of obligations of sons to fathers encouraged third-generation sons to seek more effective means of ensuring their independence.

The practice of purchasing portions of second-generation estates by third-generation sons did not necessarily foster early independence, but it did guarantee complete legal autonomy and control over the land once a deed of sale had been completed between sons and fathers. Joseph Lovejoy, for instance, sold the western part of his homestead lands for £300 in hand in December 1731 to the oldest of his two sons, a joiner, who had married in 1718 at the age of 28.[28] His

---

[26] Essex Deeds, vol. 36, p. 33. His third "well beloved Son," Nathan, also received a deed of gift for the "houseing & Lands where he now Dwelleth" with additional land and meadow on February 11, 1719. Nathan had married in 1715 at 27, receiving his deed at age 31 (Essex Deeds, vol. 73, p. 34).

[27] Essex Deeds, vol. 94, p. 158.

[28] Essex Deeds, vol. 92, pp. 102–103.

second son, a husbandman but unmarried at the age of 32, purchased the eastern part of the paternal homestead on the same day for £500.[29] He did not marry until 1737, at the age of 38. Nathaniel Lovejoy gave a deed of gift in 1734 to the third of his four sons, Ezekiel, a blacksmith, but waited until December 1746, to sell his homestead land to his eldest son, Nathaniel, Jr.[30] Since Nathaniel, Jr., a yeoman, had waited until 1743 to marry at the late age of 44, he may be assumed to have farmed the land with his father for a large part of his life, delaying his independence longer than most of his contemporaries.

The autonomy and independence which usually were achieved after the purchase of a portion often contrasted sharply with the dependence and the obligations incurred by sons receiving their land by deeds of gift.[31] In several instances, sons who were given their portions initially by deeds of gift later preferred to buy them outright from their fathers and thus escape the obligations set forth in their initial deeds. The methods used in the transference of John Farnum's estate suggest the variations that were possible. Farnum, a yeoman and a wheelwright, gave a deed of gift to his second son, David, "of Boston," for twenty-four acres of land in Andover as his full portion out of his estate in December 1716.[32] David, undoubtedly a craftsman, had married in 1713 at the age of 23. The eldest son, John, Jr., a husbandman, received a deed

[29] Essex Deeds, vol. 92, pp. 105–106.
[30] Essex Deeds, vol. 91, pp. 86–87; vol. 90, p. 84.
[31] On March 13, 1734, for instance, Jonathan Blanchard gave land in Andover to his youngest son, Stephen, for the parental love which he felt and for the "many Good Services which he has Done Me in time past" (Essex Deeds, vol. 66, pp. 72–73). Stephen had married in 1724, age 21. In 1742, Jonathan sold Stephen land for £500 in hand and secured by bond (Essex Deeds, vol. 83, pp. 157–158).
[32] Essex Deeds, vol. 40, p. 238.

for the "Dwelling House & Barne where he now Dwelleth and all ye Land he has in possession" as his full portion out of the parental estate by a deed of gift in August 1717.[33] He had married in 1710 at the age of 26. The youngest son, James, was chosen to inherit the paternal homestead, for which he also received a deed of gift in August 1717. The homestead included all of his father's unbequeathed lands and meadows and the dwelling house and barns.[34] James was 26 and unmarried; he waited until 1722, aged 31, to marry. His deed of gift provided for his father to reserve the right to improve as much of the land as he wanted for his own maintenance during his lifetime, together with his continued use of half the house and barn. His father also reserved the right to sell or convey any of the land during his lifetime. The deed of gift was little more than a promise to give James this estate as an inheritance. The son remained closely tied to the father, working the land for their mutual benefit and always risking the sale of his inheritance by his father. Not until March 1728 did the full control of the land pass from father to son. John Farnum acknowledged in a deed of sale that he had received £500 current money "in hand well and truly paid before the ensealing and delivery hereof by my Son James Farnum," husbandman, in return for which James received all of the homestead land and buildings, together with all of the livestock, husbandry tackling, and household stuff.[35] James was 37 years old; his father was 64.

Similarly, Francis Dane, a husbandman, gave a deed of gift to John, the second of his three sons, in October 1722, conveying "the whole of the farm which I am Setled upon Commonly Called Mr Danes Great Division of Land" to-

[33] Essex Deeds, vol. 36, p. 223.
[34] Essex Deeds, vol. 36, pp. 225–226.
[35] Essex Deeds, vol. 48, p. 147.

gether with thirty additional acres and a common division right "being my s⁴ Sons present Homestead," and all the housing, stock, and tools belonging to the paternal estate.[36] John was 30 years old at the time of the deed, having married in 1713 at the age of 21. His father had settled him upon family land but waited before conveying it; even then, he retained the right to sell part of the upland and to improve and use half of all the premises during his lifetime. Fourteen years later, February 6, 1736, Francis Dane received £500 from his son, who was then 44 years old, for the land and buildings, stock and tools, which had been conveyed earlier by a deed of gift.[37] Full control over the land took a long time to obtain, and the cost was considerable.

The contrast in the experiences of Samuel Farnum's two sons is very suggestive of the motivations underlying the decisions and the needs of sons in purchasing their portions of the paternal estate. On March 9, 1731, Samuel Farnum, Sr., aged 66, sold his rights to his homestead and other lands to his two sons. His eldest son, Samuel, Jr., who had married less than two months earlier at the age of 29, purchased the western half of his father's homestead, together with all of the buildings and fencing on this land; he paid his father the substantial sum of £500 for his portion. His younger brother, David, purchased the eastern half of the paternal homestead for £500 on the same day.[38] He was only 23 years old, and unmarried. This probably accounts for the fact that he signed another deed the same day reselling his half of the homestead to his father for £500, with the significant provision that if he gave his father and mother "all things needfull & Convenient for their Maintenance & Subsistence in Sickness and health

[36] Essex Deeds, vol. 39, pp. 273–274.
[37] Essex Deeds, vol. 72, p. 80.
[38] Essex Deeds, vol. 55, pp. 219, 220.

during their Natural Lives & the Life of the Longest Liver of them" without either "Delay or Deceit," the deed of sale was to become void.[39] By this device, David eventually might expect to receive his part of the paternal homestead without cost. To a 23-year-old youth such a prospect must have been appealing, but time was to prove that the personal price was higher than he probably anticipated. Unlike his elder brother, who became fully independent shortly after his marriage, David never achieved real independence. Having obligated himself to care for his aging parents, he never married. His mother died in 1747 at the age of 70, and his father died in 1754 at the age of 89. No doubt Samuel, Jr., had cause to consider the £500 spent for his land—and his independence —a worthwhile expense.

A brief series of deeds from Thomas Chandler to his eldest son, Timothy, further illustrates the burdens of family obligations and the use of deeds of sale to establish the independence of some sons. On February 4, 1724, Chandler sold his 29-year-old unmarried son all of his divisions of land in Andover, his meadow, and all of his rights to a farm in Dracut, which had belonged to Timothy's grandfather. The following October, Thomas Chandler gave Timothy a deed of gift granting all of his homestead lands, orchards, and gardens, together with his dwelling house, barn, livestock, and tools—virtually his entire estate.[40] He chose to transfer his homestead to his eldest son "For and in Consideration of Several years good Service done me by my well beloved Son," and "also in Consideration of the Obligations which my sᵈ Son is to this

---

[39] Essex Deeds, vol. 55, p. 221.

[40] Essex Deeds, vol. 43, pp. 303, 304. This accounts for the fact that Thomas Chandler died intestate. As in the cases of many others, there was no need for a last testament, all or most of his estate having been distributed by deeds prior to death.

day by firm Bonds Brought under to provide for Mary my wife so long as she shall live my widow & to pay my four youngest Children . . . Several Sums in Bills of Credit, or current money of New England." The five oldest Chandler children after Timothy already had been granted their portions out of the paternal estate. Thomas Chandler reserved the right to use and to improve the land just conveyed during his lifetime (he was then 60 and lived for another thirteen years), as well as the right to use the west end of the house for himself and his wife. Less than one week later his son Timothy married, and the couple presumably moved into the east end of their father's house. Although technically Timothy had a deed to the house and land, he was not yet his own master as long as his father retained the privilege of farming the land and as long as he was bound to pay his brothers' and sisters' portions out of the paternal estate.

Three years passed before Timothy Chandler gained his full independence. On January 2, 1728, he purchased outright, for £600 current money, all of his father's homestead lands as well as other lands in Andover, together with his father's house, barn, orchard, and garden.[41] These lands and buildings were those which he had been "given" previously. The crucial difference now was that through the payment of money to his father, whether as cash or in a bond, he freed himself of all personal obligations to his father, who no longer retained any legal rights to his former estate, and to his siblings, whose inheritances he had been bound to pay. At the age of 33 and fairly recently married, Timothy was independent at last.

The desire for full autonomy in the use and possession of land by some third-generation sons complicated the patterns

[41] Essex Deeds, vol. 63, p. 156.

of relationships between farmers and their husbandmen sons. At the same time, the fact that many fathers had also established some of their sons in trades futher complicated the patterns of relationships between the generations. Craftsmen undoubtedly could be more independent of their fathers than many of their brothers whose livelihoods depended upon family land. And trades were obviously one of the principal means which could be used by fathers to forestall the excessive parceling of their land, thereby actually augmenting their authority over some sons. At least 21 per cent, and probably more than 25 per cent, of the third generation followed a trade or craft during at least some portion of their lifetimes, although some did eventually become husbandmen as well. At least fourteen different occupations were pursued by sixty third-generation Andover men: fourteen were shoemakers, seven blacksmiths, seven joiners, six carpenters, six weavers, four tailors, three housewrights, three tanners, two millers, two saddlers, two glaziers, one mason, one clothier, and one wheelwright. Surprisingly enough, only one man appears to have been called a laborer. It is likely, though, that at least some men did work as hired hands during this period since there are others who are described as laborers in Andover during the first half of the eighteenth century.

Since in many families some sons were apprenticed to trades and some were prepared to take over the farming of paternal land, the relationships between fathers and sons must have varied considerably. As a general rule, however, sons with trades were more likely to establish their personal autonomy more readily than sons who became farmers, although many sons with trades also waited a long time to marry and even craftsmen sometimes built houses upon paternal land and waited for considerable periods before receiving titles. And as long as they remained in Andover they continued to live in close proximity to parents and siblings as well as other kindred. Their independence from paternal oversight and control was probably more often a matter of degree than of kind in comparison to their brothers who farmed. Although their ties to their families might have been looser than those of some of their siblings, these family ties undoubtedly remained an ever-present factor in their lives. Residence in Andover assured that.

The most drastic changes in the character of family life and in the nature of the relationships between the generations were experienced not by those who remained in Andover but by those who left. For all of the innovations in behavior and attitudes evident in the lives and actions of families in Andover during this period, and for all the complexities in the shapes and characteristics of their families, it is clear nevertheless that the most radically different experiences were those encountered by men and women who emigrated and resettled in other towns. The many third-generation sons who chose to migrate—leaving behind parents and kindred, leaving the community in which they had been born and raised and which had grown familiar by long experience, voluntarily moving to places where most of the people they would encounter were strangers, often living in new towns and upon new lands—these sons achieved a degree of autonomy that was impossible for those who remained in Andover. By their actions, they added yet another dimension to many Andover families.[42]

[42] The differences between the lives of people who remained settled in towns like Andover and those who left have yet to receive the attention they deserve. Indeed, the entire question of the effects of geographical mobility upon the family warrants extensive study. Richard L. Bushman's study of Connecticut provides some suggestive observations on the general subject of mobility and the psychological implications which it had for people in the eighteenth

Underlying the uprooting of so many third-generation Andover men were both economic factors and the more elusive psychological factors which traditionally have complicated the decisions of men to move. The economic motives are the most readily discernible, owing to the nature of the evidence which has survived. The limitations upon the estates possessed by most second-generation fathers, their inability to provide land for all of their sons, the less obvious but very important fact that sons could not expect to make a decent living by working as laborers and therefore were dependent upon either land or trades for livelihoods: all these factors served to limit the prospects of many of the third-generation sons who were raised to maturity in Andover.

At the time they were reaching maturity, however, many new towns and new areas began to be opened up in Massachusetts, Connecticut, and New Hampshire, thereby providing them with both land and opportunities if they were willing to move away to gain them.[43] At the time that land values in Andover were beginning to rise steeply, land was available for very little money elsewhere. In New Hampshire, for instance, land values during the 1720's and 1730's were low, adding the

century (*From Puritan to Yankee: Character and the Social Order in Connecticut, 1690-1765* [Cambridge, Mass., 1967], esp. ch. 4). The fascinating study of families in modern London by Michael Young and Peter Willmott illustrates the radical differences in the lives of the rooted and the uprooted: (*Family and Kinship in East London* [London, 1957]).

[43] The destinations of eighty-five third-generation Andover men are known, thus providing a guide to the movements of the migrants as a whole. In time, Andover men of this generation resettled in at least twenty-two towns in Massachusetts, eight towns in Connecticut, and eight towns in New Hampshire. Two men moved all the way to Pennsylvania. Thirty-two (37.6 per cent) settled in Massachusetts, twenty-seven (31.8 per cent) in Connecticut, and twenty-one (24.7 per cent) in New Hampshire.

attraction of low cost to ready availability for those willing to undertake the risks and hardships of pioneering and beginning farms of their own, just as their grandfathers had done earlier.[44] The economic inducements of new towns—cheap and abundant land—were sufficiently powerful to attract many third-generation Andover men who emigrated to Connecticut, to western Massachusetts, and later to New Hampshire. But decisions to move were not the result solely of economic considerations, important though they undoubtedly were. Other, more personal, considerations and motivations must also have played a role. Families no doubt differed in their feelings for each other, with some fathers and sons remaining on closer terms than others, with some sons willing to accept their fathers' control over the land in return for the land itself. Many men obviously preferred to remain in Andover despite a relative decline in their economic positions. A preference for family and for friends, a need for rootedness, perhaps inertia, too, were powerful forces maintaining the families of Andover. Often they could stay because others were willing to leave, and many families had sons who stayed and sons who went away. We can only surmise what personal feelings and choices entered into these very different decisions.

Families varied even in the way in which they emigrated: some evidently chose to isolate themselves altogether from kindred, settling in towns in which they were alone and

[44] Some people joined as proprietors in various New Hampshire towns; others bought land there relatively cheaply. Wilderness land during the first two-thirds of the eighteenth century generally cost about two shillings an acre and rarely as much as £1 even during the period of inflation. Improved land was more expensive, of course, but in general it was appreciably less than land in Andover. As many New Hampshire farmers were to learn, though, much of the land there was rocky and difficult to farm.

without other members of their families to fall back upon for assistance or friendship; others clearly chose to settle in places where they had members of their families living also, maintaining some degree of family connection both in their new communities and with their families remaining in Andover. But whatever the circumstances of their emigration, those who departed invariably led lives and created families which differed markedly from those who stayed in Andover.

For many families, lack of land and the prospect of poverty for the third generation were powerful agents in scattering sons to other communities.[45] The dispersal of five of George Abbot's six sons is suggestive. Abbot, the eldest of four second-generation sons of George, Sr., a tailor, followed his father's trade and settled on the sixteen acres of land which his father had given him before his death.[46] Lacking sufficient land for his own sons, he settled them in trades instead, facilitating their decisions later to move. Only the second of the six sons remained in Andover permanently. Uriah Abbot, a shoemaker, was unmarried at the age of thirty-one in October 1723 when he received a deed from his father for a new dwelling house and barn with several parcels of land.[47] The

[45] See Grant, *Kent*, pp. 98–103, and Lockridge, "Land, Population and the Evolution of New England Society," pp. 69–74.

[46] See the agreement on the division of George Abbot's estate, January 20, 1690, in Essex County Court Papers, vol. 48, p. 72. The second son, John, inherited the homestead, which he later sold in 1696, and moved to Sudbury, where he bought a house and eighty acres. His brother, Samuel, who received £70 from the paternal estate, joined him there. See Lemuel Abijah Abbott, *Descendants of George Abbott, of Rowley, Mass. . . .* (n.p., 1906), pp. 15, 54. Despite the common name, this Abbot family evidently had no kinship connection with that of George Abbot, of Roxbury, whose family in time formed one of the largest and most influential kinship groups in Andover.

[47] Essex Deeds, vol. 44, p. 172.

ollowing March, with a house and some land of his own, he
narried, inheriting "the whole and every part" of his father's
·eal and personal estate and accepting the responsibility of
:aring for his widowed mother.[48]

His brothers, in contrast, had received their portions of the
:state in money, and their livelihoods were their trades. The
:ldest of the sons, George, Jr., a blacksmith, purchased half an
ιcre of land in Cambridge in 1715 and lived there for the next
:en years. In December 1725, he sold his lot, with the house,
)arn, and blacksmith shop, and moved again with his wife and
:amily to Framingham.[49] In 1733, he acquired about 100 acres
ιs a proprietor in Hardwick, Massachusetts, near Brookfield,
where three of his brothers and two of his sisters had settled.[50]
Jacob, the third of the brothers, purchased sixty acres of land
n West Brookfield early in 1722, having settled there in 1720
ιs a carpenter. He appears eventually to have become a man
'of wealth, standing, and influence" in this community. Also
n 1722, Jacob's younger brother, Moses, a joiner, bought a
)arcel of land in Brookfield and settled, followed by their
)rother, Peter, who purchased eighty acres for £60 in 1725.
The remaining brother, Obed, a weaver, preferred to settle in
Salem initially, but in 1725 he moved to Billerica, where he
)ought about sixty-three acres of land and a house.[51] Only one
:hird-generation son remained in Andover to perpetuate this
)ranch of the family, although three brothers had resettled
:ogether in Brookfield.

Like their cousins, three of Deacon Nehemiah Abbot's five
sons also migrated from Andover and scattered to various

[48] George Abbot, will, October 1, 1724, PR 45.
[49] Abbott, *Descendants of George Abbott*, p. 70.
[50] Lucius R. Paige, *History of Hardwick, Mass.* . . . (Boston,
1883), pp. 36, 225–229.
[51] Abbott, *Descendants of George Abbott*, pp. 51, 84, 86, 76.

towns. Although Deacon Abbot had received 80 acres out of the original family estate in Andover in 1690—considerably more than his elder brother—he did not have enough land for more than two of his sons. His three tradesman sons departed from Andover. The eldest, Nehemiah, Jr., a shoemaker, bought about 64 acres of land with a house in Weston on May 11, 1714. He was then twenty-two and a bachelor. The following November, he married Sarah Foster of Andover and lived with his wife in Weston until about 1720, when he sold his property and purchased about 100 acres with a house in Lexington, where he resettled. In 1756, he sold his homestead of about 200 acres to his son; he had risen in status to a gentleman and had become an active participant in political affairs in his new town and a deacon of the church. The second son, Abiel, a carpenter, also left Andover as a young unmarried man and moved to East Windsor, Connecticut. He married at twenty-five and purchased land from his mother-in-law in 1720, to which he added until he became "one of the wealthiest, if not the wealthiest person there," with a homestead farm of 170 acres. He, too, participated actively in town and church affairs, and continued to reside in East Windsor until his death in 1758. The fourth son, John, settled as a young man in Tolland, Connecticut, where he purchased some land in 1720 and practiced his trade as a blacksmith. He married in Tolland at the age of twenty-two and died there at the age of eighty-one.[52] With three of the five sons gone before 1720, the third son, Zebadiah, remained in Andover as a husbandman and the prospective inheritor of the paternal estate. He did not marry until 1728, aged thirty-three, however, and it was not until October 15, 1747, that his eighty-year-old father sold him, for £1,000 by bond, all of his lands, mead-

[52] Abbott, *Descendants of George Abbott*, pp. 101–102, 138–139, 156.

ows, and buildings in Andover, containing a homestead of about 130 acres.[53]

The contrast between Zebadiah's life and the lives of his more independent brothers is a striking indication of the complexities of family life and of experiences characteristic of the third generation. His decision to remain left him dependent upon his father for family land to farm, a dependence which was reflected both in the late age at which he married and in the delayed acquisition of his farm. His brothers, by contrast, married young and quickly gained land for themselves; they were autonomous, distant, and cut off from kindred. Many of the emigrants had similar experiences, chosing to resettle in towns without other members of their families and often finding that their removal from Andover paid handsome economic rewards.[54] And in view of their frequent successes elsewhere, the most surprising thing of all is that more Andover men did not leave.

[53] His younger brother died in 1725 at the age of twenty-one, leaving him alone with his father in Andover. See Essex Deeds, vol. 96, p. 212, and Zebadiah Abbot's will, April 21, 1767, PR 157. No inventory is extant.

[54] Robert Barnard, for instance, the youngest of five sons and probably a craftsman, married in 1710 at the age of only twenty-one but remained in Andover until 1723, when he bought a house, a corn mill, and about 350 acres of land in Marlborough, Mass.; (Charles Hudson, *History of the Town of Marlborough* . . . [Boston, 1862], pp. 279, 313). His oldest brother, Stephen, had worked in Andover as the Reverend Thomas Barnard's "man." Similarly, Josiah Johnson, also the fifth and youngest son, a carpenter, married in 1711 at twenty-eight and later moved to Lancaster, Mass., in 1725. Two years after resettlement he died at the age of forty-four, leaving about 184 acres and buildings valued at £746, a substantial estate for this period. Both men obviously gained by their moves. (William W. Johnson, *Johnson Genealogy: Records of the Descendants of John Johnson of Ipswich and Andover, Mass., 1635–1892* [North Greenfield, Wis., 1892], pp. 15, 17).

The complete independence and the willing isolation from all members of their families characteristic of some emigrants were probably the exceptions rather than the rule among those who left Andover during the first three decades of the eighteenth century. More common, and more readily understandable, was the departure from Andover and the resettlement in other towns in the company of or preceded by other kindred and former neighbors from Andover itself.[55] The extension of kinship ties into new communities formed an important characteristic of emigration from Andover to other towns in Massachusetts, but even more to towns in Windham County, Connecticut, and Concord, New Hampshire. For many third-generation men and women, the arduous experience of resettlement and the traumas of removal were mitigated to some extent by the presence, and no doubt by the assistance, of brothers, sisters, cousins, and friends. Like their grandfathers before them, they tended to resettle in communities in which personal ties and kinship influenced their decisions in choosing one community rather than another and tempered the isolation inherent in the re-establishment of families and of roots in new communities.

The choice of Windham County, Connecticut, as a place of settlement by a number of Andover families during the first two decades of the eighteenth century was not accidental. Not only were inhabitants of other towns in Massachusetts removing their families to the northeastern part of the neighboring colony, but Andover also had an early tie through the

---

[55] For similar movements by families and groups, see Grant, *Kent*, pp. 16–18; Grant noted (p. 18) that "Kent was formed from several fragments," but that "once in Kent, the fragments tended to coalesce into a single social unit not unlike those of earlier times." See also Robert W. Ramsey, *Carolina Cradle: Settlement of the Northwest Carolina Frontier, 1747–1762* (Chapel Hill, 1964).

kindred of the Chandler family, one branch of which had remained in Roxbury after two of the Chandlers had settled in Andover during the 1640's.[56] The town of Woodstock, the earliest of the Windham County towns to be settled, was begun by a group of settlers from Roxbury, including John Chandler, who quickly became one of the leading inhabitants of the new community. This position was perpetuated in the second generation by John Chandler, Jr., an immensely wealthy landowner and magistrate in Windham County. The close connections between the Andover Chandlers and the Woodstock Chandlers is indicated by the decision of Philemon Chandler, a weaver and a second-generation Andover man, to migrate to Windham County in 1699. He was the first from Andover to arrive. Although he settled initially in Woodstock, a town dominated by his uncle, he resettled permanently in neighboring Pomfret.[57] Perhaps it was Philemon who sent word to his kindred and acquaintances in Andover telling of the abundant wilderness land available in Windham County.

Other Andover men were slow to follow, but by the early 1720's at least twenty-one members of five Andover families had migrated to Windham County, including seven Abbots, six Holts, three Prestons (relatives of the Holts), three Farnums, and two Ingallses, as well as individuals from other families.[58] The Abbots and the Holts, especially, moved to-

[56] For details pertaining to the Roxbury settlement, see Ellen D. Larned, *History of Windham County, Connecticut* (Worcester, Mass., 1874–1880), I, 18–63.

[57] See the deed, dated January 6, 1699, from Philemon to his brother William, of Andover, selling all his rights to the paternal estate for £40, in Essex Deeds, vol. 53, p. 60.

[58] For a discussion of the settlement of Windham, see Larned, *Windham*, I, 69–105; Larned noted the presence of some of these Andover families. In addition to those mentioned above, John Allen,

gether in family groups, resettling often in towns in Connecticut where other members of their families also were. Their experiences both prior to their departures from Andover and after their migrations elsewhere illustrate the persistence of family ties despite the disruptions of emigration.

Since all of the second-generation Holts had been settled upon land in Andover granted to their father, Nicholas, the inheritances of the third-generation sons were still dependent in large measure upon the distribution of the family land, which, not surprisingly, proved insufficient for their needs. For the Holts who remained in Andover, family ties were strengthened by the residences which they had established on neighboring farms, all of which were located in the South Parish. Eventually, however, seven out of the twenty third-generation sons (35 per cent) moved away from Andover to new communities, with six of the seven resettling in Windham County and remaining reasonably close together.

The first of the third-generation Holts to depart from Andover—and the only one who did not either migrate in the company of relatives or move to a town where relatives were already settled—was the younger of James Holt's two sons. Their father's premature death at the age of forty in 1690 left an estate too small to be divided profitably between the two young brothers.[59] The eldest, who stayed and married in 1705 at twenty-three, eventually bought all of his younger brother's rights to their father's land and meadow in Andover for

---

Humphrey Ballard, Caleb Johnson, John Lovejoy, Joseph Wright, and Thomas Grow, from Andover, also settled. Thomas Grow, born in Ipswich where his father had long been a resident, married Rebecca Holt in Andover in 1710.

[59] James Holt's real estate was valued at only £150, and his personal estate at about £80. He died intestate. See inventory, March 23, 1691, PR 13647.

£70, in 1712.[60] His younger brother, already a resident of
York, Maine, later moved to Reading, Massachusetts, border-
ing upon Andover, married (at the age of forty), and settled
permanently.[61] The two brothers thus eventually took up
residence within easy distance of each other.

The decisions made later by other members of the Holt
family to remove to Windham County may have been influenced by the fact that an uncle by marriage, John Preston,
had already settled there.[62] Preston, whose mother had become
the third wife of the elder Nicholas Holt in 1666, married the
widow of his own stepbrother in 1687 and resided with his
family in Andover until about 1709, when he became a proprietor at Killingly, in Windham County, and disappeared
from Andover. Preston's daughter, Rebecca, married her first
cousin and remained behind in Andover. In 1718, she remar-
ried, to Robert Holt, the fourth of Nicholas Holt II's seven
sons, and moved with him to Windham before 1722. The
connections between the Prestons and the Holts, both in
Andover and in Connecticut, were further strengthened in
1727, when the youngest daughter of Nicholas Holt married

---

[60] Essex Deeds, vol. 32, p. 83.

[61] Daniel S. Durrie, *A Genealogical History of the Holt Family in
the United States* . . . (Albany, N.Y., 1864), pp. 16, 27.

[62] This is based upon inference from Larned's inclusion of a John
Preston among the proprietors of Killingly, Conn., whose land was
granted in 1709 (*Windham*, I, 166). Since Preston disappeared from
the Andover tax lists at this time, the identity of the two Prestons
seems certain. For the genealogical details on the Holts' and Prestons'
marriages, see *Vital Records*, II, *passim*. For further details, see
Durrie, *Holt Family*, *passim*. The history of the numerous Abbot
families during this generation is similar to that of the Holts, with
twelve of thirty-three third-generation Abbot sons (36.4 per cent)
emigrating from Andover. At least one son left in all but one of the
second-generation Abbot families.

Benjamin Preston, of Windham, whose grandfather, Samuel Preston, still resided in Andover.

The Holts who migrated also maintained close connections to their families in Andover, as their marriages indicate. Abiel Holt, the fifth of Nicholas II's sons, was a resident of Windham in 1722 when he declared his intention to marry Hannah Abbot, of Andover. And his brother, Joshua, was also a resident of Windham in 1725 when he announced his intention to marry his first cousin, Keturah Holt, of Andover. Even Robert Holt returned to Andover for a second wife in 1727. The decisions by four of Nicholas Holt II's seven sons to migrate to Windham thus did not negate their sense of family connections or their ties to the community in which they had been born and raised.

Their migrations were necessary because their father's estate was insufficient to provide them with either the land or the inheritances which would have permitted them to remain comfortably established in Andover. Of the three second-generation Holts surviving beyond 1690, Nicholas was the poorest, ranking 109th among the town taxpayers in 1695; his brothers were 45th and 3rd in rank. His relative poverty, combined with his large family, made it impossible to keep more than three of his sons in Andover. His two oldest sons remained, settling upon paternal land and marrying in 1708, aged 25 and 22; the third son died in Andover unmarried at 29 in 1722.[63] The younger sons received no land but probably

[63] When Nicholas Holt died in 1756 he left 115 acres of land in Andover, most of which he had acquired by purchase during his lifetime, and a lot in Suncook, N.H. Most of his seven sons received money and trades and only one inherited his land (Nicholas Holt, inventory, January 5, 1757; will, December 29, 1752; both in PR 13680). His brother, Thomas, who died in 1767, gave his entire lands to his eldest son, and money and trades to the three other sons (Thomas Holt, will, February 11, 1760, PR 13698).

received their portions of the paternal estate in cash, which assisted them in migrating to Windham, where land could be purchased for relatively little. None left Andover, however, before the death of their father in 1715.[64]

In many respects, the families of two Farnum brothers, Ralph (1662–1737) and Ephriam (1676–1744), were comparable to Nicholas Holt's family. Both Farnums had more sons than any of their four other brothers, and both of their families were characterized by the dispersion of nearly all of their sons to other towns and colonies. Two of Ralph Farnum's seven sons moved to York, Maine, about 1712; at least three and perhaps four of his sons, including his eldest and young-

[64] Similarly, two of the eight sons of Henry Holt also immigrated to Windham after their father's death. Paul, the sixth son, sold his portion of the paternal estate to his brother, Henry, before departing for Windham (Essex Deeds, vol. 72, p. 23). He later resettled permanently in Hampton, Conn. In 1727, his older brother, George, sold his Andover property, consisting of about fifty acres of land and buildings, to his nephew by marriage, Peter Russell (Essex Deeds, vol. 53, p. 5). George Holt was then fifty years old, with five sons, the oldest of whom was then twenty-seven years old and unmarried. It is not surprising that Holt, with so little land of his own, was willing to move with his mature sons to a town where they could acquire more abundant lands.

Ramsey notes that "movement of families often occurred immediately after the death of the father or family patriarch." He also comments: "In some cases, this was evidence of filial affection; in others, it sprang from necessity, for the father customarily disposed of his lands among his faithful sons. Only by remaining until after probation of the will or other disposal of the estate could the sons obtain the shillings necessary for the acquisition of cheaper land to the south. There can be no doubt that the patriarchal position of the father in colonial America was a powerful controlling factor in the westward—and southward—movement of population" (*Carolina Cradle*, pp. 21–22). Although it is describing the emigration of people from Pennsylvania and the Cheasapeake regions, this statement could also apply to Andover in many instances. Unfortunately, Ramsey fails to pursue this important observation in his study.

est, moved to Windham, and another son eventually moved to Concord, New Hampshire, where a number of first cousins also settled. Ralph Farnum gave at least two of his sons deeds of gift for their portions of his estate in Andover shortly after their marriages. Henry, a weaver, married in December 1712 at the age of twenty-five and received a deed for twenty acres near his parent's dwelling house six months later.[65] He continued to live in Andover until about 1725, when he moved with his family to Windham, where several of his brothers already lived. The fourth son, William, had become a proprietor in Ashford, Connecticut in 1718, but subsequently established his residence in Canada Parish of Windham, where his brothers joined him.[66] In 1721, after three of his sons had departed from Andover, Ralph Farnum deeded his own homestead land and buildings to his sixth son, Barachias, a housewright, who was then twenty-four and unmarried.[67] Barachias waited three more years before marrying, carrying on the farm with his father, who continued to pay the town rates. By 1729, Barachias was considering a move to New Hampshire, since he joined in signing a petition requesting a tract of land above Pennycook on the Merrimack River.[68] About 1736, he moved to Concord, taking with him his seventy-five-year-old widowed father. In 1745, when Barachias sold his Concord

[65] Essex Deeds, vol. 28, pp. 282–283. For genealogical details concerning the Farnums, see Charlotte Helen Abbott's Farnum family genealogy, in the Memorial Library, Andover. The fifth son, Nathaniel, a husbandman, also received a deed of gift for part of the paternal homestead in 1721, only eight months after his marriage at the age of twenty-five (Essex Deeds, vol. 38, p. 235). He, too, later moved to Windham.

[66] Larned, *Windham*, I, pp. 98–99, 223.

[67] Essex Deeds, vol. 42, pp. 137–138.

[68] MS petition for land above Pennycook, 1729, in Concord Miscellaneous Papers, New Hampshire Historical Society, Concord, N.H.

homestead, he had acquired 190 acres, far more than he had owned in Andover.[69] Economically, the migration north to Concord had been advantageous, and personally, it undoubtedly had been made easier by the fact that Barachias was moving to a new community in which he already had many relatives. All but one of his uncle Ephriam's six sons had settled in Concord, and his sister, who had married James Abbot, also lived there. Like the Holts and Farnums in Connecticut, the Farnums in New Hampshire reconstituted a small kinship group as well.

The oldest of Ephriam Farnum's sons, Ephriam, Jr., had been among the original proprietors of Concord, receiving a house lot and land in the division of 1726, two years before his marriage at the age of twenty-eight. By 1731, he had built a house there and was residing in the new community, followed soon by his brothers James and Zebadiah.[70] Later during the 1730's, his two youngest brothers also moved to Concord, leaving only the second son, Timothy, a joiner and wheelwright, to inherit their father's estate in Andover. On December 20, 1726, not long after Ephriam had drawn his lot in Concord, Timothy received a tract of twenty-five acres in Andover from his father, which he may have settled upon two years later when he married at twenty-five.[71] He was the only member of his immediate family to stay in Andover. The rest preferred to undergo the labors and hardships of migration in return for the rewards which could reasonably be anticipated.

[69] His mother, Sarah Farnum, died in Andover in 1732, and Barachias appeared on the Concord tax list October 27, 1737 (Concord Miscellaneous Papers). See also New Hampshire Deeds, vol. 35, p. 190, in the New Hampshire Historical Society.

[70] Nathaniel Bouton, *The History of Concord* . . . (Concord, N.H., 1856), pp. 79, 123, 129.

[71] Essex Deeds, vol. 97, p. 107.

The settlement of Concord, New Hampshire, reflected the fact that by the mid-1720's the migrations of Andover men to Connecticut were nearly over. Attention turned to the empty lands to the north in the neighboring province. In contrast to the migrations of Andover men to Windham County—where most had gone either alone or with their families but without any direct assistance from their townsmen or from the government—the settlement of Andover men in Concord resulted from a carefully planned, carefully regulated, and skillfully organized communal effort for the creation of a new plantation in the wilderness. On May 31, 1721, a petition signed by 119 men, at least 46 of whom were from Andover, declared that "being straitned for Accomodations for themselves and their posterity," they had "Espied a tract of Land, scituate on the River Merrymake" upon which they were "desirous to make a Settlement and form a town."[72] The inaction of the General Court at this time probably encouraged some Andover men to settle in Connecticut, where towns had been established and new land was still readily available, rather than to await further developments for the northern frontier. Four years passed before the General Court granted the second petition, submitted June 17, 1725, for land at Pennycook, as Concord was first called. Thirty-two men from Andover were chosen to be among the original proprietors, together with twenty-seven men from Haverhill, nine from Newbury, seven from Bradford, and others from Salisbury, Woburn, and Chelmsford.[73] Nearly 60 per cent of the proprietors thus

[72] For a detailed narrative of the origins and settlement of Concord, see Bouton, *Concord*, pp. 52–121, and for a transcription of the proprietors' records, containing minutes of all meetings and actions of the group from 1725 to 1737, see pp. 57–121.

[73] See Bouton, *Concord*, pp. 67–68, for a list of settlers, and pp. 122–128 for details of their lands in Concord. Foremost among the leaders of the enterprise and acknowledged to be "some of the

chosen came from only two towns—Andover and Haverhill —which had been closely associated from the time of their original settlements in the early 1640's. With so many kindred and neighbors from Andover settling together, and with Abbots, Barkers, Chandlers, Fosters, Lovejoys, Osgoods, Parkers, and Stevenses representing some of the old and leading families of Andover in the new community, the new plantation in New Hampshire might well be considered an extension of Andover, an offshoot on the frontier. With the settlement of some of the third generation, and more of the fourth generation, in the new plantation, a cycle of development was about to begin again.

By the end of the third decade of the eighteenth century, the diverse experiences of the offspring of Andover's second-generation families had created an astonishing variety of family forms, corresponding to the many different experiences and decisions which had shaped their lives. Structurally, the families established by the maturing of the third generation ranged from extreme extension to isolated nuclearity, with households varying in their composition as well. In many instances, the kinship network established by the previous generation, the prolonged control over the land, and the persistence of patriarchal authority over sons continued to characterize families, and many sons remained under the domination of their fathers long after reaching maturity. Some families were still able to establish all or most of their sons upon family land in Andover and to assure that the families would remain closely knit and interdependent. Others, however, found it impossible to provide land for all sons, and chose instead to treat their sons in various ways, some receiv-

principal inhabitants" of Andover were Captain Benjamin Stevens, John Osgood, and John Chandler, whose roles testified to the persistent influence of their families in Andover's affairs.

ing paternal land and often remaining closely tied to their parents, others being established in trades, with apparent loosening in the economic bonds binding them to their parents, and some being encouraged or assisted to emigrate, thereby minimizing their connections to parents and siblings when they did not sunder them altogether. Even for many sons who remained in Andover, settled upon paternal land, an increasing desire for economic autonomy and personal independence was evident and acceded to by their fathers. But this tendency was not yet very strong, and the impressive fact continued to be the degree to which fathers and sons in Andover remained so closely related, even during the period of the 1720's and 1730's when so many sons were emigrating from the town. The extraordinary complexity of family forms and family relationships belies any simple generalization about the family in Andover during this period.

PART III

❧⁓

THE THIRD AND FOURTH
GENERATIONS

7

Change and Decline: Population and Families in a Provincial Town

Beginning about 1720 and lasting until about the beginning of the Revolution in the mid-1770's—a period which corresponded with the emergence upon the local scene of the fourth generation—many changes occurred in basic aspects of demographic and familial experiences. The demographic generalizations established for earlier generations and periods do not continue to hold true: significant differences are evident in birth rates, fertility rates, mortality rates, sizes of families, ages of marriage, and rates of emigration. Throughout the mid-eighteenth century, demographic changes fostered or accompanied other significant changes in the attitudes and in the patterns of behavior of many of the community's inhabitants, especially those affecting the relationships of fathers and sons and patterns of inheritance, which will be examined in the following chapter. What did not change significantly, however, and what continued to provide many of Andover's inhabitants with a sense of connectedness with their community and of continuity with their own pasts was the presence of numerous kindred and the extended structure of their families. During a period of appreciable and sometimes distressing changes in fundamental matters of life and death, the family still provided many of these people with a basis for stability which many other eighteenth-century Americans did not have.

If the demographic history of prerevolutionary Andover consisted solely of the numbers of its inhabitants, the period between 1700 and 1776 could be seen essentially in terms of a constant growth of population. The continuous expansion of the population is suggested by estimations based upon the town rate lists for successive decades beginning in 1685: 600 people in 1685; 710 people in 1695; 945 people in 1705; 1,050 people in 1715; 1,305 people in 1725; 1,630 people in 1735; 1,845 people in 1745; and 2,135 people in 1755. In 1764, the first census of Andover, recorded in "An Estimation of the number of Houses and Inhabitants in the Province of Massachusetts Bay in New England," revealed that the total estimated white population was 2,356, with a total population of 2,442. There were 438 families living in the town, with an average of 5.4 white children and adults per family.[1] There were 565 males under 16 years of age, 700 females under 16 years of age, 533 males of 16 years and over, and 558 females of 16 years and over. In addition there were 86 Negroes and mulattoes and no recorded Indians. Another extant estimate of the town's population reveals that in 1776 there was a total of 2,953 whites living there.[2] In 1790, however, when the first

[1] Tucker Family MSS, vol. 1 (Essex County Innholders and Miscellaney, 1680–1812), Essex Institute, Salem, Mass. This list is more complete than the 1765 list printed in Evarts N. Greene and Virginia D. Harrington, *American Population Before the Federal Census of 1790* (New York, 1932), p. 23, which includes houses and families and gives a total population of 2,462, but does not include the breakdown by age and sex found in the Tucker MSS.

[2] See "White Inhabitants, Massachusetts March 1776," Miscellaneous MSS, vol. 21, Essex Institute. For the same list, see Stella H. Sutherland, *Population Distribution in Colonial America* (1936; reprint ed., New York, 1966), p. 16.

federal census was taken, the total white population included only 2,769 whites together with an additional 94 Negroes.[3] For the first time since Andover's settlement, the population of the town had ceased to expand.

During the period in which the fourth generation reached maturity in large numbers, Andover had become one of the most populous, as well as one of the largest, towns in the colony. It ranked seventh out of twenty-one Essex County towns in 1776 in terms of its population, and it ranked sixteenth in population among all of the towns of the entire colony.[4] In 1764, the population density in the town reached approximately 41 people per square mile, with a density of about 106 people per square mile of improved land (excluding woodland). By 1776, the population density had reached approximately 50 people per square mile. Compared to most farming communities, Andover was relatively crowded by the mid-eighteenth century.

More than anything else, the persistent growth of the town's population during the prerevolutionary period distinguishes Andover from two English towns whose eighteenth-century demographic histories have been explored: Wigston Magna and Colyton. In Wigston Magna, for instance, the

[3] *Return of the Whole Number of Persons Within the Several Districts of the United States . . .* (Washington City, 1802), p. 20. Also see U.S. Bureau of the Census, *Heads of Families at the First Census of the United States Taken in the Year 1790: Massachusetts* (Washington, 1908), pp. 63–65, for Andover families.

[4] See Greene and Harrington, *American Population*, pp. 31–40, for the 1776 census figures for Massachusetts towns. For general discussions of population pressure upon land in old communities like Andover during the eighteenth century, see Kenneth Lockridge, "Land, Population and the Evolution of New England Society, 1630–1790," *Past and Present*, April 1968, pp. 62–80; and Charles S. Grant, *Democracy in the Connecticut Frontier Town of Kent* (New York, 1961), pp. 97–103.

"first half of the eighteenth century was a period of absolute stagnation in the population of the village," with "practically no increase in the population" for sixty years. Not until the period between 1766 and 1801 did the population of Wigston increase significantly.[5] In Colyton, a prolonged period of population decline between the 1640's and the 1730's was followed by a period of population stagnation between about 1740 and 1790 during which "baptisms and burials were very close to each other in number and without decisive trend." Not until after 1790 did baptisms in Colyton greatly exceed deaths, thereby increasing the actual population of the town in any marked degree.[6] Whether or not the demographic experiences of these two English towns in the eighteenth century are representative of others, they serve to indicate that the circumstances underlying the growth of the population in Andover must have been more favorable to life and fecundity than they were in these English towns during the same period. As in the seventeenth century, the balance in favor of expansion and growth was still on the side of Andover, at least until the Revolution.

Growing numbers of people alone do not tell the whole story of Andover's population during the eighteenth century,

[5] W. G. Hoskins, "The Population of an English Village 1086–1801: A Study of Wigston Magna," in Hoskins, *Provincial England: Essays in Social and Economic History* (London, 1963), pp. 200, 204.

[6] E. A. Wrigley, "Mortality in Pre-industrial England: The Example of Colyton, Devon, over Three Centuries," *Daedalus*, Spring 1968, p. 556. See also Wrigley's article "Family Limitation in Pre-industrial England," *EHR*, XIX (1966), 84, Figure 1, and 85. There are no comparable studies for the eighteenth-century American colonies except for J. Potter's excellent general study, "The Growth of Population in America, 1700–1860," in D. V. Glass and D. E. C. Eversley, eds., *Population in History: Essays in Historical Demography* (Chicago, 1965), pp. 631–688.

however. What is equally significant, particularly when viewed from the perspective of Andover's own past, is that the *rate* of growth evidently was slowing down and varied considerably from period to period.[7] Whereas the estimated total population of Andover in 1705 was 2.2 times the estimated population of the town in 1680, the estimated population in 1735 was only 1.6 times the population of 1710 (see Table 13). By 1755, the estimated population of the town was only 1.3 times that of the population of 1730; this is the lowest

Table 13. Rate of population increase, 1680–1800, based upon estimated total population

Year	Estimated population	Year	Estimated population	Total increase	Rate of increase
1680	435	1705	945	510	2.2
1710	995	1735	1,630	635	1.6
1720	1,255	1745	1,845	590	1.5
1730	1,425	1755	2,135	710	1.3
1740	1,745	1764	2,356	611	1.4
1751	1,920	1776	2,953	1,033	1.5
1776	2,953	1800	2,858	−95	0.97

rate of increase for any twenty-five-year period between 1710 and 1776. Between 1751 and 1776 however, the population increased 1.5 times, a rate similar to those earlier in the century. Crude though these rates are, they nevertheless confirm the fact that growth of population throughout this period was not steady.

[7] This is also evident in the colony as a whole during this period. See Potter, "Growth of Population," p. 648, and Table 1d, p. 639. The percentage increase in the Massachusetts population by decades is suggestive: 36 per cent from 1720 to 1730; 26 per cent from 1730 to 1740; 14 per cent from 1740 to 1750; 31 per cent from 1750 to 1760; 27 per cent from 1760 to 1770; and 21 per cent from 1770 to 1780.

Another index of the variable rate of population growth is the ratio of the excess of births over deaths in the town records in successive twenty-five-year periods.[8] Again, the last quarter of the seventeenth century is clearly one of exceptionally rapid growth, with the population increasing 2.9 times over that of the previous quarter-century (see Table 14). This rate of increase declined over the next fifty years to a low of 1.1 for the period from 1725 to 1749, indicative of an almost stagnant population. The rate of increase rose slightly,

Table 14. Rate of population increase, 1650–1799, based upon the town records

Period	Total births recorded	Total deaths recorded	Total increase	Rate of increase
1650–1674	225	38	187	
1675–1699	702	155	547	2.9
1700–1724	1,148	289	859	1.6
1725–1749	1,675	748	927	1.1
1750–1774	1,844	523	1,321	1.4
1775–1799	1,591	269	1,322	1.0

before declining again to a low of 1.0 for the last quarter of the eighteenth century.

Seen from this perspective, these variations in population increase suggest that the second and the fourth quarters of the eighteenth century were periods of demographic stagnation in Andover. Since most of the fourth generation was being born and raised in the second quarter of the century, the conditions shaping their childhood and youth differed significantly from those shaping the early years of previous generations; this indication is amply confirmed by other demographic evidence as well. The variations also suggest that the growth of the town occurred in a cyclical form, rising and falling

[8] See Appendix for data.

throughout the eighteenth century in a roughly generational pattern. They also suggest the possibility that the striking demographic decline evident during the last quarter of the century—a period of revolution and political and economic disorder—had its roots in the demographic experiences of the community during the period between 1725 and 1750. The full impact of a period of stagnation or decline in a population often is not felt for several decades afterwards, since it takes time for a generation to reach maturity and to produce another generation in its turn.

Another indication of the long-range tendency of population growth to level off and decline is evident in the failure of the numbers of recorded births to increase in magnitude continuously throughout the century. Between 1650 and 1679, for instance, the number of children born in any five-year interval never reached 100, whereas between 1680 and 1709 the numbers were always more than 100 but less than 200. After 1710 the number of births exceeded 200 but did not reach 300 until 1730. A gradual but continuous increase in magnitude had thus occurred every twenty to thirty years and one might therefore anticipate a similar increase in magnitude during the remainder of the eighteenth century. Such proved not to be the case, however: between 1730 and 1799 the number of births recorded in any given five-year period never reached 400, but usually remained above 300. What is most surprising of all, and visible on Graph 4, is that the number of births recorded in the town records began to level off in a striking fashion after 1740–1744, peaking again from 1760–1764, and then declining in a marked degree during the revolutionary period from 1770 to 1785. To the extent that population growth depended upon a steadily increasing number of births, it is evident that the second half of the century was essentially a period not of growth but of decline.

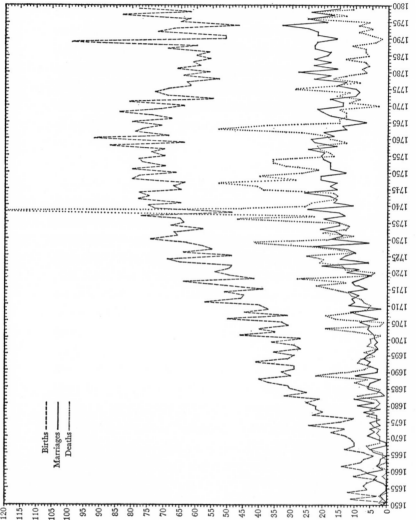

Graph 1. Annual births, marriages, and deaths in Andover, 1650–1799

Changes in the fertility index also point in the direction of a relative decline in the growth of the population during the course of the eighteenth century. The highest fertility index occurred between 1680 and 1709: the number of births per marriage was 6.0 during the 1680's; 7.6 during the 1690's; and 7.5 during the first decade of the new century. The period after 1710 is one of falling fertility, with 5.7 births per marriage between 1710 and 1719, and then fewer than 5 for the entire period from 1720 to 1789, ranging from 4.8 to a low of

Table 15. Births per marriage, 1720–1794

Marriages		Births		
Years	Number	Years	Number	B/M
1720–1729	130	1725–1734	622	4.8
1730–1739	172	1735–1744	699	4.1
1740–1749	180	1745–1754	726	4.0
1750–1759	192	1755–1764	753	3.9
1760–1769	168	1765–1774	719	4.3
1770–1779	145	1775–1784	609	4.2
1780–1789	213	1785–1794	632	3.0

3.0 (see Table 15). The trend is also evident by taking the ratio of births to marriages over longer periods: for each marriage occurring between 1680 and 1709 there were 7.0 births; for marriages between 1710 and 1739, there were 4.7 births per marriage; for marriages between 1740 and 1769, there were 4.1 births per marriage; and for marriages between 1770 and 1789, there were 3.5 births per marriage.

The significance of such figures depends, of course, upon what they are being compared with, and they can be read either negatively or positively. In comparison with some English data for this period, for example, the Andover indexes indicate relatively high levels of fertility throughout the prerevolutionary period, a fact which is worth emphasis. The fertility indexes for twelve parishes in Worcestershire between 1700 and 1800 ranged between 3.29 and 4.45; this closely resembles the range found in agricultural and industrial villages in Nottinghamshire between 1700 and 1799, which varied between a low of 3.3 and a high of 4.8.[9] This indicates that the fertility indexes for Andover throughout the first three-quarters of the eighteenth century were comparable to the highest fertility indexes found in these English communities during this century. The Andover indexes for this period, then, are low only in comparison to those in Andover itself during the last two decades of the seventeenth century and the first decade of the eighteenth century, which were extraordinarily high. The level of fertility in prerevolutionary Andover continued to be high, therefore, and indicates a potential for population growth arising from births comparable to English communities at their eighteenth-century peaks.

Calculations of birth rates for eighteenth-century Andover, although crude and little more than approximations of reality, nevertheless appear to confirm the picture derived from the fertility indexes. By estimating the population of the town at five times the number of male ratepayers on the tax lists, and by averaging the number of births in successive five-year intervals, the following birth rates (per thousand), beginning in 1710 and ending in 1760, result: 45, 48, 39, 46, 46, 40, 39,

[9] D. E. C. Eversley, "A Survey of Population in an Area of Worcestershire from 1660 to 1850 on the Basis of Parish Registers," in Glass and Eversley, eds., *Population in History*, p. 404, Table 2. This article originally appeared in *Population Studies*, X (1957) 253–279. For Nottingham, see J. D. Chambers, "The Course of Population Change," in Glass and Eversley, eds., *Population in History*, p. 333, Table 3 ("Baptisms per Marriage"). This article appeared originally in *The Vale of Trent, 1670–1800: A Regional Study of Economic Change, EHR* Supplement no. 3 (1957).

38, 39, 35, 37. In 1725, 1730, and 1735, the rates are higher than normal for England but lower than those found in Andover in 1680, 1685, and 1690—the period of the greatest growth and the highest birth rates in colonial Andover's history. The rates for the period from 1740 to 1760 correspond to the rates found in Nottingham, England, between 1725 and 1765, which varied between 36.22 and 39.73 per thousand. When the birth rate in Nottingham reached 40 per thousand in 1770, it was considered to be "explosive"; the rate reached a high point in 1790 at more than 46 per thousand.[10] It appears likely, then, that the birth rate in Andover during the first half of the eighteenth century was always at least as high as and often higher than one would expect to find in some English towns of the same period. Indeed, it is evident that when English birth rates began to reach the levels found in early eighteenth-century Andover, the birth rate was considered to be exceptionally high.

Thus, although the birth rates for Andover during the six decades preceding the Revolution declined from those of the late seventeenth century and continued to fall during the middle decades of the eighteenth century, they remained relatively high nevertheless when measured by English birth rates of this period. This suggests that although the changes in the fertility indexes and in the birth rates in Andover had some effect upon the population's growth, other factors probably played a greater role in accounting for the declining rates of population expansion and for the smaller families found in the third and fourth generations.

Among the principal factors inhibiting the expansion of the

[10] J. D. Chambers, "Population Change in a Provincial Town: Nottingham, 1700–1800," in Glass and Eversley, eds., *Population in History*, pp. 351, 349. This article originally appeared in L. S. Pressnell, ed., *Studies in the Industrial Revolution* (London, 1960).

population during the first half of the eighteenth century were the marked increase in the numbers of children dying before adulthood and the striking changes in the over-all mortality levels in Andover. Death began to strike down more and more children—and more adults as well—at much earlier ages than previously. The impact of successive epidemics was felt throughout the community, sometimes with disastrous results. The level of mortality varied greatly from year to year, of course, but periodically the numbers of deaths increased markedly, probably reflecting the visitation of an epidemic of some sort, the exact nature of which usually must be guessed since the town records rarely note the cause of death. One death from smallpox was mentioned in 1703, three in 1721, and three in 1722, with occasional references to accidents, but no mention whatsoever is made of measles, throat distemper, or other serious diseases.

All that remains are the records of the deaths themselves, but, cumulatively, these often give mute testimony to the presence within Andover of deadly diseases. Occasionally one finds families silently decimated without being able to establish the cause, as in the case of John Ballard's family: his 19-year-old daughter Sarah died in 1715 on November 27, followed by the death of his wife, Rebecca, on December 1 and the death of his 22-year-old daughter on December 2. A week passed before the death of his youngest daughter, aged 16, and John Ballard himself died nine days later, aged 62, leaving three unmarried children, aged 31, 29, and 27, to care for themselves. Other families were more fortunate, but few escaped altogether.

The graph registering deaths in Andover (see Graph 4) does not indicate an unusual peak in numbers in 1715, so that whatever caused the deaths of the five Ballards evidently was limited in its effects. In 1718, 1729, 1738, 1747, and 1763, however, the numbers of deaths recorded rose sharply; the most dramatic peak occurred in 1738, when there were 120 deaths in a single year. This is the only year in which deaths exceeded births in the entire history of Andover up to 1800 —a fact which in itself testifies to the demographic contrast between Andover and many towns in England. The numbers of deaths recorded in successive five-year intervals from 1700 to 1770 were as follows: 37, 52, 43, 85 (1715–1719), 72, 117 (1725–1729), 73, 251 (1735–1739), 105, 202 (1745–1749), 153, 91, 156 (1760–1764), 71. After 1710, not a single decade passed without a marked increase in the numbers of children and adults dying.

The most striking increases in numbers of deaths were those of children, however, with the most notable peaks in childhood deaths occurring in 1729, 1736, 1738, 1747, and 1763. Before 1729 there had never been more than 13 children's deaths recorded in any single year from 1650 to 1728, but in 1729 the records indicate that at least 30 children died, and in 1730 only 10. In 1736, 40 children died, and in 1738 there were 108 deaths, a reflection of the disastrous impact of throat distemper upon Andover, as upon so many New England towns during the mid-1730's.[11] The number of adult deaths

[11] See the excellent study by Ernest Caulfield, "A History of the Terrible Epidemic, Vulgarly Called the Throat Distemper, as It Occurred in his Majesty's New England Colonies between 1735 and 1740," *Yale Journal of Biology and Medicine* XI (1938–1939), 219–272, 277–335. Also see his "Some Common Diseases of Colonial Children," *Publications of the Colonial Society of Massachusetts*, XXXV (1942–1946), 4–65. For a more general but very useful study, see John Duffy's *Epidemics in Colonial America* (Baton Rouge, La., 1953). For the impact of throat distemper on Boston, see John B. Blake's model study, *Public Health in the Town of Boston, 1630–1822* (Cambridge, Mass., 1959), p. 107, which reveals the virtual immunity of this town to the disease, thereby heightening the contrast with towns such as Andover, which were decimated.

recorded in 1736 and 1738 (7 and 12) indicates the selective effects of the epidemic: it killed large numbers of children but spared most of the adult population of the town. The greatest effects of the epidemics clearly were upon the younger generation. Childhood mortality had increased dramatically, not only providing marked contrasts with earlier generations, but amply confirming the common assumptions about the frequency with which death decimated families in eighteenth-century towns like Andover.

The effects of the increase in the numbers of deaths, particularly among children, are evident in the increases in the proportions of recorded deaths to recorded births. Between 1660 and 1699, the number of deaths (including both children and adults) recorded had been only a little more than 20 per cent of the births. But the percentage increased to 27.4 for the decade 1710–1719, to 32.8 during the 1720's, and to 49.0 during the 1730's (signifying that half as many died as were born during that decade), and fell to 38.2 during the 1740's (still a very high proportion of deaths to births) and to 31.7 during the 1750's. The contrast between the seventeenth century and the first half of the eighteenth century is readily apparent and is indicative of the marked increase in mortality among the inhabitants of this town after about 1715.

Equally striking evidence is obtained by computations based upon data from the family reconstitution forms for death rates among the children up to 19 years of age. By limiting the rates to the numbers of children whose ages at death are known within reasonable limits, a dramatic increase is evident in the rates of death among cohorts born in successive thirty-year periods from 1670 to 1760 and ranging in age from birth to 19 years (see Table 16): of those children born between 1670 and 1699, 225 per thousand died before reaching the age of 20; of those born between 1700 and 1729, 381

Table 16. Mortality rate for persons born between 1670 and 1759 and dying before age 20

Birth cohort and age at death	Deaths (a) Male	(b) Female	(c) Total	(d) Cohort members (known deaths)	(e) c/ 1,000 d	(f) Cohort members	(g) c/ 1,000 f
1670–1699							
0–1	37	22	59	387	152	512	115
2–9	12	3	15	328	46	453	33
10–19	5	8	13	313	42	438	30
Total, 0–19	54	33	87	387	225	512	170
1700–1729							
0–1	77	50	127	540	235	838	152
2–9	18	18	36	413	87	711	51
10–19	17	26	43	377	114	675	64
Total, 0–19	112	94	206	540	381	838	246
1730–1759							
0–1	45	21	66	266	248	423	156
2–9	33	30	63	200	315	357	176
10–19	6	7	13	137	95	294	44
Total, 0–19	84	58	142	266	534	423	336

Note: Data are based upon family reconstitution forms, assuming that children known to have died young, but whose exact age is unknown, died between birth and 1 year of age. The method of computation for the tables is based upon the method used by E. A. Wrigley in "Mortality in Pre-industrial England: The Example of Colyton, Devon, over Three Centuries," *Daedalus*, Spring 1968, p. 551.

per thousand died before the age of 20; of those born between 1730 and 1759, 534 per thousand died before the age of 20. If the total number of children known to be born are included regardless of whether or not their ages at death are known (thus including many who undoubtedly lived to adulthood but who moved away and died outside Andover), the same increase in the death rates becomes evident although the rates themselves are lower: for the cohort born between 1670 and

1699, 170 per thousand died before age 20; of those born between 1700 and 1729, 246 per thousand died before age 20; of those born between 1730 and 1759, 336 per thousand died before age 20.[12] Although the rates increased in each age group after 1700, the most dramatic single increase affected the cohort born between 1730 and 1759, in which children between 2 and 9 years old died at the rate of 176 per thousand, more than three times as many per thousand as died among the previous cohort. This figure is indicative of the increased dangers to children beyond infancy but prior to adolescence—the age group which appears to have been most susceptible, among other things, to the throat distemper prevalent in the mid-1730's.

The likelihood that a child born in Andover would survive beyond his tenth year decreased during the mid-eighteenth century, as Table 17 demonstrates. The rate per thousand of children born between 1640 and 1669 and surviving to age 10 is extraordinarily high; the rate for the next cohort is still

[12] The distinction between computations based upon known ages at death and those based upon the total number of births, regardless of whether or not ages at death are known, is extremely important, since the mortality rates based upon known ages at death are seriously inflated. It would appear, therefore, that the most realistic rates are those based upon the total number of births in a given cohort, including those whose ages at death are not known, as well as those whose ages are known with reasonable certainty. The reason is obvious: Most of those whose ages are unknown almost certainly lived (most of them are recorded as marrying), but in many instances they moved away, making it impossible to determine their ages at death. The magnitude of the differences of the calculations can be seen with the birth cohort 1730–1759: 61.6 per cent of the females whose ages at death are known died before the age of 20 (58 deaths out of 94 females), whereas only 31.5 per cent of the 184 females whose births are known died before the age of 20. E. A. Wrigley discusses this problem in "Mortality in Pre-industrial England," pp. 551–553, 561–562.

Table 17. Rate of survival to age 10 for children born between 1640 and 1759

Birth cohort	(a) Cohort members (known deaths)	(b) Known survivors	(c) b/1,000 a	(d) Cohort members	(e) Probable survivors	(f) e/1,000 d
1640–1669	155	138	890	204	187	917
1670–1699	387	313	809	512	438	855
1700–1729	540	377	698	838	675	805
1730–1759	266	137	515	423	294	695

impressively high. But when, as the table shows, the rate dropped to 695 per thousand, there were still slightly more than two-thirds of the children born in this period of greatly increased mortality who managed to reach their tenth year. This figure compares closely with several for villages in southwestern France and Normandy, where 672 out of a thousand children survived to age 10 in Crulai. The rates of survival in three Breton communities during the eighteenth century were much lower, ranging between 463 per thousand to 580 per thousand, but these were areas of poverty and general unhealthiness.[13] The Andover rates contrast favorably with those of Breton and are similar to those for Crulai, another indication that, in terms of mortality, Andover had become less distinctive by the middle of the eighteenth century and more like at least some European communities.

The Andover mortality rates confirm that the chances of survival to adulthood had diminished by 1730. Of the men and women born between 1670 and 1699, 830 out of a thousand reached the age of 20, whereas of those born between 1730 and 1759, only 662 out of a thousand (two-thirds of

[13] See Pierre Goubert, "Legitimate Fecundity and Infant Mortality in France During the Eighteenth Century: A Comparison," *Daedalus*, Spring 1968, pp. 599–600.

those born) reached the age of 20. This rate, based upon the family reconstitution forms, corresponds closely with the proportion of deaths to births recorded in the town records: both indicate that about a third of the population died before adulthood.

The evidence for an increased mortality in cohorts born after 1700 is augmented by evidence based upon ages at death as well. Out of a total of 420 men born between 1700 and 1729, the ages at death of 310 (73.8 per cent) are known, of whom 198 survived at least to age 20 (see Table 18.) This group of men who survived the increased hazards of infancy and childhood fared less well as adults than had the group born between 1670 and 1699. The most striking change was in the percentage of deaths in the 20–39 age group, which

Table 18. Age at death of males born between 1640 and 1759 and surviving to age 20

Age at death	1640–1669 cohort		1670–1699 cohort		1700–1729 cohort		1730–1759 cohort	
	No.	%	No.	%	No.	%	No.	%
20–29	13	14.1	17	8.8	29	14.6	10	11.4
30–39	4	4.3	13	6.8	31	15.7	5	5.7
40–49	2	2.2	12	6.3	21	10.6	15	17.0
50–59	10	10.9	13	6.8	20	10.1	7	8.0
60–69	16	17.4	45	23.4	19	9.6	12	13.6
70–79	25	27.2	51	26.6	37	18.7	20	22.7
80–89	19	20.6	34	17.7	34	17.2	15	17.0
90–99	3	3.3	7	3.6	6	3.0	4	4.6
100 and over	0	0.0	0	0.0	1	0.5	0	0.0
Total, 20–100 and over	92	100.0	192	100.0	198	100.0	88	100.0
20–39		18.4		15.6		30.3		17.1
40–59		13.1		13.1		20.7		25.0
60–79		44.6		50.0		28.3		36.3
80–105		23.9		21.3		20.7		21.6
Total, 20–105		100.0		100.0		100.0		100.0

nearly doubled, as the table shows. Similarly, the percentage of men dying before the age of 50 also nearly doubled, with 40.9 per cent of the cohort born after 1700 failing to reach their fiftieth year, compared with only 21.9 per cent of the earlier cohort. More than half (51.0 per cent) of the men born after 1700 who survived to age 20 died before their sixtieth year, compared to 28.7 per cent for the previous cohort.

The likelihood that men born after 1700 would live lives as long as those of the previous cohort was far less than it had been for men born in the seventeenth century. This conclusion is borne out by the decline in the average age at death of men living at least to the age of 21 in successive generations: second-generation males lived an average of 64.2 years, whereas the third generation lived an average of 62.4 years and the fourth generation lived an average of only 59.8 years, indicative of the diminished chances of survival to old age during the eighteenth century. Nevertheless, it is impressive that of the group of men born during the first three decades of the eighteenth century, 39.4 per cent managed to reach the age of 70, with 20.7 per cent reaching the age of 80. The critical period, it seems, was before the age of 50—the period in which most men would be marrying and establishing families of their own. The increase in the percentage of deaths among men between the ages of 20 and 39 is particularly notable, for it meant an increased number of widows and fatherless families. The life expectancy of the generations born after 1700 was thus less than that enjoyed by their parents and grandparents.

The cohort of men born between 1730 and 1759, nearly all of whom were of the fourth generation, and 88 of whom are known to have reached the age of 20, tended to die less frequently between the ages of 20 and 39 than the earlier cohort did (17.1 per cent compared to 30.3 per cent), and fewer died before the age of 50 as well (34.1 per cent compared to 40.9 per cent). About the same percentage reached the advanced age of 80 (21.6 and 20.7 per cent). As a group, the men born after 1730 evidently stood a better chance of surviving to more advanced ages than had the group born in the previous thirty years. But whether this represents the general character of life for Andover men born after this date or only the characteristics of these particular men cannot be determined readily. It does suggest, however, the variability of lifespans and of the circumstances fostering or limiting the preservation of life in a community such as this.

In view of the common assumptions that women frequently died in childbirth and that their chances of survival to old age were relatively slight, it is surprising to discover that the percentages of women dying before the ages of 40 and 50 were smaller than those for men born during the same period. The average age at death of women in successive generations actually was far steadier than that for men. The age at death for women is more difficult to ascertain than the age for men, however, partly because of marriage and partly because of the frequency with which marriage led to their removal from Andover. Out of a total of 418 females born between 1700 and 1729, the ages at death of only 230 (55 per cent) are known, and of these, only 136 are known to have reached the age of 20. If they lived their adult lives in Andover, however, the chances were very good that their deaths would be recorded in the town records, thus permitting the determination of their ages at death. For this reason, the data on female ages at death, incomplete though they are, nevertheless provide a useful insight into the longevity of women born after 1700 and residing, for the most part, in Andover itself.

As with the men, an increased percentage of the women

Table 19.   Age at death of females born between 1640 and 1759 and surviving to age 20

Age at death	1640–1669 cohort		1670–1699 cohort		1700–1729 cohort		1730–1759 cohort	
	No.	%	No.	%	No.	%	No.	%
20–29	2	4.5	10	9.3	23	16.9	3	8.3
30–39	5	11.4	9	8.3	15	11.0	4	11.1
40–49	5	11.4	11	10.2	14	10.3	4	11.1
50–59	9	20.5	13	12.0	11	8.1	4	11.1
60–69	6	13.6	23	21.3	20	14.7	4	11.1
70–79	9	20.4	22	20.4	16	11.8	8	22.2
80–89	4	9.1	12	11.1	27	19.9	6	16.7
90–99	4	9.1	7	6.5	8	5.9	3	8.3
100 and over	0	0.0	1	0.9	2	1.4	0	0.0
Total, 20–100 and over	44	100.0	108	100.0	136	100.0	36	99.9
20–39		15.9		17.6		27.9		19.4
40–59		31.9		22.2		18.4		22.2
60–79		34.0		41.7		26.5		33.3
80–105		18.2		18.5		27.2		25.0
Total, 20–105		100.0		100.0		100.0		99.9

died between the ages of 20 and 39, rising from 17.6 per cent for the cohort of 1670–1699 to 27.9 per cent for the cohort 1700–1729 (see Table 19), but this is still less than the 30.3 per cent for men born in the same years. Similarly, the percentage of women dying before the age of 50 increased from 27.8 per cent to 38.2 per cent but still was slightly less than the percentage of men failing to reach the age of 50 (40.9 per cent). Approximately the same percentage of women lived to the age of 70 as did men (61.0 per cent and 60.6 per cent), but an even larger percentage of women reached the age of 80 (27.2 per cent compared to 21.6 per cent).

It appears, then, that the longevity of these women was appreciably greater than one might have anticipated, that the likelihood of women dying during their childbearing years was no greater than the likelihood of death for men during the same years, and that women's chances of reaching advanced ages were as good as those for men, if not somewhat better. The average age at death for women living at least to the age of 21 in the fourth generation was 61.6 years; this is higher than the average for men (59.8 years) and slightly higher than the average for third-generation women (60.8 years), and it is equal to that for the second generation. Then as now, women proved to be sturdier and longer-lived than men, folklore to the contrary notwithstanding. Even as infants, children, and adolescents, proportionately fewer females died than males, with 22.5 per cent of the total number of females born between 1700 and 1729 dying before the age of 20, compared with 26.7 per cent of the males, and with 31.5 per cent of the females born between 1730 and 1759 dying before 20, compared with 35.1 per cent of the males. The mortality rate, particularly in the early years of life, clearly had increased significantly for both women and men, and for young adults as well, after 1700. But many of those born in Andover even during the eighteenth century still managed to survive to advanced ages in sufficient numbers and proportions to testify to the relative advantages for life in this community, compared with many others, particularly in England and Europe.[14]

[14] For mortality rates in Boston, Mass., from 1701 to 1774, see Blake, *Public Health in Boston*, Appendix II, pp. 247–249. This exceptional study indicates that Boston had a mortality rate ranging from a low of 21 per thousand in 1701 to a high of 103 per thousand in 1721, but usually averaging between 31 and 46 per thousand during the entire period. These are much higher than approximations for Andover. Estimating total population by multiplying the ratepayers every five years by 5, and computing the mortality rate per thousand of population accordingly, the rates for Andover are 16 per thousand

Whatever advantages Andover might have had—and it is impossible to be certain about them until far more is known about the demographic histories of many more communities —the perceptible increase in deaths among children and young adults after 1700 must have been evident to the residents of the town and a persistent source of concern and apprehension. Measured by the increase in mortality within the community, particularly in the fourth generation, life was less secure and was cut short more often after 1700 than before.

Very little evidence of the personal effects of death upon individuals and families in Andover has survived during the eighteenth century, and this makes it exceedingly difficult to document the emotional and social impact of periodic epidemics and youthful deaths. One brief diary does remain, though, which provides some suggestive clues to the experiences and the reactions of inhabitants of the town, however unrepresentative the writer, the Reverend John Barnard, of the North Parish Church, might have been.[15] John Barnard, the son of the Reverend Thomas Barnard, the third minister of the First Church of Andover, and his successor, married Sarah Martyn, of Boston, on October 20, 1715, at the age of twenty-five. Their first child, named after John's father, was born August 17, 1716, ten months after their marriage. The second child, Sarah, was born in Andover April 28, 1719, baptised May 3,

---

in 1715; 19 per thousand in 1725; 9 per thousand in 1735; 71 per thousand in 1738 (the year of the throat distemper epidemic); 15 per thousand in 1740; and 21 per thousand in 1745. These rates are almost consistently low, but in view of the Boston rates—in a large port town rates ought to be considerably higher, or at least so one might assume—not impossibly low. I prefer, however, to rely upon the data from the family reconstitution forms, since they are generally more nearly complete than even the town records.

[15] John Barnard, Diary, 1715–1743, Essex Institute, Salem, Mass.

and "Died May. 18ᵗʰ. of Convulsion fitts." The third child, Edward, was born June 15, 1720; he survived to become a minister in Haverhill and died at the age of fifty-four. Barnard noted in his diary that "Several ffamilies in Andover were visitted with yᵉ Small pox yᵉ Latter end of Dec 1721 of which distemper There Dyed Deacon Barker, Stephen Barker, James Black. and his wife, Joseph Dane Son of Frances Dane: Lord," he prayed, "Stay thy hand, Say it is enough The wife of Jacob Tyler and their child and Ebenezʳ King dyed of abovesᵈ distemper the Same year." He observed: "Upon my Call" to the Andover church, "yᵉ Small Pox broke out in Boston and was likely to Spread and I and my Wife and Child had never had it," indicative of the apprehension which the new epidemic, of disastrous proportions in Boston, raised in those who had never suffered from it.

His brother, Theodore, died on February 16, 1725:

at about 10 oClock in yᵉ Evening having almost Compleated yᵉ 33ᵈ year of his age he lay Sick but about 6 dayes. he left a wife and 3 small children The Eldest but a Little above Six year old he gave me good satisfaction before he dyed as to yᵉ state of his soul and I mourn not without hope. I have no Naturall Fathʳ Mothʳ Brothʳ nor sister upon Earth but am left alone, but I shall not be alone if yᵉ fathʳ be wᵗʰ me Lord help me to Improve this dispensation aright Quicken me hereby to prepare for death my brothʳˢ have been short livᵈ I wᵈ not depend upon a long one Lord satisfy me with life whether longer or shorter and shew me thy Salvation.

Both before and after the death of his brother, his son John, born in 1723, had been sick and near death, but finally recovered. Although he survived long enough to enter his fourth year at Harvard College, his father sadly wrote that "My Dear and hopefull Son John died at Home Oct 1 1739 aged a Little more than 16 years and 5 months, he dyed of a Feavʳ and Flux the tenth day after he was seized therewith."

Earlier, Barnard had also lost another daughter, Elizabeth, who was born June 16, 1732, and died seven weeks later. Three years later:

Elizbith [another daughter] was born Saturday Decr 20th 1735 . . . May He who has given her to me make her his & If he Spare her life help me to bring her up (If I have an opportunity) in ye Nurture & Admonition of the Lord:—and give her an Education Suitable to her holy Dedication—dyed of Convulsion Fits Sept 21 1736 being just 9 months & 1 day old. She dyed about one Hour & a quarter after her Cousen Hannah Barnard who died of ye Feaver & Sore Throat, having entered the Thirteenth Year of her Age. Lord! help me to Sanctify thy name under these affecting visitations.

The disastrous epidemic had struck John Barnard's household, as it was to strike so many others in Andover and elsewhere as well. His hopes for his daughter and his son were dashed by their premature deaths, and however consoling his faith, their loss must have been deeply felt. His entries in his brief diary, though, were restrained: hints rather than revelations of parental grief. For nearly everyone else, however, not even this much has survived. One must imagine how a man like Benjamin Blanchard felt when the six youngest of his eleven children died in succession, four of them within one month in 1739, or Paul Faulkner, who lost four of his eight children, ranging in age from six months to thirteen years, between November 1736 and August 1737. Fortunately, few families suffered quite so many deaths so quickly.

While the emotional toll exacted among parents and young husbands and wives by the increased mortality can only rarely be demonstrated directly with surviving records, other important effects arising from changes in the mortality rates and the birth rates can be established, particularly as they affected the sizes of families. Changes in the sizes of families in the third generation, and in families resulting from marriages occurring after 1705, provide striking testimony to the other changes in rates of births and deaths, both of which independently fostered smaller families.

The decline in the birth rate, for example, coupled with an increase in the intervals between births, probably accounts for the decrease in the average number of children born to fertile couples in the third generation: including both complete and incomplete families, the average number of children per family in the first generation was 8.3; in the second generation, 8.1; and in the third generation, 7.2. A similar decrease is evident among completed families: the first generation produced an average of 8.3 births, the second an average of 8.7 births, and the third an average of 7.6 births. In part, this decline may reflect the slight increase in the average interval between births from 23.5 months for families produced by couples marrying between 1685–1704, to 26.5 months for those marrying between 1705–1724 (excluding all intervals over 59 months).

Much more likely as a significant factor in the decreased average size of third-generation families, however, is the increased average age of women at marriage, which rose from 22.3 years in the second generation to 24.5 years in the third generation. This increase occurred quite suddenly during the second half of the opening decade of the eighteenth century, when the average age of women marrying rose to 24.7 years from an average of 21.1 years for women marrying between 1700 and 1704. The increase in average marriage age persisted thereafter, dropping only between 1730 and 1734 (to 23.0 years). The effects of the increase in age are immediately evident by contrasting the average number of children born to couples married in Andover between 1685 and 1704 and the average number born to couples married between 1705

nd 1724: 8.7 births compared to 7.4 births in completed
amilies, or an average decrease of slightly more than one
irth per couple. Since the average interval between births
vas about 2 years in both periods, an average increase in
narriage age of two years ought to have had the effect of
educing the average size of completed families by about one
hild, which is precisely what happened. The correlation be-
ween increased age of marriage for women and a decreased
umber of births thus is apparent and is impressive confirma-
ion of the belief that the age of marriage, particularly for

able 20. Average family size in the first, second, and third generations

	All families			Completed families		
eneration	Number	Children born	Children living to age 21	Number	Children born	Children living to age 21
irst	34	8.3	7.2	27	8.3	7.2
econd	84	8.1	6.6	57	8.7	7.2
hird	147	7.2	5.1	93	7.6	5.5

vomen, had important demographic implications. By modern
tandards, families were still large, to be sure, but they never-
heless were smaller in the third generation than they had
een at any time since the establishment of Andover. The size
f the family, therefore, was not constant throughout the
eventeenth and eighteenth centuries. Like nearly everything
lse, family size was variable and affected by changing cir-
umstances and by changing patterns of behavior.

Changes in the rate of mortality also had important implica-
ions for the sizes of families, and these changes provided an
nportant additional factor limiting family size. Table 20
hows that the average number of children living to age 21 in
ll third-generation families, completed and incomplete, had

decreased an average of 1.5 children when compared with th
average size of all second-generation families. But the decreas
becomes even clearer if only completed families are consid
ered, since the average size of completed first- and second
generation families, measured by the number of childre
surviving to the age of 21, was 7.2, whereas the average siz
for third-generation families was only 5.5, an average decreas
of nearly two children per family. Similar decreases in the size
of completed families produced by marriages contracted be
tween 1685 and 1704 and marriages between 1705 and 172

Table 21. Average size of completed families, by date of
marriage, 1685–1744

Date of marriage	Number of families	Children born	Children living to age 21
1685–1704	37	8.7	7.2
1705–1724	62	7.4	5.3
1725–1744	17	7.5	5.3

confirm the generational differences (see Table 21). Thes
differences also continued to be evident in marriages con
tracted between 1725 and 1744, in which the average numbe
of children surviving to age 21 (5.3) is approximately 2 les
than the number of children born in these families, and ap
proximately 2 less than survived in families established durin
the period 1685–1704. The contrast between the first- an
second-generation families, established for the most part dur
ing the seventeenth century, and those of the third generatior
established largely in the eighteenth century, is strikingl
clear: the size of the family had declined. Fewer childre
were being born, and fewer still were surviving. Individua
families thus reflected the larger changes in the town's birt

and death rates and in the ages at which women were marrying.

The decreases in family size can be demonstrated in
another way by comparing the percentages of families of
various sizes in different generations. Measured by the number
of children born to completed families, 25.9 per cent of first-
generation families had six children or less, compared to 22.8

Table 22. Number of children born to completed first-, second-, and
third-generation families

No. of children	First-generation families		Second-generation families		Third-generation families	
	No.	%	No.	%	No.	%
0–4	2	7.4	8	14.0	13	14.0
5–7	5	18.5	10	17.5	34	36.6
8–11	18	66.7	27	47.4	38	40.8
12–20	2	7.4	12	21.1	8	8.6
20 or more	0	0.0	0	0.0	0	0.0
Total, 0–20 or more	27	100.0	57	100.0	93	100.0
0–6	7	25.9	13	22.8	33	35.5
7–20	20	74.1	44	77.2	60	64.5
Total, 0–20	27	100.0	57	100.0	93	100.0

per cent of the second generation, and 35.5 per cent of the
third-generation families (see Table 22). Even more strikingly, though, 40.7 per cent of the first-generation families
had six children or less surviving to age 21, and 38.6 per cent
of the second-generation families had this many children surviving (see Table 23), which indicates that nearly two-thirds
of the second-generation families had seven or more children
surviving. By contrast, only one-third of the third-generation
families (33.3 per cent) had seven or more children surviving,
and two-thirds had fewer than seven children surviving. Out

Table 23. Number of children living to age 21 in completed first-, second-, and third-generation families

No. of children	First-generation families		Second-generation families		Third-generation families	
	No.	%	No.	%	No.	%
0–4	6	22.2	10	17.5	27	29.0
5–7	7	25.9	22	38.6	45	48.4
8–11	14	51.9	22	38.6	21	22.6
12–20	0	0.0	3	5.3	0	0.0
20 or more	0	0.0	0	0.0	0	0.0
Total, 0–20 or more	27	100.0	57	100.0	93	100.0
0–6	11	40.7	22	38.6	62	66.7
7–20	16	59.3	35	61.4	31	33.3
Total, 0–20	27	100.0	57	100.0	93	100.0

of a total of ninety-three third-generation completed families, only eight had twelve or more children born, and none had twelve children surviving to adulthood. By comparison, 21.1 per cent of the second-generation families had twelve or more children born (twelve out of fifty-seven families), although only three of these families ultimately succeeded in raising twelve or more children to maturity. The largest second-generation completed family produced eighteen children (the next largest had fourteen), but the largest number of children surviving to age 21 in any family was only thirteen. The largest third-generation family produced only fourteen children, and the largest number of children surviving to age 21 in a third-generation family was only ten. For families to have contained between fifteen and twenty-five children, therefore, remarriage for men was the only likely cause. The normal family, however, was always much smaller.

The long-range effects of the decreased size of third-gener-

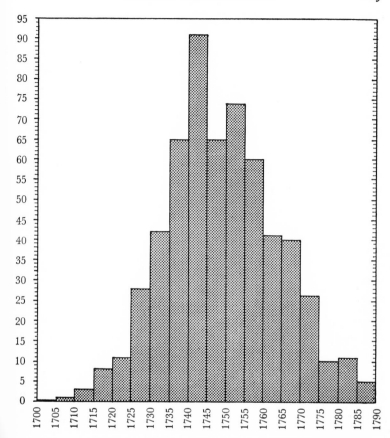

Graph 5. Fourth-generation marriages in consecutive five-year intervals

ation families began to be evident when the fourth generation
reached maturity during the middle decades of the eighteenth
century. The distribution of fourth-generation marriages
through time indicates a long generational cycle, beginning in
1705 and ending in 1790 (see Graph 5); but the number of
marriages rose significantly between 1730 and 1769, and the
generational peak occurred during the 1740's, when there

were 156 marriages. Within the town as a whole, however, the number of marriages recorded after 1730 failed to increase at a steady pace, tending instead to level off for nearly three decades before reaching another brief peak between 1755 and 1759, after which the numbers of marriages dropped continuously to a low point between 1770 and 1774 (see Graph 4). In any single year between 1700 and 1780, the number of marriages recorded in Andover exceeded 25 only once, in 1744. In successive five-year periods, the numbers of marriages recorded between 1720 and 1779 were as follows: 64, 66, 85 (1730–1734), 88, 88, 92, 87, 105 (1755–1759), 88, 80, 65 (1770–1774), and 80. Measured by recorded marriages, therefore, the population of Andover was not growing as it had during the earlier periods. That this should be so is not surprising in view of the evidence presented earlier on births, deaths, and family sizes. What is most impressive is the fact that the full impact of demographic experiences often was not felt until many years after the events themselves. Andover during the 1740's, 1750's, and 1760's was still being affected by the demographic histories of families in the 1720's and 1730's. The lives of the fourth generation clearly were being shaped in ways unfamiliar to their parents' and grandparents' generations.

A further indication of the novelty of their experiences is the fact that the average age at marriage of men dropped significantly during this same period, beginning after 1730. Taken as a whole, the average age of marriage for fourth-generation men declined to 25.3 years from the high average of 27.1 years for their fathers' generation; this is the first significant departure in Andover from traditional characteristics of male marriage ages in England and most of western Europe. Fourth-generation men clearly were marrying at younger ages than either their fathers or their grandfathers (see Table

Table 24. Age at marriage of second-, third-, and fourth-generation males

Age	Second generation		Third generation		Fourth generation	
	No.	%	No.	%	No.	%
Under 21	5	4.8	6	2.7	17	5.8
21–24	36	34.6	72	32.1	122	41.5
25–29	39	37.5	87	38.8	119	40.5
30–34	17	16.3	39	17.4	27	9.2
35–39	4	3.8	12	5.4	6	2.0
40 and over	3	2.9	8	3.6	3	1.0
Total	104	99.9	224	100.0	294	100.0

24), with higher percentages marrying between the ages of 21 and 24 and between 25 and 29 than had done so in previous generations. Nearly half of the fourth-generation men (47.3 per cent) married before reaching the age of 25, compared with 34.8 per cent of the third generation and 39.4 per cent of the second generation. Only 12.2 per cent of the fourth-generation men married at the age of 30 or later, compared with 26.4 per cent of the third generation and 23.0 per cent of the second generation. Birth order made relatively little difference in the marriage ages of fourth-generation men, with 114 eldest sons marrying at an average of 25.2 years, 77 second sons marrying at an average of 25.3 years, 69 youngest sons marrying at an average of 24.0 years (compared with the average of 27.2 years for youngest sons in the previous generation, a striking drop in average age), and 42 sons with trades marrying at an average of 24.5 years. Youngest sons and sons with trades thus tended to marry younger than older brothers and brothers who farmed, but not by much. Out of a total of 393 fourth-generation men, only 14 are known to have lived at least to the age of 25 and to have remained bachelors, but since the marriages of 70 men cannot be determined, it is possible that others also remained unmarried. The likelihood, however, is that the great majority of these men married outside Andover.

The over-all decrease in the average age at marriage for the fourth generation persisted, for the most part, from 1730 to at least 1770; the average ages in successive five-year intervals, based upon the data from the family reconstitution forms (thus excluding fifth-generation males) were as follows, beginning in 1720: 27.1, 26.9, 25.8, 26.5, 25.6, 26.7, 24.9, 25.3, 25.6, 25.9. The tendency thus was for marriage ages of men to be lower than they had been throughout most of the second half of the seventeenth century and the first two decades of the eighteenth century.[16] In their marriages, as in their births and deaths, the experiences of fourth-generation men were dissimilar to those of earlier generations.

The average age at which fourth-generation women married does not reflect a decrease as striking as that for men; the average age did decline to 23.2 years from the previous generation's high of 24.5 years, but it still remained above the average of 22.3 years for the second generation. Nearly 70 per cent of the fourth-generation women married before reaching

[16] This does not appear to be the case with sons of later-comer families who married between 1720 and 1759. For most of these men, the average age at marriage actually increased during this period, from an average of 26.2 years for men marrying between 1700 to 1719 to an average of 28.3 years for men marrying between 1720 and 1739, and an average of 27.5 years for men marrying between 1740 and 1759. Since most of these marriages involve men who either remained permanently in Andover or who at least stayed there an appreciable period of their lives, the rise in marriage age after 1720 reflects both the generational phenomena (many are actually third-generation Andover men since their grandfathers had settled later than the families of the first settlers) and the fact that many of their families were relatively poorer than many of the inheritors of the first settler families. The delays in their marriages highlight the earlier marriages of the fourth generation of the settler families.

the age of 25, and about 90 per cent married before the age of
30 (see Table 25). The youngest to marry was 14, but most
did not marry until they reached 17, and 31.9 per cent married before the age of 21. The oldest woman to marry was 46,
but only five women married between 35 and 39, and only
four married at 40 or older. Only fourteen are known to have
remained spinsters after the age of 26. On the average, the
difference in ages between husbands and wives in the fourth
generation was only 2.1 years, slightly less than the previous

Table 25. Age at marriage of second-, third-, and fourth-generation females

Age	Second generation		Third generation		Fourth generation	
	No.	%	No.	%	No.	%
Under 21	29	35.8	58	27.6	90	31.9
21–24	32	39.5	74	35.2	105	37.2
25–29	14	17.3	48	22.9	60	21.3
30–34	3	3.7	12	5.7	18	6.4
35–39	2	2.5	10	4.8	5	1.8
40 and over	1	1.2	8	3.8	4	1.4
Total	81	100.0	210	100.0	282	100.0

generation's 2.6 years, but appreciably less than the 4.4-year
gap separating husbands and wives in the second generation.

What is most striking about the average ages of fourth-generation Andover women, as with previous generations, is their
relative youth at marriage compared with women in villages
such as Colyton, in Devon, where the mean age for women at
first marriage reached a high of 30.7 years between 1700 and
1719, dropping to 27.2 years during the next 20 years, and
then to 26.3 years between 1750 and 1769.[17] Not until the
period 1825–1837 did the mean age at marriage for women in

[17] E. A. Wrigley, "Family Limitation in Pre-industrial England,"
p. 87, Table 2.

Colyton approach the average for fourth-generation Andover women. The limited data for eighteenth-century France also indicate that women tended to marry somewhat later there than in Andover (ranging from 24.7 to 26.2 years in five communities).[18] The fourth-generation women thus married at slightly younger ages than the preceding generation, and at considerably younger ages than many European women during the same period.

Marriages between men and women resident in Andover accounted for a somewhat smaller proportion of all the marriages recorded between 1720 and 1749 than had been the case during the first two decades of the century. In at least 238 out of the 482 marriages recorded (49.4 per cent), both partners were residents of Andover; and 56.0 per cent of those partners whose origins can be reasonably ascertained were both from Andover during this period, compared with 66.5 per cent of those marrying between 1700 and 1719 (see Table 26). As the table shows, proportionately fewer men married wives from outside Andover after 1720 than before, but a much higher proportion of women married men from outside Andover after 1720 than before. In view of the rough balance in the proportions of men and women surviving to adulthood during this period (51.2 per cent male, 48.8 per cent female), the increased proportion of women marrying husbands from outside Andover after 1720 quite probably reflects the outward mobility of substantial percentages of third- and

[18] Louis Henry, "The Population of France in the Eighteenth Century," in Glass and Eversley, eds., *Population in History*, p. 454, Table 10. On the other hand, fourth-generation women married somewhat later than did women in eighteenth-century Bristol, R.I., where the mean age before 1750 was 20.5 years and after 1750 was 21.1 years (John Demos, "Families in Colonial Bristol, Rhode Island: An Exercise in Historical Demography," *WMQ*, XXV [1968], 55, Table 9).

Table 26. Residential origin of marriage partners, by date of marriage, 1650–1749

Date of marriage	Both from Andover		Husband from outside		Wife from outside		Marriages recorded	Origin of partners known
	No.	%	No.	%	No.	%		
1650–1699	78	48.1	30	18.5	54	33.3	173	162
1700–1719	99	66.5	9	6.0	41	27.5	152	149
1720–1749	238	56.0	126	29.6	61	14.4	482	425

fourth-generation men and the concomitant influx of men from outside Andover into the community. The increased tendency of women to marry men from outside Andover almost certainly was accompanied by the likelihood of marriage outside Andover for men who moved away; their marriages, though, are not reflected in the town's own records. The rough ratio was about half marrying partners from Andover, and half marrying outside, although exactitude in this matter is impossible to achieve.

Despite the effects of a decline in the rate of birth and a rise in the rate of mortality in Andover during the period after 1725, and despite the shrinkage in the average sizes of families, the proportion of emigrants leaving Andover in the fourth generation increased by the same percentage as had been the case a generation earlier. Less than half of the fourth-generation men who reached the age of twenty-one chose to remain permanently in Andover, with a maximum of 224 out of 398 men (56.3 per cent) moving away at some point in their lives (see Table 27). The percentage of men remaining in Andover thus continued to decline and was only 43.7 per cent in the fourth generation. While it must be emphasized that this represents the minimum percentage remaining in Andover (since the data reflect the assumption that men whose marriages and deaths are unrecorded in the town records proba-

Table 27. Geographical mobility of second-, third-, and fourth-generation
males living to age 21

Generation	Men living to age 21	Men living in Andover		Men moving	
		No.	%	No.	%
Second	129	101	78.3	28	21.7
Third	287	175	61.0	112	39.0
Fourth	398	174	43.7	224	56.3

bly survived and moved away, and it is always possible that a proportion actually died in childhood, thereby augmenting the mortality rates and diminishing the extent of geographical mobility), the proportion of fourth-generation men leaving Andover almost certainly was half.[19]

The emigration of the fourth generation reflected an increased tendency toward widespread dispersal, rather than the frequent concentration of resettlement in the cluster of towns in Windham County, Connecticut, or in Concord, New Hampshire, which marked the migrations of many in the third generation. After the mid-1720's, the path of emigration shifted north to New Hampshire and west toward the middle of the Bay Colony, where two new towns, Lancaster and Lunenburg, attracted at least ten fourth-generation Andover men. Eighteen other towns in Massachusetts also attracted

[19] The imbalance in the rate of mobility in the North and the South Parishes was less striking in the fourth generation than in the previous generation, but it continued nevertheless. Although 46.2 per cent of the fourth-generation males were born in families residing in the North Parish, only 43.8 per cent of the emigrants were from the North Parish families, compared with 56.3 per cent from the South Parish. The percentage of men moving from the North Parish, however, increased from 32.1 per cent in the third generation to 43.8 per cent in the fourth generation. Perhaps this accounts for the continued disparity in the number of ratepayers in the two parishes, the North being larger throughout the period from 1715 to 1765.

emigrants from Andover who are known to have resettled in these towns either alone or in very small numbers.[20] Several fourth-generation men moved to towns in Windham County already settled by earlier Andover emigrants. But the majority of the emigrants moved to New Hampshire, where some

[20] The mobility of the third and fourth generations in Andover evidently corresponded to increased mobility in other Essex County communities during this period, judging by the increased numbers of men appearing on the Andover tax lists from outside the town. Most of these men were transients, although some settled permanently in Andover, usually as craftsmen. Others, however, were laborers, and very mobile. These migrants also often ended up in New Hampshire, and also discovered that their geographical movement could foster economic gains. In 1742, for instance, John Cristy "of Andover . . . Labourer" bought fifty acres of land in New Hampshire for £28, after which he moved to Londonderry, N.H., where he became a husbandman, and bought another tract of forty-five acres in Windham, N.H., in 1745 (New Hampshire Deeds, vol. 30, pp. 333-334; vol. 47, p. 362, in the New Hampshire Historical Society). The following year, John Christy "of Windham . . . Husbandman" bought more land there, leaving an estate in 1767 in Windham worth £998, of which £655 was in real estate (see New Hampshire Deeds, vol. 47, p. 363, and John Christy, inventory, June 16, 1767, New Hampshire Probate Records, vol. 18, pp. 482-483 in the New Hampshire Historical Society). Others who came to Andover also bought land in New Hampshire but did not leave Andover immediately.

The inventories of some of these outsiders who died in Andover generally reveal them to be poor. William Baxter, for instance, left no real estate in 1752, with a personal estate of about £3, with money due for services at Cape Breton, totalling £23 with £13 in debts (William Baxter, inventory, PR 2155). Similarly, Samuel Dillaway left no real estate at his death in 1756, with £45 in personal estate, but £67 in debts, thus dying insolvent (Samuel Dillaway, inventory, PR 7696). Some of these men were husbandmen with small estates, such as John Danford, who left about thirty-seven acres in Andover and eight in Tewksbury in 1758 (inventory, PR 7140), or Phineas McIntire, who left a house, "The Fraim of a Small Barn" and "about Six Acres of Land & Meadow" in 1759, with a total estate worth £25, and £16 in debts (inventory, PR 18115).

resettled in Concord, Pembroke, and Wilton, and others reestablished themselves in at least sixteen additional towns. Andover men also moved into at least seven towns in the northern part of Massachusetts which is now included in Maine, and eventually at least one fourth-generation man made his way to Vermont. Altogether, these emigrants resettled in at least fifty-two different communities in Massachusetts, Connecticut, New Hampshire, Maine, and Vermont.

The mobility of half of the fourth-generation men is indicative of the increasing proportion of nuclear families from Andover scattering about New England during the mid-eighteenth century. At the same time, the number of men coming to reside in Andover during this period also indicates the presence of nuclear families in the town itself. Out of twenty men born outside of Andover but appearing on a rate list of 1755, for instance, nine appear to have been unmarried, presumably young; five were either already married or were later to be married to women with no kindred in Andover.[21] Nathan Frazier, for instance, married Elizabeth White, of Boston, in 1756 but continued to reside in Andover at least until 1768, when the last of six births in his family was recorded, forming a nuclear family without known kindred in Andover. Phineas McIntyre probably married before coming to Andover, and he had three children baptised in 1752 but no relatives in the town in 1755. These men and their families in Andover were comparable to many of the fourth-generation men who left Andover to reside elsewhere.

In some instances, men from outside Andover acquired kindred through marriage to an Andover girl, some of whom

[21] See the Province tax rate list, October 10, 1755, in Andover, Town and County Tax Lists, 1717–1768. For vital data on these newcomers, see *Vital Records, passim.*

had extensive groups of kindred in the community.[22] At least five men on the 1755 list from outside married into Andover families, including the Abbots, Barkers, Faulkners, Fosters, and Stevenses. Within the context of the extended family networks of mid-eighteenth-century Andover, nuclear families were usually the result of having come into the community from outside and not marrying into families already established there. For families to be truly autonomous and completely isolated from kindred in Andover was relatively rare.

The pervasiveness of the kinship network which came to dominate the family structure of prerevolutionary Andover is revealed by the large numbers of men bearing old family names who paid rates in the town from decade to decade. The continuity of these kinship networks is reflected in the consistency with which descendants of the majority of the families of early settlers continued to reside in the town. Some of these family groups were very extensive in numbers, as Table 28 indicates, and their numbers alone would serve to reveal the presence of several widely extended families; the most notable were the Abbots, Holts, Stevenses, Osgoods, Johnsons, Fosters, Barkers, Blanchards, Chandlers, Farnums, Fryes, Parkers, and Poors, all with at least ten ratepayers in 1767. Other old settler families were smaller in numbers, such as the Barnards, Ballards, Faulkners, Martins, Russes, Russells, and Tylers. Relatively few of these families increased their num-

[22] Elizabeth Lovejoy, for instance, married William Baxter in 1742. After his death, she informed the probate judge that she was "Under poor Sorcomstances and no way Capeable of Administaring on the Estate . . . but I have Take advice of my frinds and Neighbours and they Recommend my Honoured Oncle M[r] Henry Phelps," her deceased mother's brother. See petition, Elizabeth Baxter to Judge Thomas Berry, PR 2155.

Table 28. Males on tax lists, by families, 1730–1767

Family	1730	1740	1750	1760	1767
Abbot	23	24	31	34	33
Allen	1	3	1	0	0
Aslet	0	0	0	0	0
Ballard	6	5	5	2	4
Barker	15	15	13	11	12
Barnard	4	3	5	6	3
Blanchard	9	10	7	9	10
Bradstreet	0	0	0	0	0
Chandler	8	10	13	9	11
Dane	3	2	3	3	6
Farnum	12	11	9	10	10
Faulkner	4	1	2	1	1
Foster	10	11	12	18	17
Frye	9	13	14	11	11
Holt	15	23	28	25	25
Ingalls	7	6	10	10	9
Johnson	12	13	16	15	16
Lovejoy	14	14	9	8	8
Martin	3	3	5	6	3
Osgood	13	12	15	13	13
Parker	6	7	8	9	12
Poor	5	5	7	10	11
Russ	1	1	0	0	1
Russell	3	4	5	4	4
Stevens	15	14	19	17	19
Tyler	1	1	2	3	2
Total	199	211	239	234	241

bers on the rate lists between 1730 and 1767, with most remaining fairly constant numerically throughout this period. This is scarcely surprising in view of the number of fourth-generation men who departed. But what it indicates is the persistence of a considerable number of extensive family groups, and of many extended families, within the community during the lifetimes of the third and fourth generations.

The largest of these extended families, the Abbots, car

serve as an example of the complexities of kinship binding families together and forming a substantial portion of the entire community into a closely-knit social world of grandparents, uncles, aunts, and cousins, both within the family itself and among other related families in the town as well. On the town rate list of 1755, for example, there were thirty-one male Abbots, all descendants of George Abbot I. Twelve of them were third-generation, nineteen were fourth-generation, and none on the list was fifth-generation. The majority of the men were over thirty years old, with only two under twenty; nine were in their twenties, six in their thirties, two in their forties, four in their fifties, six in their sixties, two in their seventies, and none any older than seventy-nine. Two were deacons in the South Parish Church, two were captains in the militia, one was a lieutenant, and one was an ensign. At least ten of the fourth-generation men had their fathers living still, and at least fourteen had their mothers living still in 1755. Only six of the thirty-one men were unmarried. Of the rest, four married Lovejoys, two married Holts, one married another Abbot, and others married into the Stevenses, Allens, Blunts, Danes, Fosters, Farringtons, Farnums, Fryes, and Ballards of Andover.[23] Eight married women from outside Andover.

The great majority of the Abbots were residents of the same general area in the South Parish, with nineteen of them living on the eastern side of the Shawsheen River and nine on the western side. Only three of these Abbots lived in the

---

[23] Out of a total of sixty-eight marriages of Abbots of the third and fourth generations (including both men and women) which took place before the end of 1755, fifty-one were to members of other Andover families, including fifteen to other Abbots, six to Lovejoys, four to Holts, and involving them altogether with twenty other Andover families. Only seventeen of their marriages were to outsiders.

North Parish. Closely connected by ancestry and by residence, the Abbots formed a large and impressive group of kindred within the South Parish of the town. Their marriages into other Andover families only added to their already extensive numbers of relatives within the community itself. The widely extended family was a persistent reality of immense importance in shaping the characteristics of families in mid-eighteenth-century Andover.

Equally important, however, is the fact that the degree to which families were extended in their structures varied considerably, depending in part upon the number of members who resided within Andover and in part upon the extent of their connections with other families in the town. For families with no more than five men paying rates in Andover, the extent of their probable kinship relations was relatively narrow compared to large and complex families like the Abbots and Holts, or even the Barkers, Farnums, and Osgoods. The Ballards, for instance, were represented by six male ratepayers in 1755, one of whom was third-generation and five of whom were fourth-generation. Josiah Ballard, the only one of four third-generation brothers still paying rates in Andover (two were dead and the oldest, Uriah, 71, was being maintained by his son, who paid the rates), had only one of his sons paying rates. His eldest son married outside Andover and moved away, and his youngest son married in 1756 and then moved away. His daughters married into two Chandler families (their mother was a Chandler also and still alive until 1779) and into the families of the Johnsons, Holts, and Lovejoys, of Andover, as well as the Danas of Cambridge, and the Clarks. Two of their cousins also married Chandlers. Uriah, Jr., had married into the Dane and Barker families with his first two wives, and then he married a Danforth from outside Andover in 1754 and later moved away. Their marriages thus often established or consolidated kinship connections with other Andover families, thereby extending the boundaries of the Ballard family as a whole within the town. Their smaller numbers made it less widespread than some of the larger families in Andover, but no Ballard living in Andover was completely isolated from other close relatives or relatives by marriage. Taken as a whole, this family, like nearly all of the old established families in the town, was extended in its structure.

The kinship network within Andover also accounted for the extension of family connections in the case of James Allen, the only fourth-generation member of this old settler family paying rates in the town in 1755. James Allen, aged 42, had married Deborah Poor in 1736 at the age of 23, thereby allying himself to the extensive family of Daniel Poor, whose wife, the daughter of John Osgood, had died in 1752 at the age of 80. The Poors were married to members of the Osgood, Faulkner, Farnum, Stevens, and Russ families in Andover. James Allen's mother, Mary Dane Allen, was still alive in 1755, aged 63, thus maintaining her connections with the Danes, and with the Osgoods, Graingers, and Fosters through the marriages of her brother and sisters. Two of James Allen's brothers had left Andover to resettle elsewhere, and one of his brothers died in 1745 at the age of 24. His family thus was minimal in extent in Andover, yet was not isolated in terms of kinship with the other inhabitants of the community. James' marriage assured that he would remain closely connected to other families in Andover. Before the end of 1758, however, James was dead at the age of 45, leaving his widow and children residing in Andover in the company of a considerable number of relatives.

For the most part, households in Andover in the middle of the eighteenth century continued to be nuclear in structure as they had been in previous generations, with the majority of married couples residing in houses of their own apart from parents or other kindred. During the course of the middle decades of the century, though, it became increasingly common for households to be extended in their structures by the residence of married children in the houses of their aging parents, thus forming trigenerational households. The census of 1764, for instance, reveals that 438 families in Andover lived in only 360 houses, which suggests that 78 families must have shared houses with other families.[24] Some of these probably were unrelated, boarding or renting their space in other households. Others, however, were clearly constituted of grandparents, children, and grandchildren, as evidence from wills and deeds confirms. Such extended households remained the exception, but they evidently were becoming more and more common in Andover during the lifetimes of the third and fourth generations.

In mid-eighteenth-century Andover it was almost impossible for the families of descendants of early settlers to be completely nuclear so long as they remained settled in the community. Whether their own particular households consisted of two or three generations—and thus were either nuclear or extended in their structures—they were nearly always parts of larger networks of kindred. Collectively, these households formed the extended families which remained a permanent part of the familial experiences of descendants of the settler families through the lifetimes of at least four generations. Even when men married wives from outside Andover but continued to live in Andover, their own kindred within the town—including their parents, some of their siblings, uncles, aunts, and cousins, both in their own particular family

[24] See Greene and Harrington, *American Population*, p. 23.

and in the families related to them by other marriages—provided them with a complex web of family relationships and connections.

What matters most, however, is not simply that so many of these families were extended in structure, but that the degree of extension varied so widely. Depending upon many factors —some demographic, some economic, some residential—these families could expand or contract in size. Nearly everyone was a part of a kinship group, to be sure, but the kinship world of an Abbot or a Holt was more extensive than that of a Chandler or a Frye, and far more extensive than that of a Ballard or an Allen. In this sense, the structures of their families were varied and variable, responsive to the changing circumstances of life and of actions governing individuals and families in the third and fourth generations. But—equally significantly—what did not change appreciably over time was the persistence of these extended families within this particular community. They provided a basic source of stability and continuity in the midst of many profound changes reshaping the lives of Andover's inhabitants in the mid-eighteenth century.

8

Independence and Dependence in Mid-Eighteenth-Century Families

The changing circumstances underlying the patterns of experiences that shaped the lives of the maturing fourth generation were reflected most strikingly in changing relationships between generations. Although some fathers continued to act like patriarchs and to prolong their control over their maturing sons, many no longer did. In retrospect, it is apparent that this generation was increasingly independent.

A combination of circumstances probably fostered the relatively early autonomy of many fourth-generation sons and encouraged their fathers to assume that their sons ought to be on their own as soon as possible. The rapid expansion of new settlements and the emigration of many third-generation Andover men had amply demonstrated the opportunities which existed outside Andover for those willing and able to leave their families and begin life for themselves elsewhere. The diminished landholdings of many families and the constantly rising prices of land in Andover during the first half of the century also put great pressure upon sons who wished to remain as farmers in Andover and made it imperative that many sons take up trades instead or move elsewhere for the land they needed. Less obvious (but surely no less important) must have been the heightened sense of the impermanence of life itself, reflecting the diminished chances for survival in childhood and youth among the fourth generation. Perhaps this, too, might have encouraged fathers to let their offspring establish their own independence sooner than they themselves had generally done. By examining their actions in transmitting their estates to their sons and in settling their sons in livelihoods of their own, such elusive developments can be demonstrated. For the history of the family, the loosening of the ties binding the generations together was of the utmost importance, distinguishing the fourth from earlier generations.[1]

For the fourth generation, as for earlier generations, the family provided the principal source of support in making the transition from youth to adulthood. Sons continued to need substantial assistance in the form of money or land in order to be able to assume responsibility for families of their own. Parents still played an indispensable role in the lives of their maturing children. The principal difference was that many had grown more willing to let go of the economic bonds tying their children to them. They now offered help without the strings binding earlier generations together. And this, more than any other single thing, is what distinguished their families from those of earlier generations.

As earlier, the relationships between fathers and sons and the characteristic structures of families depended in large measure upon the economic resources at the disposal of particular families. The amount of land owned by a family as well as the particular attitudes of fathers toward the use and trans-

[1] For a general perspective upon social, economic, and psychological changes occurring in the mid-eighteenth century, see Richard L. Bushman, *From Puritan to Yankee: Character and the Social Order in Connecticut, 1690–1765* (Cambridge, Mass., 1967). Unfortunately, Bushman's suggestive study is not based upon an analysis of specific individuals, families, or communities, and thus is difficult to use for purposes of comparison with studies such as this.

mission of their land shaped the alternatives open to third-generation families as their fourth-generation sons reached maturity and required settlements. On the basis of surviving probate records, it is evident that most third-generation estates contained at least 30 acres of land, with more than half ranging in size between 30 and 109 acres (34 out of 61, or 55.7 per cent), and more than a third ranging between 110 and a maximum of 611 acres (23 out of 61, or 37.7 per cent). The proportion of probated fourth-generation estates containing between 30 and 109 acres was only slightly greater than in the third generation, with 59.7 per cent (43 out of 72) in this range, but the proportion of large estates exceeding 110 acres was considerably smaller than before, totaling 25.0 per cent, of which only one estate contained more than 300 acres.

Despite the trend toward somewhat smaller estates, what is most interesting is the tendency for estates to remain above 30 acres in size, indicative, it would seem, of a common conviction that less than this would not be sufficiently profitable to provide a living for a family—to say nothing of a surplus for cash or credit. In effect, the character of the agrarian economy combined with the interests and the desires of families to limit the parcelling of the land beyond a certain point.

The values of probated third-generation estates reflect an increased disparity of wealth when compared to the estates of the second generation. This can be seen in the differences in the value of the estates of the wealthiest and the poorest men. The values of fourth-generation estates indicate that an increasing proportion of men were unable to maintain the levels of wealth of the preceding generation; Table 29 shows a sharp increase in the proportion of very modest estates and a sharp decrease in the proportion of very substantial estates. One quarter of the second-generation estates were valued at less than £200 compared with only 9.3 per cent of the third-gen-

Table 29. Total value of estates in inventories for four generations of men

Value (in £)	First generation		Second generation		Third generation		Fourth generation	
	No.	%	No.	%	No.	%	No.	%
0–99	0	0.0	3	8.6	3	4.0	10	10.8
100–199	1	6.7	6	17.1	4	5.3	11	11.8
200–399	8	53.3	12	34.3	16	21.1	27	29.0
400–599	5	33.3	5	14.3	9	11.8	13	14.0
600–799	1	6.7	1	2.9	15	19.7	9	9.7
800–999	0	0.0	3	8.6	5	6.6	5	5.4
1,000–1,999	0	0.0	2	5.7	15	19.7	7	7.5
2,000 and over	0	0.0	3	8.6	9	11.8	11	11.8
Total	15	100.0	35	100.1	76	100.0	93	100.0

eration estates. By the fourth generation, however, the percentage of estates below £200 in value increased again to 22.6 per cent, with a similar increase in the proportion of estates valued at less than £600 (42.2 per cent in the third generation, 65.6 per cent in the fourth). Whereas 31.5 per cent of the third-generation estates were valued at more than £1,000, only 19.3 per cent of the fourth generation estates were valued this high (only 5 per cent more than in the second generation). In terms of the total values of their estates, the second and the fourth generations appear to be surprisingly close, with a higher percentage of the third generation evidently being wealthier and possessing more ample estates. In the case of the fourth generation, however, these changes appear to indicate a declining standard of living for those who remained in Andover.

Perhaps one of the most striking differences between the periods in which the third and fourth generations reached maturity, apart from the events of the time, was the great disparity in the value of land in Andover between the first and second halves of the century. The period between 1710 and

1750 evidently was one of almost continuous inflation of value
for land of all sorts, but particularly for land which could be
improved for tilling, mowing, or pasturage. The average value
of all land in Andover had increased markedly every decade
after 1710, having remained remarkably constant throughout
the seventeenth century and into the first decade of the eighteenth century. The 1730's and 1740's, however, were the decades of greatest value, with mixed land averaging about £9
during the 1730's and about £11 during the 1740's; the average suddenly plummeted to only about £4 during the 1750's
and about £4½ during the 1760's, and rose to about £5½
during the 1770's and 1780's. In effect, during much of
the period in which fourth-generation Andover men were
maturing and acquiring land for their own livelihoods, the
value of land in Andover itself fell sharply from the previous
period. The average value of upland and arable land, for
instance, dropped from about £10 during the 1740's to about
£5 during the 1750's, with the maximum values dropping
from about £21 per acre to about £9 per acre. Similarly, the
maximum values for meadow in Andover dropped from about
£20 per acre during the 1740's to about £5 per acre during
the 1750's, a level closely aligned with that for the period
prior to 1710. Even the value of unbroken land in Andover
returned to seventeenth-century levels after 1750.

In general, then, land cost appreciably less after 1750 than it
had before 1750, with the result that the great disparity between land values in Andover and in newer towns in New
Hampshire during the 1720's, 1730's, and 1740's, became less
striking during the 1750's and 1760's. This resulted in part
from the general decline in land values in Andover and in part
from the general rise in land values in the New Hampshire
towns which had already been settled for a decade or more.

In terms of land values, therefore, it appears that much of

the pressure upon the local economy lessened after 1750. Undoubtedly part of this can be accounted for by factors reshaping and affecting the economy of the entire colony, although very little is yet known about the general economy; perhaps part also can be accounted for by the relative decrease in the size of families and in the slowing rate of growth of the town's population; in addition, though, a psychological predisposition toward movement out of Andover by the fourth generation, reflected in the increasing percentage of emigrants, might have had an effect in reducing the value of land in the community. Lacking any concrete evidence, such speculations must serve until much more is known about the economy of the colony in general during this period.

Fourth-generation sons, like their fathers and grandfathers before them, often were dependent upon their fathers for the inheritances which constituted a substantial portion of their livelihoods and which would provide them with at least an initial start in life, whether in the form of land, money, education, or a trade. An even larger proportion of third-generation estates were transmitted intact to the fourth generation than had been the case in the previous generation, thus augmenting the trend toward impartible inheritances.[2]

[2] The inheritances of the fourth generation represent an early stage in the tendency toward imparitable inheritances noted during the 1830's by Alexis de Tocqueville. As he observed: "The laws of the United States are extremely favorable to the division of property; but a cause more powerful than the laws prevents property from being divided to excess. This is very perceptible in the states which are at last beginning to be thickly peopled. Massachusetts is the most populous part of the Union. . . . But in Massachusetts estates are very rarely divided; the eldest son generally takes the land, and the others go to seek their fortune in the wilderness. The law has abolished the right of primogeniture, but circumstances have concurred to re-establish it under a form of which none can complain and by which no just rights are impaired." These observations were followed by

Whereas 95.7 per cent of first-generation estates and 75.0 per cent of second-generation estates had been divided among all or most sons in families with at least two surviving sons, only 58.3 per cent of third-generation estates were divided among two or more sons. Out of 43 yeoman families, 24 chose to divide their land among several of their sons, giving some land to 67 out of 93 of their surviving sons (72 per cent), in contrast to 19 yeoman families having more than one son but preferring to bestow their entire landed estates upon one son only, with the result that only 19 out of their 68 sons received inheritances in Andover of their fathers' farms (27.9 per cent). Of the 8 gentlemen whose actions are known in dividing their estates among two or more sons, only 2 left their entire landed estates to one son and a total of 17 out of 25 fourth-generation sons of Andover gentlemen inherited a portion of their fathers' Andover farms (68 per cent). Out of a total of 74 third-generation fathers, 60 had to provide inheritances for two or more surviving sons, 13 had only one son surviving and one had no sons for whom to provide. Out of a total of 226 fourth-generation sons at least 152 were given land from their fathers' estates (67.3 per cent), with at least 46 receiving deeds of gift for their portions or buying them with deeds of sale, and with 106 sons receiving their land either by wills or by the actions of probate courts in those cases in which their fathers died intestate. About two-thirds of the inheritances of paternal land by will alone involved the paternal homestead, the majority of inheritors being eldest sons.

---

comments about American mobility, and the connections between patterns of inheritance and the uprooting of Americans were very evident to de Tocqueville, although they have been ignored by most later historians. See *Democracy in America*, ed. Phillips Bradley (New York, 1956), I, 293.

The average age at marriage for sons inheriting their fathers' land by will was 25.2 years, and their average age at the time of inheritance was 30.4 years, indicative of frequent delays between marriage and inheritance of land in Andover. Slightly more than three-fifths of the fourth-generation sons waited less than ten years to receive their inheritances, having gotten their land before marriage in 38.9 per cent of the cases. On the other hand, an equal percentage waited more than ten years before becoming full owners of their share of the paternal land, a reflection of the longevity of many of their fathers, forty-seven of whom died at an average age of 69.5 years.

A larger percentage of sons receiving deeds of gift for their portions married before the age of thirty than had done so in the previous generation (60.9 per cent instead of 40.7 per cent). A somewhat smaller percentage (53.4 per cent) of those buying their portions by deeds of sale married before thirty, but this was considerably more than the 42.1 per cent in the third generation. A larger percentage of the fourth generation receiving deeds of gift for their portions received them either before marriage or within five years of their marriage than had been true for the third generation (85.7 per cent versus 54 per cent), although the percentage of fourth-generation sons buying their portions within five years of their marriages was similar to that for the previous generation (57.1 per cent versus 54.5 per cent). It evidently was still difficult for men to acquire the capital or to achieve a position from which to purchase their portions of the paternal estates. The large percentage of sons receiving deeds of gift to their lands so quickly after marriage, if not before, does suggest a tendency for fathers to establish some of their sons independently at earlier ages and with less delay than had been apparent during the previous generation.

The sharp drop in the average age of marriage, the rising

proportion of impartible inheritances, and the tendency to convey land by deed to sons of younger ages and without undue delays all suggest the willingness on the part of third-generation fathers to permit and to encourage many of their sons to establish themselves economically on the land as independent farmers sooner than most second-generation fathers appear to have done. When these factors of inheritance are linked to the increased rate of mobility among fourth-generation sons, the evidence points toward the increasing independence of sons, the loosening of family ties binding the older and the younger generations together in Andover, and an increased awareness of, and willingness to take advantage of, economic opportunities outside of Andover itself. The changing patterns of inheritance thus suggest other changes within the families of the community as well.

The maintenance of the old patterns of partible inheritances and the establishment of all or most of one's sons on family land in Andover depended in large measure upon the amount of land which could be divided among the younger generation. For the most part, if estates could be divided at all and remain viable farms for the inheritors, they were divided into two or three parts. Occasionally an individual such as David Abbot (1689–1753) owned enough land to anticipate being able to settle all of his sons upon his own land, thereby keeping most of his children closely attached by their residences to their paternal family and extensive kindred in Andover itself, where the Abbots formed one of the largest single family groups in the South Parish. Although David Abbot had himself waited until the age of twenty-nine to marry, having previously followed the trade of housewright, his fortune was made by the transference by deed of gift from his mother of her share in the former Bradstreet estate, con-

taining about 350 acres, to which Abbot later added by purchasing "y° Greater part of a Certain Farm" which also had
been originally a part of the Bradstreet estate.[3] When he
bought this land in 1731, David Abbot was called a husbandman, indicating that he had given up his craft in favor of
farming; this change is readily understandable in view of the
fact that at his death at the age of sixty-four in 1753, he left
more than 579 acres of land in Andover, with real estate
worth a total of £1552—far more land than most men of his
generation had been able to accumulate either through inheritance or purchase.[4]

His estate was ample and could easily provide settlements
of land for his five sons, unless, of course, he chose to settle
the entire estate, or a substantial portion of it, upon a single
son, a choice which some men of equal wealth preferred.
Abbot, however, stated his desires in the will which he wrote
only seven days before his death.[5] Noting that he was "weak
of Body but of a perfect mind and Memory," he bequeathed
to his "Dearly and well Beloved Wife" the use and improvement of one-third of all his real estate, the use of the east end
of his dwelling house, and various other items. Less than a

---

[3] Essex Deeds, vol. 43, p. 87; vol. 92, pp. 59–60. David Abbot and his
three brothers formed a closely-knit group after the early death of
their father, Benjamin (1661–1703), and their mother continued to
act in his place, providing her sons with land which she purchased
and gave them. See Essex Deeds, vol. 94, p. 131 for her deed to
Samuel. These brothers often acted in partnership in the buying and
selling of land, and their family transactions may be seen in the
following deeds: vol. 43, p. 88; vol. 94, pp. 130–136.

[4] David Abbot, inventory, December 4, 1753, PR 28. His personal
estate was worth £210.

[5] David Abbot, will, November 7, 1753, PR 28. For the actual
division of the real estate, see the "Division of the Reall Estat David
Abbott late of Andover dec⁴ 1754," PR 28.

year before, Abbot's eldest son, David, Jr., had married at the age of twenty-four, having already been given a deed of gift from his father for a parcel of about twenty-three acres on the west side of the family homestead as a "part of his portion"; this deed established him independently on land of his own at a young age but kept him close by the family, nevertheless.[6] After his father's death, David, Jr., received an additional portion which added substantially to his initial grant, amounting finally to about 156 acres. The second son, "my Beloved Son Solomon," inherited about 160 acres, a portion equal to that of his elder brother but greater than those given to the three youngest sons. Their portions (ranging from 107 to 118 acres each) were later divided among them, although David, Sr., simply bequeathed the remainder of his land and buildings to his three youngest sons and his two daughters without specifying their particular portions. Two days after making his will, David Abbot's youngest son, ten years old, died, followed five days later by his own death, and the next day by the death of his third son, aged seventeen, thereby leaving only three sons to inherit and to divide the land with their widowed mother and their sisters. The widow Abbot, however, proved to be a hardy woman, living in the east section of her son Jonathan's house until 1788, when she died at the age of ninety-one, still surrounded by her surviving sons who continued to live nearby, and cared for by her son in the house which he had inherited.

Similar choices were evident in the documents remaining to illuminate the actions taken and anticipated by another wealthy Andover farmer, Lieutenant John Frye (1672–1739), whose estate at the time of his death included about 611 acres, nearly all of it in Andover, with buildings, valued

[6] Essex Deeds, vol. 100, pp. 115–116.

at £3,987.[7] Although he was sixty-five when he died, Frye had not yet written a will explicitly stating his wishes, and he died leaving an intestate estate to be divided by the court among his widow and ten surviving children. Five of his seven sons had survived (the eldest, John, Jr., had died at the age of twenty and the fifth son at the age of twenty-three), and three followed trades, one as a blacksmith and two as hatters. Frye had established his second surviving son in the hatter's trade, giving him a deed of gift in 1724 in token of his parental love for his dutiful son to the four and one-half acres of land upon which Joshua had already "Sett up a house and a Shop."[8] One month later, at the age of twenty-three, Joshua married, already established in a separate household with full control over his own livelihood and the property essential to his craft. The following year, Isaac, the eldest surviving son, married at the age of twenty-five; two months earlier he had received a deed of gift for ten acres "together with the dwelling house that I the said John Frie & my said son Isaac Frie hath built," a token of parental love for another dutiful son.[9] The third son, Abiel, did not marry until 1732, aged twenty-nine; he did not receive a deed for any property, but had to wait to inherit the land which his father settled him upon and upon which he evidently built a house. Similarly, the fourth

[7] His personal estate was relatively small in value, £219, but his estate had few debts, which totalled £169.6.4 (John Frye, inventory, September 1, 1739, PR 10303). Only the estate of Timothy Osgood, inventoried in 1748, was greater in value than Frye's, although much of the difference reflected the inflation of the period. Osgood left more than 450 acres, with an estate valued at a total of £8,131, to be divided between his only surviving son and his grandson; (Timothy Osgood, will, December 5, 1743, and inventory, September 29, 1748, PR 20282).

[8] Essex Deeds, vol. 42, pp. 224–225. Later he sold Joshua another two and one-half acres (Essex Deeds, vol. 48, p. 172).

[9] Essex Deeds, vol. 44, p. 244.

son, Joseph, who married at twenty-one, built a house apparently without receiving a deed. The youngest of the sons,
eighteen years old, died the year after his father, thus leaving
four brothers to inherit the bulk of the estate, the inventory of
which included twenty-seven acres of land "where his Son
Abiel Frie Liveth," indicative of the continued possession by
the elder Frye.

Thus Lieutenant Frye, by virtue of his extensive landholdings, was able to establish all of his sons upon his own land,
just as many fathers had done in the past. And like many
fathers in the past, he chose to retain control over the extensive acres which he had accumulated, giving only a token
amount to two of his sons. His sons, in turn, stayed in Andover, settled upon land given or promised to them by their
father, willing to await the time that they would gain full
titles to their inheritances.

As in previous generations, the division of this large estate
left all the inheritors relatively poorer than their father had
been. When Abiel Frye died in 1757, at the age of fifty-four,
for instance, he left only about 92 acres, with real estate
valued at £535 and a total estate worth £838, quite ample
for one family, yet far less than that left by his father.[10]
Similarly, when Joshua Frye died in 1767, he left about 127
acres, of which three-quarters was settled upon his eldest son
and one-quarter was given to his second son, whose mother
had been instructed "to give my s^d Son a Liberal Education &
a Handsome Decent Support 'till he arive to the Age of
Twenty one Years."[11]

The actions taken by Henry Holt, another wealthy gentle-

[10] Abiel Frye, inventory, April 13, 1758 and will, June 28, 1755, PR
10273. He divided his land equally among his three sons.

[11] Joshua Frye, will, March 14, 1764, and division of estate, May 27,
1771, PR 10314. No inventory survives.

man, in dividing his real estate among his sons, were similar to
those taken by Lieutenant Frye. At the age of seventy-six,
Henry Holt sold a substantial portion of his estate to two of
his four sons, one of whom married at thirty in 1735 and the
other in 1736 at twenty-nine, and both of whom were husbandmen.[12] Although Holt sold his second son in 1742 a small
parcel of upland and meadow containing about fifteen acres,
he waited until 1749 before selling him his major portion of
the paternal farm for the sum of £1,000 old tenor, or about
£250 new tenor. Although Henry Holt had been styled
"husbandman" earlier, he now was a "Gentleman" and his son
a "yeoman" in the deed of sale, which conveyed over 160
acres. Another deed of sale, signed the same day, conveyed
for £2,000 old tenor, or about £500 new tenor, a substantial
sum, "the Land which my Said Son has lived on & improved
for some years past" containing about thirty-five acres together with an additional twenty acres elsewhere. His son was
then forty-four years old. Similarly, Holt had sold his third
son, Henry, Jr., fifteen acres of upland and meadow in 1742,
but waited until 1749 before selling him his own homestead
lands and house in addition to other lands and a share in a
sawmill. On May 31, Holt received £3,000 in bills of credit,
old tenor, paid to him in hand before signing the deed to his
son, Henry, Jr., turning over to him full title to forty acres of
homestead land by Holt's dwelling house, which also adjoined
the homestead of his brother Josiah Holt, together with the
land upon which his house stood and all of the housing, barns,
and orchards which he had in his own possession, thereby
literally selling the roof over his own head to his son. For an

[12] For the deeds from Henry Holt, Sr., to his two sons, Benjamin and
Henry, Jr., see Essex Deeds, vol. 88, p. 110; vol. 93, p. 188; vol. 94, pp.
188–189, 212–221; vol. 95, p. 34. Neither a will nor an inventory exists
for Henry Holt, Sr.

additional £1,500 old tenor, Holt sold his son 180 acres of upland, meadow, and swamp and one-quarter share in the saw mill and dam which he owned. To complete the transference of his estate to the son who bore his name, he also sold for £500 old tenor all of his husbandry tools and utensils, carpentry tools, and most of his livestock.

Since Henry, Jr., had waited until the age of twenty-nine to marry, and eventually purchased his father's own homestead and house, the implication is that he acted in partnership with his father and lived within the same household as his parents, both before and after his marriage. Insofar as he evidently had no land whatsoever of his own, apart from that sold to him by his father, the inference seems justified. It is further supported by the inventory taken on December 3, 1754, three months after his death at the age of forty-eight and only three years after the death of his aged father.[13] Henry, Jr., left a homestead of about 45 acres with the buildings, originally his father's, together with more than 152 acres and an interest in a sawmill—clearly this was essentially the estate which he had purchased from his father. Although according to the deeds he had paid his father approximately £1,250 new tenor, his own estate was valued at £826, less £152 in debts owed by his estate. There can be little doubt that he had paid his father the full value of the land and housing which he obtained. Yet he had stayed and he had paid or promised to pay this much for part of the paternal estate in Andover.

His younger brother, Ephraim, also stayed in Andover, although it is not clear how he acquired the land which he left at his death in December 1749 at the age of thirty-six. He had married in 1735 at the age of twenty-two, and left his widow and children a house and about 78 acres in Andover, valued at

---

[13] Henry Holt, Jr., inventory, December 3, 1754, PR 13640. He died intestate.

£229 new tenor, with a personal estate worth only £30 and debts amounting to £53.[14] Presumably this land had also been conveyed to him by his father, whose estate was clearly one of the largest in Andover at this time and more than enough to justify him in styling himself a gentleman. Henry Holt, Sr., had divided at least 465 acres among two sons, and he may have had more than 540 acres if Ephriam's land had also been his originally. But like other Holts before him, he kept most of his land in his own name until old age made it necessary to convey it to his sons, three of whom remained in Andover, the eldest having left to live in Maine.[15]

[14] Ephraim Holt, inventory, May 28, 1750, PR 13637. He died intestate.

[15] A similar reluctance to part with control of the land is evident in the case of Oliver, the brother of Henry Holt, Sr., who faced the problem of settlements for eight sons. At least three were given trades, and four moved away from Andover. Just before his death at 76 in 1747, Oliver Holt sold part of his land to three of his sons. The eldest, Oliver, Jr., a blacksmith, had married in 1722 at 24 and settled upon his father's land, but waited until 1747 for a deed, paying his father £550 for the land "whereon his Dwelling House & Barn Now Stands" with some additional land as well (Essex Deeds, vol. 87, pp. 273–274). At his death in 1761, aged 63, he left only fifty-six acres of land (inventory, March 10, 1761, and will, May 2, 1760, PR 13681). David Holt, also a blacksmith, married at 24 and died at 39, leaving a house, barn, and thirty-two acres (inventory, October 28, 1747, PR 13631). The fourth son, Jonathan, married at 23, settled upon paternal land, which he purchased at the age of 36, including the land which he had built upon. The fifth son, Jacob, married in 1737 at 23 and ten years later bought most of the paternal homestead, including the buildings, for £700, together with part of the sawmill and livestock and husbandry tackling. When he died in 1761 at the age of 47, Jacob left seventy-two acres of land and the buildings that had belonged to his father, with an estate worth a total of only £362 and with debts amounting to £180 (inventory, March 27, 1761, PR 13645). He died intestate. The three youngest sons moved away from Andover, one to Lancaster and the others to Lunenburg. For the deeds from Oliver Holt to his sons, see Essex Deeds, vol. 87, pp. 273–274; vol. 91, pp. 46–47.

Other fathers, with considerably less land and less valuable estates, also chose to divide their land among as many sons as they could, thereby keeping many close by on land which in many instances had belonged to their grandfathers and great-grandfathers as well. Stephen Abbot, for instance, settled his three sons upon his Andover estate, which probably contained between 150 and 190 acres at the time of his death in 1766.[16] His eldest son had married at the age of twenty-four but died intestate in 1745 at the age of thirty-five, leaving a wife and three small children, and an estate worth a total of only £57.19.9 new tenor, which consisted of two acres of land, a barn but no house, eleven assorted animals, and a small personal estate.[17] It is evident that he owned neither the house in which he lived nor the farm which he probably cultivated, both of which, however, were to be inherited eventually by his son, whose grandfather left him the land and buildings which his father had used during his lifetime. Stephen Abbot's youngest son, Samuel, married in 1754 at the age of twenty-eight, but died four years later, leaving an intestate estate with a total value of £117, consisting of a dwelling house but no land.[18] Presumably he had built his own house upon his father's land, but had not yet received a title to his portion of the paternal estate, although his two daughters did eventually inherit land from their grandfather, which presumably was their father's portion of the estate.

The dependence of these Abbot sons upon their father for the land which they used was further demonstrated by the fact that virtually all of the land which the remaining son,

[16] No acreage is given in the inventory, and the estimate is based upon the average value of mixed land in Andover during this period (Stephen Abbot, inventory, July 7, 1766, PR 132).

[17] Ephraim Abbot, inventory, June 27, 1745, PR 40.

[18] Samuel Abbot, inventory, November 28, 1758, PR 122.

Stephen, Jr., had in his possession in 1768, when he died at the age of fifty-nine, had been inherited two years earlier from his father. When Stephen, Sr., died in 1766, at the advanced age of eighty-eight, he finally bequeathed his only surviving son all of the land not intended for the children of his two deceased sons, and the buildings in which he lived, together with half a corn mill that he had in partnership with two other men. His real estate was valued at £796, including the buildings, but his personal estate was worth only £40.[19] Two years later, his son's real estate was was valued at £555, consisting almost entirely of the land inherited from the original paternal estate. About all the property that his fifty-nine-year-old son had managed to acquire on his own was one Negro boy.[20] Stephen, Jr., a yeoman, had married in 1743, at the age of twenty-five; his father was then sixty-five and might have

[19] Stephen Abbot, will, November 3, 1759, and inventory, July 7, 1766, PR 132.

[20] Stephen Abbot, Jr., inventory, February 27, 1769, PR 133. At the time of his death, he was in debt to forty-six people, owing a total of £227, with the total debt incurred by his estate reaching about £345. The administrators of his estate estimated that the income from the real estate amounted to £25.9.4 for one year, which provided a return on the total investment of 4.6 per cent, about average for farms during this period. Jackson Turner Main (*The Social Structure of Revolutionary America* [Princeton, 1965], p. 105) found that "the great majority of farms" in all sections of the colonies "produced only a small cash surplus, and that the return on the value of the property . . . was low—probably seldom over 4 percent." This seems to hold true for Andover as well, although specific evidence is rare. The only other instance is the income for David Stevens' estate for one year, £5.6.8, with real estate valued at £106.17.6, which provided an annual return of 4.7 per cent. But Stevens, too, died heavily in debt in 1752, aged 29, leaving seven acres of land, a house, a barn, and a joiner's shop, twenty-nine shillings in cash, £110 in debts (see David Stevens, inventory, January 15, 1753, and account of administration, May 27, 1754, PR 26316).

been willing to share the burden of farming with his son, who must have continued to act in partnership with his father and probably even lived with his father and his mother, who died in 1750 at the age of seventy. Nevertheless, the elder Abbot, unwilling to transfer the legal control of the land over to his three sons during his lifetime, remained the owner of his entire landed estate until his death.

Similarly, Timothy Holt, a yeoman, died in 1758, at the age of seventy-five, in full control of his own estate. He bequeathed the east end of his house to his wife, who lived until she was eighty-one in 1765 and who was to be provided for by their second son, Timothy, Jr., who finally inherited the paternal homestead and buildings after nearly twenty years of marriage.[21] The eldest son, James, had been married twenty-three years before inheriting "all that Land whereon the Building Stands where he now dwells," the building itself, and additional land. Both sons, though, had married in their mid-twenties. Holt's estate consisted of approximately 150 acres, which were divided between his two oldest sons. The youngest son, Joseph, who had married in 1747 at twenty-seven, inherited £16 in silver money, some bedding, "with what he has already received in Books & house hold moveables and the Expense I have bin at for his learning." Joseph had attended Harvard, graduating in 1739.

Finally, Francis Ingalls, who died in 1759 at sixty-five, left 134 acres with real estate valued at £623. Included in the inventory was "His House where Eben' Live' at," which his eldest son, who married at the age of twenty-eight a decade earlier, received by his will, together with half of the real and personal estate.[22] The second son, Francis, who married in

[21] Timothy Holt, will, June 6, 1754, and inventory, March 28, 1755, PR 13700.

[22] Francis Ingalls, will, January 5, 1759, and inventory, February 26, 1759, PR 14499.

1754 at the age of twenty-three, inherited the paternal house and barn, together with the remaining half of the estate, except for one-third of the house reserved for his mother, who was to receive one-sixth of the income from the real estate during her lifetime as well. The youngest son, a carpenter, had already been given most of his portion, presumably in the form of money. All three sons remained in Andover.

In families such as these, the old patterns of partible inheritance, delayed control of the land by fathers, and the settlement of several sons upon paternal land in Andover continued to persist, which indicates both the viability of paternal influence over the lives of mature sons, and the presence of families which were extended in structure, as so many had been in the past. Even in the middle of the eighteenth century, in other words, families such as these were to be found in a town like Andover despite the high rate of mobility among fourth-generation sons, and the obvious economic advantages of cheap and abundant land in countless new communities throughout New England during this period. Some fourth-generation Andover sons evidently were content to remain in the town in which their parents and grandparents and great-grandparents had lived, and were content to settle upon paternal land without gaining full legal possession of the land which they had built upon and farmed until relatively late in their lives, just as earlier generations had done.

Such instances of prolonged paternal control over the land and over the lives of the younger generation were becoming less and less characteristic of father-son relationships, however. Increasingly, it appears, sons were seeking and gaining control over their estates and their inheritances before their fathers died and while they were themselves relatively young. Many did so by acquiring their land by deeds of gift or sale, and others established their autonomy even more visibly by the distances which they put, sometimes with the active help of their parents, between themselves and their parents and siblings in Andover. Among the most suggestive indications of this tendency are the increasing preference for impartible inheritances, the lower age of men at marriage, and the mobility of so many fourth-generation sons.

By the time that Deacon John Abbot died, aged eighty in 1754, he already had given away most of his estate to his sons, spending its substance for the provision of their settlements and for their establishment as independent adults.[23] His eldest son, John, Jr., was designated heir to the entire paternal real estate in Andover, half of which (including half of the paternal house and barn and about thirty acres) he purchased from his father, receiving a deed six days before his marriage at the age of twenty-eight. Eight years later, he purchased additional land from his father for £265, largely the other half of the land which he had obtained in 1732.[24] By his father's will, dated August 12, 1747, John, Jr., inherited all of the homestead lands and buildings, other parcels of land, together with the land which had been conveyed to him previously by deeds. The land and buildings thus became his exclusive inheritance. His father had transferred half of his estate at the age of fifty-eight, and most of the remainder by the age of sixty-six. His eldest son had waited, it appears, until he could be firmly in control of his own land, or at least a substantial portion of his father's land, before marrying. But by the time that he did finally marry, he evidently was no longer dependent upon his father. However, he continued to be responsible for his aged mother, who outlived her husband by two years, since she inherited the use of the west end of the paternal

[23] At his death, Abbot left about thirty-nine acres with his homestead buildings, valued at £255, with a total estate worth £353 (inventory, February 14, 1754, and will, August 12, 1747, PR 67).

[24] Essex Deeds, vol. 80, pp. 17, 255; vol. 81, p. 199.

house and was to be provided with all the necessities of life by her son.

With the transference of the paternal homestead to only one son, though, other alternatives had to be found for the settlements of the three younger sons. The second, Barachias, inherited one-quarter of his father's livestock, a little gun, "together with y° Trade that I helped him into" and the sum of £250 "wherewith I purchased the Land which he is now setled upon" and which he had received by deed. Barachias, a cordwainer or shoemaker, had married in 1733 at the age of twenty-six, having been given about 32 acres by his father.[25] The third son, Abiel, was sent to Harvard College, class of 1737, but died in 1739 at the age of twenty-three.[26] The youngest son, Joseph, who married his cousin in 1741 at the age of twenty-two, inherited one-quarter of his father's live-stock, half of the husbandry tools "which he now hath," and an old musket, "together wth Four hundred pounds in bills of Credit, some years since by me Bestowed upon him," his father noted, "and where with he purchased a Tract or Tracts of Land In Lane [New Hampshire] for his Settlement." This constituted his full portion. Having thus settled his eldest son upon his land in Andover, having given his second son a trade and money, having provided an expensive liberal education

[25] Essex Deeds, vol. 77, p. 179. This is actually a deed of sale rather than a deed of gift, but according to John Abbot's will, the money for the purchase was itself a gift, part of Barachias' portion of the paternal estate.

[26] Clifford K. Shipton, *Biographical Sketches of Those Who Attended Harvard College* [*Sibley's Harvard Graduates*] (Boston, 1873–   ), X, 112–113. See also the sermon preached at his funeral by John Barnard, minister of the North Parish Church, with a preface by Samuel Phillips, minister of the South Parish Church: John Barnard, *The Expectation of Man disappointed by the Great God. A Sermon . . . Occasioned By the much lamented Death of that hopeful Young Gentleman, Mr. Abiel Abbot . . .* (Boston, 1739).

for his third son, and money for land in New Hampshire for
his fourth son, Deacon Abbot felt impelled to add the following note to his will:

And here let it be further Observed that it is upon mature
Deliberation and for Sundry good & weighty Reasons that I have
Bequeatted & Willed to my Said Eldest Son as above Expressed,
and therefore I Expect, and my Will is, that my other Children
. . . be fully Satisfyed & Contented with what I have in time past
bestowed upon them, together with what I have now Bequeathed
to them.

There could be no mistake about his considered intention to
settle his entire landed estate upon only one of his sons. He
must have known full well what this decision meant in terms
of his family and his relationships with his sons. They had all
been settled independently both in and out of Andover long
before his death. As far as one can tell, this was his conscious
intention and choice. Other fathers made similar decisions.

A similar readiness to see sons established independently
upon the land is evident in the willingness of John Dane to sell
portions of his estate to three of his four sons when he himself
was only fifty-six years old. Although Dane did not die until
1763 at the age of seventy-one, he divided and sold most of his
estate to his sons in 1749.[27] His eldest son, John, Jr., who
married at twenty-three in 1739 and who thus was thirty-
three at the time of purchase, paid £200 for a tract of land
"with my Buildings on it" together with an additional forty
acres. The second son married at the age of twenty-seven
about one year after purchasing about thirty acres of his
father's farm for £150 and the third son also waited until
after purchasing about twenty acres of the paternal farm
before marrying at the age of twenty-three. All three sons

[27] See Essex Deeds, vol. 93, pp. 193–196, for their deeds.

were husbandmen, and only the fourth and youngest, who married in 1760 at the age of twenty-five, evidently moved to New Hampshire. At the time of his death, John Dane, Sr., had almost completed the transference of his estate to his sons since he left no house of his own and only twenty-six acres of woodland.

Some fathers established their sons on land of their own out of affection and as a free gift. James Ingalls, for example, gave his eldest son, a housewright, a gift of twenty-nine acres shortly after his marriage at the age of twenty-two in 1744, but later sold another of his sons, a yeoman, a tract of twenty-one acres.[28] Joseph Ballard gave his eldest son all of his buildings and much of his land as his full portion out of the estate, only reserving the use of one end of the house for himself and his wife during their lifetimes.[29] His son was then unmarried, probably in his mid-twenties, and married two years after receiving the deed of gift to his father's house and land. Similarly, William Barker divided his own house in half, deeding the "one half of our Dwelling house," and half the cellar and barn, together with six parcels of land, "with liberty to pass and repass across our land and out and in at our doors at all Occasions," to the third of their five sons, as a token of their parental love.[30] Their son had married two months earlier at the age of twenty-five, and both father and son were farmers. Several years earlier, in 1734, Barker had given the second of his sons, then a husbandman of Rumford,

[28] Essex Deeds, vol. 91, p. 161. In 1747, Ingalls, Sr., a gentleman, sold his son twelve and one-half acres for £420 old tenor (Essex Deeds, vol. 90, p. 192). A month earlier, he had sold about twenty-one acres to his son, Joseph, for £400 old tenor (Essex Deeds, vol. 90, p. 170).

[29] Essex Deeds, vol. 47, p. 242.

[30] Essex Deeds, vol. 74, pp. 153–154.

New Hampshire, all of his rights to land in Rumford.[31] Again, the father had purposefully settled one of his sons at a considerable distance from Andover and provided him with the land which he was to farm, giving him full title to his inheritance as a young man of twenty-eight. In these two instances, both sons could be considered fully independent of their father as far as the ownership of land was concerned, yet one son continued to share a roof with his father and mother, literally dividing the paternal house in half, while the other established himself and his own wife and children many miles away. Although each was financially independent, their places of residence made their lives significantly different, adding to the complexity of relationships and family structure evident throughout this period.

The frequent decisions of fathers to settle their entire Andover real estate upon only one of their sons required that the others be settled in trades, in professional careers in the ministry or commerce, or on land not owned by the family and often not even in Andover. All of these fostered the autonomy of sons by freeing them from the need to wait until their fathers were willing and able to divide their own land with them. Particularly important, though, is the willingness of many third-generation fathers to assist some of their sons to settle outside of Andover, usually upon land either bought for them by their father or with money provided by him for the purpose. Such actions took foresight and planning as well as conscious choices by parents with the concurrence, presumably, of their sons as to which would be given which portion of the estate and in which form it would be given: land in Andover, land outside Andover, or a trade.

Ebenezer Stevens, a husbandman of Andover, evidently

[31] Essex Deeds, vol. 67, pp. 30–31.

had begun to be concerned about land for his sons as early as 1726, when he first joined with the prospective proprietors of the new frontier town of Concord to the north.[32] With five sons to provide settlements for, but too little land to divide among them, Stevens evidently recognized the need for other alternatives.[33] By 1731, he had cleared his land and built a house in Concord, and between 1730 and 1732 he added to his initial holdings there by purchasing additional land in the community.[34] When Ebenezer's second son, Aaron, recorded his intention of marriage to his cousin, Deborah Stevens, of Andover, which took place May 4, 1732, he was already a resident of Concord, and almost certainly settled in the house which his father had built there and beginning to farm the land which his father had so assiduously acquired over the last six years. On March 26, 1732, Ebenezer Stevens, still a husbandman in Andover, gave Aaron a deed of gift to his rights to land in New Hampshire, together with two additional house lots, thereby giving him all but one of his pieces of property there.[35] Thanks to his father's foresighted efforts and generosity, Aaron Stevens migrated and settled permanently in the neighboring province.

With his departure, four sons remained to be provided for. The eldest son, Jacob, who did not marry until 1748 at the age of forty, was picked to inherit the largest portion of

---

[32] Similarly, John Chandler, gentleman, gave his eldest son and youngest son land in Rumford, N.H., bequeathing his entire Andover real estate to his second son. (John Chandler, will, April 20, 1741, PR 4940).

[33] Stevens probably owned about 135 acres before dividing it among his sons. At his death, his real estate consisted of about 38 acres with a house and two barns, valued at £214 in 1757 (inventory, June 10, 1757, PR 26324).

[34] See the following Essex Deeds: vol. 88, p. 135; vol. 89, pp. 68, 78.

[35] Essex Deeds, vol. 89, p. 56.

Ebenezer's Andover estate, including the homestead land an
buildings.[36] The third son, Ebenezer, Jr., waited until 1741 t
marry at the age of twenty-seven, and waited until 174
before receiving a deed of gift from his father for abou
forty-four acres of land in Andover.[37] The youngest son, Asa
a yeoman, received a deed conveying about thirty-six acre
three years after marrying at the age of twenty-five in 1745.[38]
The fourth son, Phineas, received a liberal education, whicl
enabled him to enter the ministry, after which he became th
minister ordained at Boscawen, New Hampshire, where h
eventually accumulated over 240 acres of his own.[39]

Humphrey Holt, with four sons and only a modest amoun
of land in Andover, settled his entire real estate, both land an

[36] See Ebenezer Stevens' will, November 17, 1750, PR 26324, whicl
specified that Jacob was to pay his widowed mother £60, to allow
her the use of half the dwelling house, and to provide her with the
necessities of life annually. In return he received all of his father'
remaining land and buildings and his personal estate, together with a
bond for about £63 which he had owed his father.

[37] Essex Deeds, vol. 92, pp. 131–132; vol. 93, p. 57. When Ebenezer
Jr., died in 1755 at forty-one, he left a house, barn, and shop witl
eighty-three and one-half acres valued at £441, and a total estate
worth £584. His debts, however, amounted to almost half the value
of his entire estate, being about £226 (Ebenezer Stevens, Jr., inven
tory, January 25, 1755, PR 26323).

[38] Essex Deeds, vol. 89, pp. 215–216; see vol. 93, p. 58 for ar
additional deed of sale for five and one-half acres. At his death in
1755, Asa left about seventy-three acres and an estate valued at £630
(Asa Stevens, inventory, May 8, 1756, PR 26288).

[39] Although Phineas died before Ebenezer, Sr., his children were
given some land in Rumford, N.H., with the comment that the
reason they were not given more was that their father "by his
Education & otherwise" had received the greater part of his portior
"heretofore" (Ebenezer Stevens will, PR 26324). For Phineas Stevens' inventory, May 1, 1755, see the New Hampshire Probate
Records, vol. 19, p. 373, New Hampshire Historical Society, Concord, N.H.

buildings, upon his eldest son, Fifield, who married at
twenty-four and inherited at thirty-seven.[40] The second son,
William, received a portion of only two shillings from his
father "which to geather with a Tract of Land which I gave
him for his Settlement at Lunenburg," a new settlement in
Massachusetts to the west of Andover, "and other helps wher
with I help't him in Settling" constituted his full inheritance.
The youngest son also received two shillings together with a
tract of land in Lunenburg "which I gave to him for his
Settlement." The third son, Humphrey, Jr., had already received the sum of £187 from his father as his portion of the
estate; he married at twenty-two in 1745 and eventually died
in Andover at the age of sixty-three. Two sons stayed in
Andover and two were settled elsewhere with the help of
their father.

One final example illustrates the variety of alternatives used
by fathers in providing settlements for their sons. Ephriam
Abbot, with six sons to provide for, settled his entire Andover
real estate upon his third son, who previously had been given
the trade of blacksmith. In 1747, about a year before
Ephriam's death at the age of sixty-six, he sold part of his
homestead land, containing about twenty acres, with half of
the parental dwelling house, the west end of which was reserved for Ephriam's own use, half the barn, and other small
parcels of land, "only reserving liberty for my brother Ebenezer Abbot and his heirs to pass and repass to his land where it
may do the least damage."[41] His son, Daniel, was then
twenty-three and unmarried, waiting until four years after his

---

[40] Holt had about fifty-six acres with buildings at the time of his
death in 1754, worth £265, and a personal estate worth only £37. See
his inventory, November 29, 1754, and his will, July 25, 1754, both in
PR 13643, for further details.

[41] Essex Deeds, vol. 89, pp. 209–210.

father's death and his full inheritance of the estate before marrying at the age of twenty-eight. The eldest son, Ephriam, Jr., a husbandman, had already sold all rights to his portion of the paternal estate to his brother Daniel, who paid him £600 by a deed made the same day that Daniel purchased part of the paternal homestead.[42] Ephriam had married in 1740 at twenty-two and evidently moved to Amherst, New Hampshire, sometime after 1745. By his father's will, he received the token sum of five shillings together with the £600 which had been paid by his brother.[43] The second son, Joshua, who married at the age of twenty-seven, after his father's death, inherited a division of land "Lying in a Township Called New Ipswich" in western Massachusetts, and later moved away. To his son, Josiah, who was nineteen at the time he wrote his will, he left £60 in bills of credit "togather with a trade which I order him to have or what he can procure by his Endostry togather with what shall fall to him of my household goods." His two younger brothers also were given £60 each and ordered to take up trades, with one becoming a shoemaker, marrying at twenty-one, and dying at forty, and the other presumably also following a trade, marrying at twenty-three, and also dying at forty. Ultimately, four of these six sons moved away from Andover.

For the most part, the migrations of the fourth generation can be seen and described from the extant sources, but the motivations and concerns which prompted them, and the effects which their migrations had upon their lives, can only be approached indirectly, surmised rather than documented.[44]

[42] Essex Deeds, vol. 89, p. 209.

[43] For details, see Ephriam Abbot's will, March 12, 1747, PR 41. Also see his inventory, September 1, 1748, PR 41, which valued his homestead land and buildings at £175, with a total estate at £218.

[44] Mobility evidently proved economically rewarding in many

One suggestive and tantalizing exception to this generalization exists, however, in the form of several almanac diaries kept by the Reverend Samuel Chandler (1713–1775). He was the third of Josiah Chandler's seven sons and the only one educated at Harvard and entering the ministry.[45] Like many fathers in Andover at this time, Josiah Chandler chose to settle his entire real estate in Andover upon only one of his sons, giving the others trades, money, or education instead of land. The result was the dispersal of his family, as several of his sons, including Samuel, moved away to other towns.

Three years before his death at the age of sixty-nine, Josiah Chandler wrote his will.[46] After providing for the maintenance of his wife, who outlived him by two years and also died at the age of sixty-nine, Chandler gave the sum of £40, besides what had previously been given, to his eldest son, who

---

cases, if some of the surviving probate records are any indication. William Barker, for instance, who died at thirty-eight in Rumford, N.H., left an estate which included more than 127 acres of land, with real estate valued at £421 in 1743, and a total estate worth £598 (William Barker, inventory, N.H. Probate Records, vol. 15, p. 266). His cousin, Abiel Chandler, who died at thirty-three in 1750, left more than 162 acres, with a total estate worth £1384 old tenor, or about £346 new tenor (Abiel Chandler, inventory, N.H. Probate Records, vol. 16, p. 108; vol. 25, p. 231). James Osgood, the second of three sons, left more than 230 acres, 10,000 bricks, 4 Negroes, and a total estate in Rumford in 1757 worth £7,179 when he died at the age of fifty (James Osgood, inventory, N.H. Probate Records, vol. 20, p. 280; also see his will, vol. 20, pp. 170–171).

[45] Six of Samuel Chandler's Almanac diaries for the years 1746, 1749–1751, 1752–1753, 1756–1758, 1761–1764, and 1769–1772, are located in the Essex Institute, Salem, Mass. For printed extracts from several of his diaries, see George Chandler, *The Chandler Family* . . . (Worcester, Mass. 1883), pp. 190–202, *passim*. For printed extracts from his diaries of 1751–1764, see John J. Babson, *Notes and Additions to the History of Gloucester* (Salem, 1891), pp. 6–64.

[46] See Josiah Chandler, will, February 18, 1749, PR 4957. For other details relating to the family, see Chandler, *Chandler Family*, *passim*.

had settled in Suncook, New Hampshire, and who evidently followed the trade of carpenter. The second son, Josiah, Jr., who had become an innholder in neighboring Bradford, Massachusetts, also received a legacy of £40, together with previous gifts. Samuel, who had graduated from Harvard in 1735, received the token sum of twenty shillings "with a Liberal Education which I have Given him at the University in Cambridge" as his full portion. To the fourth son, Abijah, who died at the age of thirty-five, he left £300 old tenor and a cow, explaining that his portion was given because of "my Said Son having been helpful to me in the Management of my affairs for Several Years since he came of age." Abijah did not marry until 1750, at the age of thirty-one. To the youngest son, Daniel, he left the sum of £120 old tenor and a good cow, but Daniel died five months before his father, unmarried at the age of twenty-five. Since Daniel's estate consisted only of a bible, a shoe knife, a hammer, a last (which suggest that he followed the trade of shoemaker), and several notes of hand, all of which was valued at only slightly more than £12, it is evident that he had not yet been given his portion of his father's estate in cash. Seven years earlier, his brother, Jonathan, had died at the age of twenty-three, leaving about £18 in cash, a gun worth £1 and a psalm book valued at eight pence, making his estate worth about £19 in all, with nearly £5 in debts.[47]

Both Daniel and Jonathan died poor, with neither land nor the resources to provide for families of their own. Their meager estates demonstrate once more the crucial importance of paternal assistance in establishing sons with sufficient economic resources to become independent adults capable of providing for their own livelihoods and for the maintenance

[47] Daniel Chandler, inventory, June 2, 1755, PR 4925; Jonathan Chandler, inventory, May 23, 1755, PR 4943. Jonathan died in 1745.

of families of their own. Fathers still owned most of the initial resources which the fourth generation had to have in order not to begin their own adult lives in poverty. Josiah Chandler's family was no exception.

Although a yeoman, Josiah Chandler did not have enough land to provide farms in Andover for more than one of his sons.[48] His real estate, valued at £450, consisted of about eighty-eight and one-half acres, with a dwelling house. He therefore decided to settle his entire real estate upon his sixth son, David, who married in 1750 at the age of twenty-six and inherited his father's estate two years later. Chandler wrote in his will, made the year before his son's marriage: "I give Unto my Son David Chandler (who for Several Years hath been in my Service at all times Acquiting himself faithful and in Confidence of his being a Comfort to me in my old age and in Consideration of what I have willed him to do for my Beloved wife and my other Children . . .)," all of his lands and buildings in Andover, together with all of the stock and tools, and all money and notes of hand due to him, in return for which David was obligated to provide his mother with all the necessities of life during her lifetime.

With all of the Andover land thus given to only one son, with several sons established in trades, and with one son given an expensive education in preparation for the ministry, the Chandler family clearly could not remain closely knit, settled upon family land, and dependent upon an aging father for support. Instead, the family had dispersed, indicative of the loosening of ties between members of the family. However, Samuel Chandler's diaries indicate that so long as their parents lived, connections between the generations were never entirely severed.

[48] See his inventory, November 20, 1752, PR 4957.

For Samuel Chandler, as for nearly all emigrants, life away from Andover was very different from life in Andover, where Chandlers were numerous, and where kindred abounded and neighbors were long familiar. Life tended to revolve around the concerns of his own immediate family in the community in which he had chosen to settle, a nuclear family living in the midst of relative strangers. Yet despite the distance from York, Maine, where Samuel had settled as minister, to Andover, kinship connections and old friendships were maintained by frequent trips and visits back and forth.

Occasionally such trips were prompted by sickness or death, as one of the earliest recorded visits in Samuel Chandler's diary indicates. On December 10, 1745, Chandler's father-in-law, Captain Pecker of Haverhill, journeyed to York to bring the news of his brother Jonathan's death in the expedition to Louisburg. Upon hearing the news, Samuel wrote "Letters to my parents and brethren," and then, on December 23, he set out on his journey to Andover, stopping in Amesbury to lodge with his brother Benjamin, then riding the next morning to Haverhill where he "dined at brother Websters." On the way to Andover, he "Stop^d at Several places, got to grand-mothers at 7 clock tarried till 8, got to fathers at 9, sat up til 12." His mother, he discovered, was "disconsolate," and his sister complained "of declension and deadness." His father, in a rare but extraordinarily revealing comment, "says he has been much distressed for land, for his children, too much—one is taken away and needs none. Bewails that he took so much care."[49] This single comment epitomizes the consuming concern of Andover fathers to see that their sons were settled upon land—either their own or land somewhere else—because the possession of land repre-

[49] Samuel Chandler, diary entry for December 23, 1745, quoted in Chandler, *Chandler Family*, p. 192.

sented so much that these men valued. Josiah Chandler spoke for most of his generation, whose actions confirmed his words.

So long as Josiah Chandler and his wife lived, Samuel Chandler had reason to return frequently to Andover, to maintain contacts with his parents and kindred, and to remain concerned about the lives of the many people he had known so well in Andover. His diaries recorded his continued visits during the 1740's and early 1750's, particularly after 1751, when he moved from York to Gloucester, Massachusetts. In March 1752, his brother Daniel, died "of a fever after fifteen days illness," and "all the Brethren" came to his funeral except for the oldest brother, who lived too far away to attend.[50] Daniel had boarded with Ebenezer Osgood before his death, rather than with his parents—another indication of the independence of the fourth generation, reflecting the fact that men did not have to move away from Andover in order to separate themselves from their parental homes.

The Chandler family was growing increasingly distant, and the bonds holding it together appear to have been becoming more and more tenuous. With the deaths of Josiah and his wife, Samuel Chandler ceased to be as concerned with life in Andover; he visisted less frequently and focused his attention upon his own family in Gloucester and his duties as minister there. Earlier, in January 1746, Samuel Chandler had just returned from a visit to Andover when he noted in his diary: "I studied all day. Wrote the Genealogy of my family."[51] This action speaks eloquently of the concerns of a man cut off from his parents and kindred by distance, and conscious of the

[50] Samuel Chandler, diary entry for March 30, 1752, quoted in Chandler, *Chandler Family*, pp. 194–195.
[51] Samuel Chandler, diary entry for January 9, 1746, quoted in Chandler, *Chandler Family*, p. 193.

need to preserve his memory of them on paper. In setting down his family's history, Samuel Chandler secured from the silent oblivion of forgetfulness and ignorance the names, and perhaps something of the lives, of kindred whom his own children would scarcely know or remember. As Andover faded into the past, Samuel Chandler's genealogy became a monument to the dead, rather than a guide for the living. Distance, time, and the deaths of members of the immediate family were powerful forces cutting the ties of emigrants to the place of their birth and to the kindred who had remained behind. Their children, the new generation, raised away from their parent's birthplace, knew little about their family's past. To break their ties to their families and their pasts completely, they had only to move once more.

For the history of the family, much obviously depended upon the extent to which men were rooted to the places where they had been born and raised and where other members of their families also lived, and the extent to which men departed, resettling at a distance from their original home, usually without close kinship ties to people living in the new towns to which they moved. Just as Samuel Chandler and his brother David must have led lives which were very different in terms of the human experiences of daily life—Samuel returned periodically to Andover to see parents, kindred, and friends, and David lived with his parents and close by many of his relatives and friends from childhood—so too did the lives of other members of this generation differ. Those who remained permanently in Andover more often than not settled upon land which had been passed from generation to generation from the original family grants in the seventeenth century and which often continued to be transmitted through successive generations during the nineteenth century and sometimes even into the twentieth century. Family land thus provided a permanent basis for the maintenance of family continuity in Andover for more than a century. As a result, the kinship networks which had been established during the first and second generations were maintained and extended as successive generations married cousins, neighbors, and other inhabitants of the town, as well as people from outside the community, and these networks of family relationships persisted in the two parishes with remarkable consistency.[52] A number of households were extended in structure, having three generations living together in a single house, which was often divided in half to provide a settlement for a son and his own wife and children. Often, too, fathers still proved to be reluctant to part with their own control over land which they themselves had inherited and which they farmed, continuing to make at least one or more of their sons wait until middle age before taking full control of the families' land in Andover. Sons still settled and built upon paternal land in Andover, much as earlier generations had done.

It had grown increasingly rare, however, to find many sons in a single family settled on family land in Andover; too few estates could bear to be divided into very many portions. For many sons who remained in Andover, proximity to parents and even settlement upon paternal land no longer indicated

[52] One of the few surviving family letters for the mid-eighteenth century demonstrates the importance of the extended kinship group very clearly. As twenty-year-old Benjamin Farrington wrote to his father and mother on June 23, 1757, from "Foart Edward," where he evidently was stationed: "Ever Honored Father [and] mother after my duty to you and my Love to my Brothers and Sisters I would Inform you that I am well and in good Helth." He concluded: "So Remember my love to my ouncls and ants and to all my Cusens and frinds But I Remain your Dutiful Son Benjamin Farington" (letter, June 23, 1757, in the William A. Trow Collection, Andover Historical Society, Andover, Mass.).

necessarily their prolonged dependence upon the older generation. On the contrary, very often they were established as independent adults while relatively young. The predisposition to see sons settled on their own, with full control over their own land and their own estates, and often marrying at younger ages than either their fathers or grandfathers had done before them, seems to be one of the most significant factors in changing the lives of the fourth generation.

The continued viability of family life in Andover during the mid-eighteenth century clearly demanded that many sons would have to leave and establish themselves elsewhere. The willingness of fathers to help sons settle outside of Andover testifies to their awareness of this necessity and to their concern for their offspring. In this sense, Andover, having grown old and crowded, served as a seedbed for the new communities being established elsewhere. They, in turn, would provide land and livelihoods for many people for several generations. The recurrent process of migration, resettlement, stability of residence, and then migration again served as a web of experience binding together many people otherwise separated by time and space. But though many left, many also stayed. Their lives, and their differing families and experiences, form two persistent poles in colonial American history. Neither the rooted nor the uprooted alone can tell the whole story of family life in colonial Andover.

PART IV

❧⚜❧

CONCLUSION

9

Historical
Perspectives on the Family

Despite the novelty of historical demography and of historical family studies, enough research already has been done to permit some educated guesses about the nature of family life and the character of family structure in Elizabethan and Stuart England and in modern England and the United States. The dual perspectives of past and present thus can be used to augment our understanding of families in colonial Andover and to indicate the potential relevance of the experiences of these Andover families for other studies of families. This final chapter will be a speculative, and quite tentative, attempt to probe the relationship of this one local study to some of the broader interests of scholars in various disciplines who also are concerned about the history and the nature of the family and the relationship of the family to other aspects of life in the modern Western world.

Since the history of Andover properly begins in England, the history of English families during the late sixteenth and early seventeenth centuries forms an essential background for an evaluation of familial experience in colonial Andover. Yet until recently, owing to the dearth of credible evidence about family life in England during this period, historians seeking to place early American experiences in perspective and to assess the changes which occurred as Englishmen migrated to the New World often based their conclusions on unproven hypotheses about families and communities in rural Stuart England.

Many historians probably would agree with Peter Laslett's description of communal life in villages scattered throughout the English countryside:

As a community the village consisted of households in association. To the facts of geography, being together in the one place, were added all the bonds which are forged between human beings when they are permanently alongside each other; bonds of intermarriage and of kinship, of common ancestry and common experience and of friendship and co-operation in matters of common concern.[1]

Such were the circumstances of life which Bernard Bailyn probably had in mind when he described life in England prior to the emigrations of the colonists:

[1] Peter Laslett, *The World We Have Lost* (New York, 1965), pp. 78–79. For a similar picture, see W. G. Hoskins, *The Midland Peasant: The Economic and Social History of a Leicestershire Village* (London, 1957), p. 194. As Hoskins' study amply demonstrates, however, even a village such as Wigston Magna was constantly changing so that such a picture might not apply to another period. Oscar Handlin frequently assumes that rural villages in Europe during this period were continuously stable and cohesive. For a classic statement of this view, see Oscar Handlin, *The Uprooted: The Epic Story of the Great Migrations That Made the American People* (Boston, 1951), esp. ch. 1. More recently, Handlin asserted: "The villagers and townsmen of Europe looked back to a past unbroken in its continuity. They believed that they were where they were because their ancestors, to a time out of mind, had been there; and they could see everywhere about them the monuments of their heritage. They did not have to wonder, as Americans did, what had been the meaning of lives interrupted in mid-course" (*The Americans: A New History of the People of the United States* [Boston, 1963], p. 59).

For so elaborate was the architecture of family organization and so deeply founded was it in the soil of stable, slowly changing village and town communities in which intermarriage among the same groups had taken place generation after generation, that it was at times difficult for the child to know where the family left off and the greater society began. The external community, comprising with the family a continuous world, naturally extended instruction and discipline in work and in the conduct of life.

For Bailyn, as for others, the nature of communal and agrarian life had profound implications for the family, which he defined in the following terms:

The family familiar to the early colonists was a patrilineal group of extended kinship gathered into a single household. By modern standards it was large. Besides children, who often remained in the home well into maturity, it included a wide range of other dependents: nieces and nephews, cousins, and, except for families at the lowest rung of society, servants in filial discipline. In the Elizabethan family the conjugal unit was only the nucleus of a broad kinship community whose outer edges merged almost imperceptibly into the society at large.

The interconnections between these extended families and their communities become vitally important in accounting for the stability of family life in England, particularly if one believes, with Bailyn, that

Disruption and transplantation in alien soil transformed the character of traditional English family life. Severe pressures were felt from the first. Normal procedures were upset by the long and acute discomforts of travel; regular functions were necessarily set aside; the ancient discipline slackened. But once re-established in permanent settlements the colonists moved toward recreating the essential institution in its usual form. In this, despite heroic efforts, they failed.[2]

Thus Englishmen who dared to cross the ocean to the New World forsook the stable, orderly, ancient peasant families and villages of the Old World to experience instead disruption, disorder, constant uprootedness, nuclearity of families, and ultimate failure in their attempts to recreate a familiar society.

From this point of view, the history of the family in America during the seventeenth century is the history of declension, the falling away, often involuntarily, from the standards and the modes of behavior of earlier times and places. Beneath many of the recent descriptions of colonial families, one detects a sense that a certain disintegration of family life explains some of the most fundamental characteristics of existence in early America.[3] The images of stability in England and disor-

[2] Bernard Bailyn, *Education in the Forming of American Society: Needs and Opportunities for Study* (Chapel Hill, 1960), pp. 17–18, 15–16, 22. Bailyn's essay is still the most suggestive commentary on the family in America to appear during the past decade. It is, and will remain, a landmark in the historical study of both the family and colonial American society.

[3] This is particularly true of the work of Oscar Handlin. See, for instance, his provocative, but undocumented, essay, "The Significance of the Seventeenth Century," in James Morton Smith, ed., *Seventeenth-Century America: Essays in Colonial History* (Chapel Hill, 1959), pp. 3–12, esp. 6–9. Handlin said: "The terms of American existence compelled frequent and serious deviations from the norms of behavior accepted by the men who peopled the colonies. Every aspect of their existence combined to produce disorder." In America: "The lack of permanence, the constant mobility that shifted individuals and families about through the continent exacerbated all these tensions [within families and communities]. By contrast, the old homes of the Old World in retrospect came to embody orderliness. Often, in thinking of what they had left in Europe, the colonists expressed a poignant sense of separation from the source of stability and culture" (pp. 6, 8). Also see Handlin's *The Americans*, esp. pp. 28–29, 36–37, 40–42, 59–63.

der in America form the counterpoints in our assessment
of the changes which took place in the seventeenth-century
colonies. But just as the image of declension may not be appropriate to describe the changing religious experiences of
Puritans in New England, neither may the images of failure
and disorder be adequate to describe changes in family life.

There are many reasons to believe now that even if early
American families were nuclear, uprooted, and unstable, these
characteristics in no way set them apart from numerous families in England during the same period. Far from changing in
the American environment, such families represented forms of
familial continuity remarkably consistent with many English
experiences. The evidence for such continuity has been
mounting, and now, as far as England is concerned, it appears
to be convincing.

Far from being permanently rooted in the soil of the same
villages from time beyond the memories of men, countless
rural English families in the late sixteenth and early seventeenth centuries were uprooted, mobile, and nuclear, dependent upon the soil yet independent of particular places. So
extensive was the mobility of the rural population in Elizabethan and Stuart England that, as an English historian has
estimated, by 1641 "only 16% of our agricultural population
had a hundred years in the same village behind them."[4] This
general conclusion has been further confirmed by the analysis,

[4] E. E. Rich, "The Population of Elizabethan England," *EHR*, II
(1950), 261. As Rich said, in an observation which has been over-
looked too long: "Between migration and emigration there is but a
small difference. The Irish plantations and the mass Puritan emigrations of the next generation became the sensible and commonplace
actions of ordinary people—and this lack of distinction is probably
the most important thing about the peopling of British North
America. The distance across the Atlantic and the virgin soils were
for most of the emigrants the only new factors. . . . They and their
families were already accustomed to migration; emigration held few
additional terrors" (pp. 263–264).

undertaken by Laslett and Harrison, of Clayworth from 1676 to 1688 and Cogenhoe from 1618 to 1628, which demonstrated that in both of these small rural Northamptonshire villages the mobility of the population was astonishingly high. Furthermore, this study showed that the structures of families in these villages were not extended, as they were expected to be, but nuclear, with households ordinarily consisting only of husband, wife, and children, with occasional servants, but rarely with additional kindred; nor do there appear to have been extensive kinship networks in these villages.[5] Judging by the descriptions, these seem to be classically nuclear families: impermanently attached to a place, small in size, very mobile, and isolated from their kindred and neighbors. Their lives were short, difficult, and lonely.[6]

---

[5] Peter Laslett and John Harrison, "Clayworth and Cogenhoe," in H. E. Bell and R. L. Ollard, eds., *Historical Essays, 1660–1750, Presented to David Ogg* (London, 1963), pp. 166–168, 177. As they remarked about their own discovery on the mobility of the population, "So surprising is it that we do not yet know quite what to make of it" (p. 174). We are still trying to find out. At various times, the population of Wigston also was very mobile. See W. G. Hoskins, "The Population of an English Village, 1086–1801: A Study of Wigston Magna," in Hoskins, *Provincial England: Essays in Social and Economic History* (London, 1963), 190–193, 195. More recently, Julian Cornwall, in "Evidence of Population Mobility in the Seventeenth Century," *Bulletin of the Institute of Historical Research*, XL (1967), 143–152, studied Malling, East Sussex, from 1580 to 1640 and found evidence for some mobility. Most of the people studied lived their lives in the counties in which they had been born, however, and nine out of ten died within ten miles of their birthplaces; this contrasts sharply with the Laslett and Harrison findings. Only an extensive study of mobility can establish the frequency and the extent of population mobility, although it is probable that considerable variation will be found.

[6] For a general discussion, see Carl Bridenbaugh, *Vexed and Troubled Englishmen, 1590–1642* (New York, 1968), esp. chs. 2, 3, 10, and 11.

Under such circumstances, it is most unlikely that patriarchalism could flourish, for there was little in the lives of these families which might provide a viable basis for the prolonged exercise of paternal authority and influence over mature sons.[7] In any case, there has yet to be an actual demonstration of the patriarchal nature of the families of farmers, craftsmen, and laborers in seventeenth-century England. What has been demonstrated quite satisfactorily, however, is that in the seventeenth century, English society often was disrupted, disorderly, and conducive to profound anxiety among many of its members. Whatever difficulties might await the thousands of immigrants to America during this time, there was little to

---

[7] In Peter Laslett's view, "European society is of the patriarchal type, and with some variations, of which the feudal went the furthest, it remained patriarchal in its institutions right up to the coming of the factories, the offices and the rest." Yet Laslett recognized that "European patriarchalism" was "of a rather surprising kind, for it was marked by the independence of the nuclear family, man, wife and children, not by the extended family of relatives living together in a group of several generations under the same patriarchal head" (*World We Have Lost*, p. 21). Unfortunately, Laslett never clarifies his conception of patriarchalism sufficiently. As I pointed out in my review of his book, I find an inherent contradiction between the demographic and familial evidence presented by Laslett and his argument for traditional, patriarchal forms of family and society; see Philip J. Greven, Jr., "Historical Demography and Colonial America," *WMQ*, XXIV (1967), 449–453. Patriarchalism, however, has been a theme of Laslett's work for the past two decades: see "The Gentry of Kent in 1640," *Cambridge Historical Journal*, IX (1948), 148–164; his introduction to *Patriarcha and other Political Works of Sir Robert Filmer* (Oxford, 1949); and his essay with John Harrison, "Clayworth and Cogenhoe," esp. pp. 180–181. One of the basic questions yet to be answered is how mobile nuclear families in England or America managed to be patriarchal, if in fact they did. The extent to which families were patriarchal is bound to be variable, just as it proved to be in Andover during the lifetimes of the first four generations.

make them overly nostalgic about their old communities or the circumstances of life in England.

To an extent which few historians have appreciated as yet, the circumstances of life in early New England towns like Andover proved to be remarkably suited to the establishment and maintenance of orderly and stable families and communities.[8] Despite all the physical hardships of life in the wilderness, the first generation, after an initial period of uprootedness, movement, and resettlement, re-established their families more permanently than historians have thought possible. Because of our frequent assumption that Americans have been a permanently uprooted and mobile people from the beginning, we have failed to take into account the lives and the families of people like those who settled Andover. With abundant land for themselves and their offspring, the first generation established extended patriarchal families, in which fathers maintained their authority over their mature sons, mainly by withholding control over the land from them until late in their lives. The delayed marriages of sons testified to their prolonged attachment to paternal families, and their residence in houses built upon their fathers' lands sustained close relationships with parents and siblings. The result was a commu-

---

[8] Recently, however, several studies have pointed in this direction: Kenneth A. Lockridge, "The Population of Dedham, Massachusetts, 1636–1736," *EHR*, XIX (1966), esp. pp. 323–324, 344; John J. Waters, Jr., "Hingham, Massachusetts, 1631–1661: An East Anglian Oligarchy in the New World," *Journal of Social History*, I (1968), pp. 351–370; and Waters' multigenerational study, *The Otis Family in Provincial and Revolutionary Massachusetts* (Chapel Hill, 1968), esp. pp. ix–x, 21n., 48–50, 73–75. Andover, Dedham, and Hingham all contrast sharply with Boston during its early period, as analyzed in Darrett B. Rutman's *Winthrop's Boston: Portrait of a Puritan Town, 1630–1649* (Chapel Hill, 1965).

nity which became closely integrated and which grew more so with each successive generation.

Indeed, Andover came to resemble in many significant ways the ancient villages which may once have dotted the English countryside, where family names and family lands passed from generation to generation and where countless human lives formed the complex chain of continuity that structured the community and provided it with substantive forms of familial and social stability. Most of the families which first settled in Andover became as deeply rooted to the land and the community as it is possible for families to be. Many of these families are in Andover still. Their desires to re-establish themselves permanently in a place, to farm, to provide land and settlements for their children, to be patriarchs surrounded by dutiful sons and daughters, were amply fulfilled in the new community which they established. If their experiences differed from those of English families and villages, it was largely because life in many parts of England had already made such forms of families and communities unlikely.

Equally significant, and equally unexpected by historians, is the demographic experience of seventeenth-century Andover which provided a fundamentally important basis for the stability and orderliness of life in the town. During this period, the evidence reveals that people were extraordinarily healthy, lives were unusually long, and women were exceedingly fecund. Nothing like this has yet to be found during the second half of the seventeenth century in England, where the demographic data point in almost the opposite direction: available evidence indicates that the mortality rates had risen sharply over those of the late sixteenth century, that lifespans were relatively short—and shorter than they had been in earlier periods—and that families were relatively small in size. The population in many communities in the old country had ceased to grow at the rates found in earlier decades of the century, either stagnating or actually falling in numbers; both indicate a period of demographic decline.

In Andover, the experiences of the first three generations were profoundly different, and the population of the town as a whole grew more rapidly than at any other time in its colonial history. Husbands and wives lived longer and shared the responsibilities of parenthood together into old age. The survival to adulthood of most of their offspring meant a large number of children to provide for and to establish as adults. The delays in the marriages of men until their middle and late twenties also suggests that their own families would be formed when they were themselves mature and economically well-established. What this might have meant for parent-child relationships and for the fundamental security of the families themselves is not clear, but it is worth pondering. What the basic demographic characteristics of life in seventeenth century Andover imply altogether, though, seems clear enough: stability and health. Serious and frequent disruptions within families, and the accompanying emotional stresses of loss and anxiety owing to early deaths of children and adults, proved to be far rarer in early Andover than in English communities of the same period or even in Andover itself later.

Taken together, the fundamental elements shaping the characteristics of family life in seventeenth-century Andover were profoundly important factors in transforming the utopian ideals of community and social order set forth by Governor John Winthrop into practical reality. However difficult or impossible it might have been to institute such ideals in the town of Boston, with its commerce and its fairly disparate population, the small rural agricultural towns like Andover probably proved to be excellent places in which to realize the goals of order, hierarchy, and the closely-knit community.[9] The rapidity with which the new settlers recreated the effective basis for patriarchal families integrated into a coheisve and enduring social fabric testified, perhaps, to the intensity of their desires for such order and stability, as well as to the role which economic factors, especially the possession of abundant land, played in permitting these goals to be realized. But the history of Andover probably was not unique among the experiences of other rural communities in the Massachusetts Bay Colony during this period. The remarkable success with which Andover's first generation rerooted themselves in the soil of New England and maintained their families for generations to come reflects the opportunities for the establishment of orderly and cohesive families and communities in the midst of the American wilderness. In no significant sense were the lives of the first and second generations in disorder, once their permanent roots had been firmly established in early Andover.

Throughout the early and middle decades of the eighteenth century, Andover as a whole continued to be remarkably stable and orderly despite the rapid growth of its population and the numerous changes which reshaped the nature of families within the community. The kinship networks established during the lifetimes of the first two generations expanded and grew more complex until they involved not only families within Andover itself but, through marriages, numerous families in other towns as well. The experiences of many third-

[9] See Rutman, *Winthrop's Boston*, esp. pp. 274–279. Too much of early New England history has been seriously warped by a Boston bias. In due course, however, studies of other towns ought to alter our perspectives and refocus our attention upon the agricultural communities in which so many people lived.

generation sons and some fourth-generation sons in the middle of the century demonstrated the continued viability of patriarchalism in many families. During the early decades of the century especially, the late marriages of men, the delays in the transferences of many estates from fathers to sons, and the frequent prolongation of paternal controls over lands conveyed to sons indicate the strength of paternal authority and the acceptance of filial dependence and obedience. The third generation, however, also proved to be distinctive insofar as many sons began to seek ways of limiting their fathers' control over their inheritances and found practical ways of establishing their independence, although not too often as young men. Also, at the same time that the third generation reached maturity, the demographic characteristics of the town began to alter in important ways, reflecting increased rates of mortality, decreasing rates of fertility, and reduced sizes of families.

By the time the fourth generation began to reach maturity during the middle decades of the century, much had changed. Not only were their lives cut short more often than in past generations, but they also reached maturity sooner, married younger, established their independence more effectively and earlier in life, and departed from the community with even greater frequency than in earlier generations. The ties binding men to their parents and to their families were loosening. Yet families still continued to accept their responsibilities for the nurture and the establishment of their sons in livelihoods and often upon land of their own, and the evidence suggests that most sons still were dutiful and respectful to their parents. But the actions which fathers and sons took imply a changing attitude toward one another and a different conception of maturity itself. One of the principal clues is the younger ages at which people married; another is the willingness of fathers to transfer complete control over inheritances while sons were relatively young men.

If patriarchalism was not yet gone, it had been made less viable by the changing circumstances. The earlier economic basis which had sustained the attempts by fathers to establish and to maintain their control and influence over the lives of their sons no longer was to be found among the majority of families living in Andover. Only the wealthy and only those with sons who were willing to accede to their fathers' wishes regarding the possession and ownership of the land could still consider themselves to be patriarchs. For the majority, another conception of their roles and their authority as fathers had become necessary, and the evidence suggests that most adjusted, whether reluctantly or willingly. By the middle of the eighteenth century, many families in Andover accepted the early independence and autonomy of their sons.

Closely related to many of the factors responsible for the changing characteristics of family life in Andover was the extent to which people were geographically mobile. As this study of four generations demonstrates, the extent of mobility was not constant throughout the seventeenth and eighteenth centuries; it varied from generation to generation, from period to period, and from community to community. The close interrelationship between demographic and economic circumstances was clearly of fundamental importance in determining the extent to which successive generations might be mobile. At the same time, it is also clear that although many families faced common problems in terms of the transmission of estates and the settlements of their children, their individual reactions to such problems varied considerably; cultural, psychological, and familial considerations also must have played an influential role in shaping individual responses to the basic question of whether to remain in Andover or to emigrate from Andover to another community. Judging by the actions taken by successive generations in Andover, however, a long-term trend appears to indicate an increased readiness within each generation to leave family and community and an increased willingness to establish sooner the maturity and autonomy of those sons who stayed as well as of those who left. Undoubtedly this reflected a general response both to circumstances within families in Andover and to the general increase in mobility of the third and fourth generations.

In other agricultural communities, similar patterns of experience arising from similar circumstances, with successive periods of mobility, stability, and renewed mobility, have been found to correspond closely with the lifetimes of successive generations.[10] The changes which occurred in communities like Andover usually occurred in generational cycles, reflecting the subtle and flexible rhythms inherent in the life cycle

---

[10] In particular, see Kenneth A. Lockridge, "Dedham, 1636–1736: The Anatomy of a Puritan Utopia," (Ph.D. diss., Princeton University, 1965), and "Population of Dedham," pp. 328, 341–342; see also Charles S. Grant, *Democracy in the Connecticut Frontier Town of Kent* (New York, 1961), pp. 98–103. Some of the general implications of such local studies, including mine, have been considered by J. M. Bumsted and J. T. Lemon in their article "New Approaches in Early American Studies: The Local Community in New England," *Social History*, II (1968), 98–112, and esp. pp. 110–111, which offers a model corresponding closely to my own. The forthcoming study by John Demos, *A Little Commonwealth: Family Life in Plymouth Colony* (New York), provides a striking contrast with my own study of Andover both in terms of methodology and in terms of conclusions about the nature of the family. Demos has chosen not to use a generational approach. I am convinced, however, that methodological choices have a profound importance for our interpretations of the nature and history of families. I am also convinced that only by studying the family through time, and through successive generations, can some of the most basic changes in family life be determined.

itself. Other communities may also have been shaped by the actions of the first generation in founding the town, settling down, acquiring land, and raising children; by the tendency of the second generation to remain in the community which their parents had established, settled upon land which their parents often bestowed upon them; and then by the tendency of the third generation to be forced by demographic and economic pressures to move away in appreciable numbers in search of more abundant land and opportunity elsewhere. However, only by studying a number of communities over time, with a close examination of the lives and actions of several successive generations, can such fundamental patterns be established and their variations explored and explained. Such studies are essential if we are to put together a solid basis for accurate generalizations and for meaningful comparisons of families, communities, and colonies in early America. For the time being, therefore, any attempt to determine whether or not Andover was "typical" of other towns or to generalize extensively about other families and communities in early America must remain largely in the realm of intuition and speculation.

But some speculation about the potential contributions which specific studies such as this might make to research in fields other than social history might be suggestive and may point in unexpected directions. Does the history of the family have any relevance for an understanding and an analysis of religious and political history, for instance?[11] Do the varying

[11] Curiously, Peter Laslett, one of the principal exponents of demographic and familial history, does not appear to see any significant relationship between the family, population, and politics in England during the mid-seventeenth century: "Nothing in economic organization or in social arrangements seems to have come about which would have led of itself to political crisis, and the changes that did go on seem to have been gradual over the whole period rather than

demographic and familial experiences of a community such as
Andover have any general implications for the study of evangelical piety, in particular, or did they contribute to the readiness with which many colonists ultimately accepted independence from England?

Since the ultimate sources of religious experiences and especially of Puritan piety in the seventeenth century are still
extraordinarily elusive, speculations are certainly in order.
The most promising avenue of exploration, so far completely
neglected, is the history of the family and its connections with
the history of religious experience and thought. Indeed, there
is every reason to believe that the history of the family is
central to the history of pietism and orthodoxy, to the sect
and to the church.[12] Perhaps one of the principal reasons why
such potential connections have not been pursued by histori-

---

sudden" (*World We Have Lost*, p. 158). His argument for the basic
social stability of England during the pre–Civil War era seems
dubious, however, and I find his general argument for the disconnec-
tion between political, social, and familial experience unconvincing.
For his views, see *World We Have Lost*, ch. 7, pp. 150–169. Far more
persuasive is Michael Walzer's study, *The Revolution of the Saints:
A Study in the Origins of Radical Politics* (Cambridge, Mass.,
1965); Walzer sees a close connection between familial, social, religious, and political experiences.

[12] In this monograph, I have quite consciously chosen *not* to
consider the relationship of the family to religious experience and
church membership. In a subsequent study, however, I intend to
pursue this problem extensively, partly through a comparative analysis of family structure and mobility in particular communities, and
partly through a general study of the experiential and intellectual
aspects of evangelical piety in seventeenth- and eighteenth-century
America. An initial exploration of this question was made in a paper
which I delivered at the Southern Historical Association Meeting,
November 7, 1968, in New Orleans, La., on "Family, Mobility, and
Revivalism in Early America: Some Perspectives and Hypotheses"
(mimeo.).

ans as yet is our failure to understand the histories of families in the Old World and the New.

If, for instance, the emergence of Puritanism in England in the late sixteenth and early seventeenth centuries coincided with a period of rapid population growth, extensive population mobility, and large numbers of nuclear families, and if many families and communities in England were profoundly disrupted, with many people cut off from old roots and old ties to kindred and communities, then the emergence of new and radically different forms of religious experience—centered about conversions, covenants, congregations, and sects instead of the established ceremonies, traditions, orthodox beliefs, and church—might be closely linked to the actual experiences of families. The nature of the family might have much to do, therefore, with an explanation of the origins and character of English Puritanism itself.[13]

But what happened to these Puritans when they left England and resettled in the New World? The story of Puritanism in America may seem too familiar to need retelling, for it is thought to be one of the rapid decline of piety and the rapid extension of the congregation into virtually a form of inclu-

[13] Some recent works on English Puritanism and society in the seventeenth century point in these directions. In particular, see Michael Walzer, *Revolution of the Saints*, esp. pp. 14, 47–50, 184–198, 311–316; Lawrence Stone, "Social Mobility in England, 1500–1700," *Past and Present*, April 1966, esp. pp. 49–50; Christopher Hill, *Society and Puritanism in Pre-revolutionary England*, 2nd ed. (New York, 1967), esp. pp. 482–500. Hill observed: "The old geographical communities, with their rough-and-ready but effective hierarchical subordination, their traditional ceremonies, their succession of popular seasonal festivals, with the nominated priest in theory directing the spiritual life of the community: these were passing. The new communities of the sects which ultimately emerged were voluntary. . . . Contract communities had succeeded status communities" (p. 491).

sive church in many New England towns. What has not yet become a familiar story, however, is what happened to many of the families that resettled in New England towns like Andover. The rapidity with which they rerooted themselves and created extended patriarchal families in the context of orderly and closely-knit communities dramatically reveals just how profoundly different were the circumstances shaping their lives from those shaping the lives of many of the English Puritans. Above all, their new circumstances seem unlikely to have fostered the acute anxieties and the disruptions of experience characteristic of Puritans elsewhere. Without in any way ceasing to be deeply religious, people living in towns like Andover probably would have found that their religious experiences and concerns would have changed as their personal and familial experiences stabilized during the course of their lives in many New World communities. Certainly it is demonstrable that their families had changed their characters in the course of their lifetimes—from being mobile and nuclear, in many instances, to being rooted and extended. Thus it is likely that there was a link between the changing character of the family, the shifting circumstances of life, and the changing character of religious experience itself.[14]

[14] Richard L. Bushman's study, *From Puritan to Yankee: Character and the Social Order in Connecticut, 1690–1765* (Cambridge, Mass., 1967), points in this direction, but fails to probe the actual circumstances of families in terms of their structures, relationships, and the extent of their mobility. As he says (p. 187) of the Great Awakening of the early 1740's, "A psychological earthquake had reshaped the human landscape." But his answer to the specific sources of this transformation is not altogether convincing (see pp. 187–195). Alan Heimert almost completely ignores the role of the family and of social and demographic change in religious thought and experience, focusing upon intellectual history instead. The result is descriptive history, but not a convincing analysis. See his *Religion and the American Mind from the Great Awakening to the Revolution* (Cambridge, Mass., 1966).

This possibility is strengthened by the changing character of life generally and of families in particular during the early and mid-eighteenth century in Andover. The changing experiences of the third and especially of the fourth generation might prove to be of great significance for changes in religious experience and expression during this period. The increasing mobility of these generations, for instance, indicates that many people who had been born into a well-established community of closely-knit families spent much of their adult lives in new communities and in towns where they had few kindred or friends. There might very well be a close connection between their physical mobility, with all that it implies of the uprooting, the dislocations, the anxieties experienced by those who left, and their heightened religious needs and religious experiences.[15] The probability of such a connection is suggested by the fact that many of the people who left Andover moved to towns in Massachusetts, Connecticut (Windham County), and New Hampshire, towns which later were caught up in the revivals of the 1720's and 1740's. In contrast, many of those who remained behind in Andover failed to be touched by the Awakening, and Andover itself was an Old Light, nonrevivalist town during the 1740's. That there were such perceptible differences in the religious experiences of members of the same families, some of whom stayed and others of whom left, does suggest that their familial experiences might have been of critical importance in shaping their religious needs and responses.

The relevance of the history of families goes beyond the realm of religious history, of course, and extends into the realms of political thought and behavior, too.[16] It is not incon-

[15] See Bushman, *From Puritan to Yankee*, chs. 4 and 5, for some suggestive observations and evidence.

[16] The question of the relationship between families and local and provincial politics is an important one that has only occasionally

ceivable, for example, that the slow and subtle, but nevertheless tremendously important, changes in the relationships between fathers and sons might have been connected closely
with the movement for independence itself during the third
quarter of the eighteenth century—that period in which the
fourth generation in Andover was coming to maturity and
establishing its own independence from fathers and families.
Though it might seem absurd to some to try to link the
changing patterns of inheritance and the methods of transmitting estates during this period with essentially political and
ideological issues and events, we nevertheless must confront
the extraordinarily difficult question of the experiential basis
for the political responses of thousands upon thousands of
Americans who supported the cause of independence.[17]

To Andover sons in 1685, the thought that a man might
become fully independent in his youth from his father and
mother and from his familial duties and responsibilities would
have been difficult to conceive. Their late marriages and their
prolonged dependence upon their aging fathers for financial
support and land surely would have inhibited such assumptions. In a world of closely-knit, extended families, with dutiful, dependent sons and strong, patriarchal fathers, independence—particularly as a consequence of emerging out of

received the attention it merits. Most New England towns appear to
have been dominated by relatively few families in terms of local
offices of importance. The general subject of families in politics
warrants very careful and ample attention. See the excellent study by
John J. Waters, Jr., *The Otis Family in Provincial and Revolutionary Massachusetts* (Chapel Hill, 1968) for one suggestive approach.
[17] See, for instance, Gordon S. Wood, "Rhetoric and Reality in the
American Revolution," *WMQ*, XXIII (1966), 25–31. Wood points
in a similar direction, trying to locate the source of political paranoia,
and the forms of political thought and expression, in the basic structure of society itself, one component of which, of course, was the
family.

adolescence—would have conflicted sharply with experience. By the middle decades of the eighteenth century, however, the maturing fourth generation would not have found the idea of independence from parental authority at a relatively early age foreign to their own experience. Men were marrying significantly earlier than in previous generations; they were able to establish earlier, and with far less apparent hesitation and difficulty, their economic independence from their fathers; their autonomy often was accepted and even fostered by their parents: these facts suggest that their attitudes toward parent-son relations had changed significantly from those of their fathers' and their grandfathers' generations. For Andover's fourth generation, Thomas Paine's call for independence in 1776 from the mother-country and from the father-king might have been just what Paine claimed it to be—common sense.[18] In their own lives, this generation had come to take for

[18] I owed this hypothesis originally to the fact that I was asked to criticize Winthrop D. Jordan's paper, "Familial Politics: The Killing of the King, 1776," delivered on April 27, 1967, at the Organization of American Historians Meeting in Chicago. Although Jordan's reading of Thomas Paine's *Common Sense* and my own reading of it were fundamentally different, we agreed upon the richness of the source in its familial imagery and psychic meaning. What I discovered by rereading Paine in response to Jordan's version of the significance of the "subliminal" message of *Common Sense* was simply that Paine took for granted the presumption that young men gained their complete independence from parents when they reached maturity. When Paine asserted, "as I have always considered the independency of this continent, as an event which sooner or later must arrive, so from the late rapid progress of the continent to maturity, the event could not be far off," he spoke to the experiences of Andover's fourth generation, not to those of its second generation (Thomas Paine, *Common Sense and the Crisis* [New York, 1946], p. 29). For a more extended discussion, see Philip J. Greven, Jr., "Comments on 'Familial Politics: The Killing of the King, 1776,' by Winthrop D. Jordan" (paper delivered at the Organization of American Historians Meeting, April 27, 1967, Chicago, Ill.).

granted that young men ought also to be independent men—
freed of ties to their parental families, freed often of responsibilities to aging parents, economically independent, and able
to follow their own interests. Surprising though it may seem,
political independence in 1776 might have been rooted in the
very character of many (but not all) American families. At
levels which are very elusive (because our sources rarely
reveal the relevant evidence directly), the nature of the family probably was one of the determinative factors shaping the
responses of people to the most important issues of their
times.[19]

If the history of the family is relevant for the study of
politics and religion in the seventeenth and the eighteenth

[19] This assumption has been confirmed recently by the fascinating
evidence on the relationship of the family experience of James Otis,
Jr., to his political behavior provided by Waters in *Otis Family*, esp.
pp. 128–134. The elder Otis was seen by his sons as "an awesome,
overbearing, and jealous *pater familias* intent upon retaining control," leaving them with both "the motivation to succeed" and "a
feeling of personal inadequacy" (p. 131). According to Waters,
James, Jr.'s sister may have "perceived that the model for James's
love-hate relationship with George III was her own father. After all,
had not the elder Otis been both king and tyrant, father and antago-
nist to his own sons?" (p. 133). Otis "wanted to keep a connection
with Britain but saw that the imperial violations of colonial rights
would bring about an independence that he could not face. Independence from the parent state, he opined, 'every good and honest
man would wish delayed for ages, if possible, prevented for ever.'
The act of separation constituted Otis's political and psychological
stumbling block" (p. 134). The linkage between patterns of family
relationships, an individual psyche, and political affiliations could
not be delineated more succinctly. Other such studies are essential.
For more general observations on the relationship of familial
experiences and political actions and beliefs, see: Walzer, *Revolution of the Saints*, esp. pp. 149, 183–198; R. W. K. Hinton, "Husbands, Fathers, and Conquerors, II: Patriarchalism in Hobbes and
Locke," *Political Studies*, XVI (1968), 55–67; and Laslett's introduction to Filmer's *Patriarcha*, esp. pp. 21–33.

centuries, it is essential for studies of modern families. The nature and functions of modern families have preoccupied the attention of many sociologists, anthropologists, and psychologists whose theoretical and empirical studies have laid the basis for our understanding of contemporary families. Yet their work has been carried out in a historical vacuum, owing to the dearth of reliable information and useful assessments of families in the past. Although we now know in considerable detail how the modern family in the United States and western Europe is structured and how it functions, we cannot yet determine the extent to which such forms of family life and experience are unique to our particular social, economic, and cultural circumstances. We cannot be entirely certain, therefore, about the correlations of family forms with other determinants of behavior. The only way to establish what is unique about modern families is to compare them with families in the past.[20] For this reason, the history of the family is of fundamental importance if we are to understand ourselves and our societies.

Until recently, most students of the modern family in the contemporary United States and in Europe generally agreed that the central characteristics of families in urban industrial societies included nuclear structures, a high rate of social and geographical mobility, and a persistent isolation of nuclear households from their kindred. In addition, many sociologists evidently assumed that the nuclear family had arisen historically as a result of the industrial revolution, and that the changes occurred in a linear development from extended to nuclear families as agrarian society was industrialized. The

[20] I explored this question at some length in a paper, "An Historical Perspective on Family Structure," delivered at the Social Science Research Council Conference on the History of the Family, October 26–27, 1967, Washington, D.C. (mimeo.).

history of the family thus was thought to show profound change and striking contrast between modern and traditional forms of family life and family structures: industrialization and urbanization had made the older forms of extended family life impossible, and the nuclear family became the only viable form in our societies. Such assumptions implied that nuclear families were not to be found in preindustrial societies, either in America or Europe, and that they were not characteristic of agrarian communities. The emergence of the nuclear family was thought to be one of the distinguishing developments of the modern social order.[21]

During the past decade, however, such common sociological theories have been challenged by empirical studies of families in urban communities in both England and the United States.[22] Collectively, these studies have been demon-

[21] See Talcott Parsons' articles, "The Kinship System of the Contemporary United States," *American Anthropologist*, XLV (1943), pp. 22–38, and "The Social Structure of the Family," in Ruth Nanda Anshen, ed., *The Family: Its Function and Destiny* (New York, 1959). A more theoretical statement appears in Talcott Parsons and Robert F. Bales, *Family, Socialization and Process* (Glencoe, Ill., 1955), esp. ch. 1. A general study that reflects similar assumptions is John Sirjamaki's *The American Family in the Twentieth Century* (Cambridge, Mass., 1953), esp. pp. 192–193. William J. Goode, *World Revolution and Family Patterns* (New York, 1963), pp. 10–26, discusses "The 'Fit' Between the Conjugal Family and the Modern Industrial System."

[22] In particular, see Michael Young and Peter Willmott, *Family and Kinship in East London* (London, 1957), and Colin Rosser and Christopher Harris, *The Family and Social Change: A Study of Family and Kinship in a South Wales Town* (London, 1965). The persistence and the importance of kinship networks and extended families in the modern United States have been demonstrated by the following studies: Herbert J. Gans, *The Urban Villagers: Group and Class in the Life of Italian-Americans* (Glencoe, Ill., 1962), esp. pp. 45–46; Eugene Litwak, "Occupational Mobility and Extended Family Cohesion," *American Sociological Review*, XXV (1960), 9–21, and "Geographical Mobility and Extended Family Cohesion," *American*

strating that earlier assumptions about the modern family are at best only partially valid, and that there is actually a considerable amount of evidence pointing to the continued viability of the extended family, however it is defined, in the setting of urban industrial societies. Studies of English families, in particular, have demonstrated the persistence of widespread kinship groups and extended family structures in the midst of crowded London and other cities as well.[23] Some English families are still dependent upon their kindred for support and

Sociological Review, XXV (1960), 385–394, two very important articles; Marvin B. Sussman and Lee G. Burchinal, "Kin Family Network: Unheralded Structure in Current Conceptualizations of Family Functioning," Marriage and Family Living, XXIV (1962), 231–240, and "Parental Aid to Married Children: Implications for Family Functioning," Marriage and Family Living, XXIV (1962), 320–332, both of which are reprinted in the useful collection edited by Bernard Farber, Kinship and Family Organization (New York, 1966). See also Sidney M. Greenfield, "Industrialization and the Family in Sociological Theory," American Journal of Sociology, LXVII (1961), 312–322, reprinted in Farber, ed., Kinship and Family Organization, pp. 408–417; and Goode, Family Patterns, pp. 70–76.

[23] See Young and Willmott, Family and Kinship, esp. pp. xv–xvii, 66, 81–93, 108, 127, 136–137. This study is surprisingly relevant to the study of families such as those in colonial Andover: the fundamental patterns of kinship, residence, and mobility and their effects appear to be extraordinarily similar. The families of East London and the suburban town of Greenleigh, however, are our contemporaries, and the study of their lives is based upon direct observations and interviews. By understanding their lives and their families, a historian is better prepared to understand and to reconstruct the nature of family structure and family relationships from evidence that is indirect, incomplete, and dependent upon inference and intuition for its meanings. Studies such as Young and Willmott's of working-class families in London, or Rosser and Harris' of middle-class families in a Welsh town (Family and Social Change) are immensely suggestive, and I am convinced that studies of contemporary families must play a major role in our efforts to understand families in the past. Whatever the dangers (and there are some) in the use of analogy, modern sociological and psychological studies of the family provide an invaluable perspective upon families in the past.

for essential human relationships, and the extension of family ties is actually a reality of the utmost importance in modern English families, just as it was for Andover families. In addition, studies of rural communities in England have demonstrated the continued viability of patriarchalism in the twentieth century, with delayed marriages, delayed inheritances, and delayed control over the land still characteristic of at least some English farming families today.[24] In the United States, recent studies have demonstrated that many families, including many mobile families, still depend to a significant degree upon the kinship relations which bind generations and relatives together. Even here the extended family has continued to function. Although there is as yet too little evidence concerning kinship networks and extended families in modern America, there is little reason to doubt that it will be forthcoming.

When studies of modern families in urban industrial communities are juxtaposed with this study of four generations of families in rural, preindustrial Andover, modern families

[24] In particular, see W. M. Williams, *The Sociology of an English Village: Gosforth* (London, 1956), and *A West Country Village, Ashworthy: Family, Kinship and Land* (London, 1963), esp. pp. 53–64, 84–98. Both of these studies have had a great influence upon my own awareness of the significance of the patterns of family life and land transmission which I found in Andover. It is rather astonishing to find in mid-twentieth-century England, patterns of relationships binding fathers and sons together on the land almost identical to those found in seventeenth- and eighteenth-century Andover; yet they are there and are still just as important as they were earlier. Although I tend to emphasize Williams' studies because of their close analogies with Andover experiences, no study of farmers or of men's use of land can be ignored, since all can add to our understanding of the variety and the complexity of the experiences of men living upon the land. It is not easy for urban dwellers to appreciate the role and the significance of land in the lives and feelings of farmers. The simplicities of rural family life are largely a figment of our urban imaginations.

begin to look curiously traditional. Indeed, it is now apparent that there has been an astonishing degree of continuity in the forms of families in communities and societies, whether traditional or modern, rural or urban, agricultural or industrial, in England or in the United States. Under many different circumstances, from the mid-sixteenth through the mid-twentieth centuries, one can find nuclear households and extended households, nuclear families and extended families, mobility and rootedness, autonomy and dependence. Many basic characteristics of families thus have remained remarkably unchanged during the past four centuries. There has been more fundamental continuity in human experience than one might assume from most historical accounts. The fact that such basic forms of continuity are rooted in the family itself seems to be of the utmost importance for further analysis of behavior, thought, and experience, past and present.

Yet equally striking and equally important is the impressive degree of discontinuity and change which has also existed in the formal structures of families and in the types of relationships between members of families. What this study of Andover families demonstrates beyond reasonable doubt is that family structure is variable and complex, and that families are usually in a slow but almost continuous process of change through time.[25] The process of change, though, is far more

[25] So far, the only serious attempt to trace general changes in the structure and functioning of the family through time has been Philippe Ariès' brilliant and imaginative study, *Centuries of Childhood: A Social History of Family Life,* trans. Robert Baldick (New York, 1962). No one who reads Erik H. Erikson's *Childhood and Society* (New York, 1950) can doubt the importance of childhood and the family for social history. Owing to the dearth of sources for towns like Andover, however, the subject is very difficult to explore. John Demos, in his forthcoming study, *A Little Commonwealth,* provides a rare, and quite remarkable, insight into many of the innermost areas of childhood and of family life. Hopefully others also will be able to pursue this vitally important problem.

complex than we have generally assumed; it is not simply a long-term change from the extended family to the nuclear family, coinciding with industrialization or urbanization. Changes in family structure usually occur *within* definite periods, within particular places, whether rural or urban, and within particular societies, whether agrarian or industrial. The shapes and the natures of families depend upon the circumstances in which they are functioning and upon the wishes, assumptions, and actions of the people involved. In a sense, families often experience a fluctuating process of expansion and contraction, with the structures of families usually being built upon nuclear households, but with the degree of extension varying according to particular demographic, economic, and social circumstances. In some periods and places, the majority of families undoubtedly are nuclear in structure; in others, the majority are extended in structure; and in yet others, the structures of families will be found to be variable in the extent of their complexity and in the density of their kinship connections.

The history of the family has scarcely begun to be explored. Yet it may hold a key to many aspects of experience, behavior, and thought of men in the past, just as it clearly does for men in the present, and it may also hold a key to meaningful comparisons between different periods, places, and societies. Since the history of the family necessarily involves the study of countless thousands of ordinary people, it must also provide us with new insights into the basic circumstances of life which shaped behavior and thought among people in general. Most of all, though, the history of the family ought to demonstrate to historians, to sociologists, and to others as well, that history still is useful and relevant to us. I am convinced, and I trust that this study of four generations of families in colonial Andover will convince others as well, that the history of the family has a direct bearing upon our understanding of families in our own time and our own society. Equally significantly, our understanding of families in the modern world has a direct bearing upon our understanding of families and of societies in the past. By exploring the histories of families we can establish, with greater precision, clarity, and understanding than we have achieved so far, what actually have been the recurrent and distinctive experiences shaping the lives of countless generations of men and women in Europe and in America.

APPENDIX
BIBLIOGRAPHY
INDEX

Appendix: General Demographic Data

Births, marriages, and deaths recorded in the Andover
town records, in five-year intervals, 1650–1799

Period	Births	Marriages	Deaths
1650–54	28	5	6
1655–59	32	8	1
1660–64	43	14	3
1665–69	44	9	15
1670–74	78	20	13
1675–79	90	18	22
1680–84	125	26	20
1685–89	168	29	46
1690–94	163	24	42
1695–99	156	20	25
1700–04	179	24	37
1705–09	196*	34	52
1710–14	239	54	43
1715–19	247	40	85
1720–24	287	64	72
1725–29	289	66	117
1730–34	333	84	73
1735–39	328	88	251
1740–44	371	88	105
1745–49	354	92	202
1750–54	372	87	153
1755–59	365	105	91
1760–64	388	88	156
1765–69	377	80	71
1770–74	342	65	52
1775–79	311	80	84
1780–84	298	108	41
1785–89	344	105	35
1790–94	288	118	30
1795–99	350	99	79
Total	7,185	1,742	2,022

* Estimated by the author. For explanation, see note
6 in Chapter 1.

Bibliography

PRIMARY SOURCES

Town and County Records

ANDOVER, MASSACHUSETTS

The manuscript town records are located in the Town Clerk's Office, Town Hall, Andover, Mass. (microfilm copies are also available): Ancient Town Records, 1656–1708; Births, Marriages, Deaths, and Intentions, 1701–1800; Old Tax and Record Book, 1670–1716; Proprietors' First Book of Records: Meetings, 1714–1789, Land Grants, 1717–1760; Proprietors' Second Book of Records: Meetings, 1800–1824, Land Grants, 1719–1819; A Record of Births, Deaths, & Marriages, begun 1651 Ended 1700; Record of Town Meetings, 1709–1808; Record of Town Roads and Town Bounds, 1698–1852; Town and County Tax Lists, 1717–1768. Vital records of the town have been published in *Vital Records of Andover Massachusetts to the End of the Year 1849*, 2 vols. (Topsfield, Mass., 1912).

The manuscript records of the North Parish and of the North Parish Church, Unitarian, are located in the North Andover Historical Society, North Andover, Mass.: A Book of Records for the North Precinct in the Town of Andover, 1708; Journal Kept by Rev. Thomas Barnard, Rev. John Barnard, and Dr.

Symmes from 1687 to 1810 of Church Matters, Baptisms, and Weddings.

The manuscript records of the South Parish and of the South Parish Church, Congregational, are located in the vault of the Merrimack Valley National Bank, Andover, Mass.: Assessors' Rate Book, South Parish, 1710–1749; A Book of Records for the South Precinct in Andover, 1708; Rev. Samuel Phillips' Record Book, 1711–1722; South Parish Treasurers' Records, 1711–1732; South Parish Treasurers' Records, 1763–1836.

CONCORD, NEW HAMPSHIRE

The manuscript records of the town are located in the New Hampshire Historical Society, Concord, N.H.: Concord Miscellaneous Papers; Concord Proprietors' Records, vols. I–III, 1725–1781; Records of the Congregational Church in Concord, Commencing 1730 (1730–1825); Walker Papers.

HAVERHILL, MASSACHUSETTS

The manuscript records of the town are located in the City Clerk's Office, Haverhill, Mass.: Haverhill Town Book Number 1; Haverhill Town Book Number 2; Haverhill Town Book Number 3.

NEWBURY, MASSACHUSETTS

The manuscript records of the town are located in Town Hall, Newbury, Mass.: Births, Marriages, and Deaths, Newbury, 1635–1735; Newbury Town Records, 1637–1692; Newbury Town Records, 1635–1681 (MS copy); Proprietors' Records from 1635.

ESSEX COUNTY, MASSACHUSETTS

The manuscript deeds and probate records are located in the Registry of Deeds and Probate Court Building, Salem, Mass.: Essex County Deeds, bound transcriptions, seventeenth and eighteenth centuries (indexed); Ipswich Deeds, bound transcriptions, seventeenth century; Probate Records, individually filed original MSS (indexed); Probate Records, bound transcriptions, seventeenth and eighteenth centuries (photostat copies, indexed). Some probate records have been published in *The Probate Records of Essex County Massachusetts* (1635–1681), 3 vols. (Salem, Mass., 1916–1920).

The court records are located in the Office of the Clerk of the County Court, Essex County Court House, Salem, Mass.: County Court, Ipswich, September 1682–April 1686; County Court, Ipswich, 1682–1692; County Court, Salem, 1679–1692; County Court, Salem, June 1682–November 1685; Court of General Sessions, 1696–1718; Court of General Sessions, 1719–1727; Court Papers (57 vols.); Court of Pleas, Ipswich and Salem, September and November 1686; Court of Pleas and Sessions, 1688–1689; Inferior Court of Pleas, December 1692–September 1695; Inferior Court of Pleas, December 1695–September 1698; Inferior Court of Pleas, December 1698–June 1704; Inferior Court of Pleas, September 1704–September 1726; Inferior Court Book begun July 1719; Miscellaneous Ancient Papers (4 drawers, basement vault); Sessions, July 1692–September 1709; Verbatim transcriptions of Records of Quarterly Courts of Essex County, Mass. (compiled by the Works Project Administration, 1936, typed MSS, 57 vols.); Verbatim transcriptions of Salem Witchcraft Papers (compiled by the Works Project Administration, 1938, typed MSS, 3 vols.). Some court records have been published in *Records and Files of the Quarterly Courts of Essex County Massachusetts*, ed. George F. Dow, 8 vols. (Salem, Mass., 1911–1921)

SUFFOLK COUNTY, MASSACHUSETTS

The Suffolk County Probate Records are located in City Hall, Boston, Mass.

Provincial and Other Public Records

MANUSCRIPT

Andover, Province Tax Rate List, 1767. Mass. Archives. Vol. 130, pp. 34–50.
New Hampshire Deeds. New Hampshire Historical Society. Concord, N.H.

New Hampshire Probate Records. New Hampshire Historical Society. Concord, N.H.

Valuations Towns, 1781–1785. Mass. Archives. Vol. 162.

"White Inhabitants, Massachusetts March 1776." Essex Institute, Salem, Mass. Misc. MSS, vol. XXI.

PRINTED

Documents and Records Relating to Towns in New Hampshire, ed. Nathaniel Bouton et al. Vols. IX–XIII. Concord, N.H., 1875–1884.

Greene, Evarts N., and Virginia D. Harrington. American Population Before the Federal Census of 1790. New York, 1932.

Records of the Governor and Company of the Massachusetts Bay in New England, ed. Nathaniel B. Shurtleff. 5 vols. Boston, 1853–1854.

Return of the Whole Number of Persons within the Several Districts of the United States, According to "An Act providing for the enumeration of the Inhabitants of the United States;" Passed March the first, seventeen hundred and ninety-one. Washington City, 1802.

United States, Bureau of the Census. Heads of Families at the First Census of the United States Taken in the Year 1790: Massachusetts. Washington, 1908.

Private and Personal Records

MANUSCRIPT

Barnard, John. Diary, 1715–1743. Essex Institute, Salem, Mass.

——. Sermons. Historical Society of Pennsylvania, Philadelphia. Original MSS, vol. 32.

Barnard, Thomas. Personal Account Book, 1688–1707. Essex Institute, Salem, Mass.

——. Sermons. Historical Society of Pennsylvania, Philadelphia. Original MSS, vol. 32.

Buckley, Joseph. Account Book, 1693–1701 (Boston). Massachusetts Historical Society, Boston.

Chandler, Samuel. Almanac Diaries, 1746, 1749–1751, 1752–1753, 1761–1764, 1769–1772. Essex Institute, Salem, Mass.

Corwin, George. Account Books, 1653–1655, 1655–1658, 1658–1663, 1663–1668. Essex Institute, Salem, Mass.

Corwin, Jonathan. Ledger, 1685–1691. Essex Institute, Salem, Mass. Corwin Papers.

English, Philip. Ledgers, 1664–1718. 6 vols. Essex Institute, Salem, Mass.

Farrington, Benjamin. Letter to Parents, June 23, 1757. Andover Historical Society, Andover. William A. Trow Collection.

Higginson, John, Jr. Account Book, 1678–1689 (Salem). Essex Institute, Salem, Mass.

Hull, John. Account Book, 1685–1689 (Boston). Baker Library, Harvard University, Cambridge, Mass.

Lovejoy, Nathaniel. Almanac Diaries, 1762–1799. American Antiquarian Society, Worcester, Mass.

Phillips, Samuel. Almanac Diary, 1744. American Antiquarian Society, Worcester, Mass.

——. Letter to Samuel Phillips, Jr., August 26, 1746. Historical Society of Pennsylvania, Philadelphia. Simon Gratz Collection, Case 8, Box 24.

——. Letters to Samuel Phillips, Jr., August 26, 1746, and November 10, 1755. Historical Society of Pennsylvania, Philadelphia. Simon Gratz Collection, Case 8, Box 24.

——. Letter to South Parish, March 5, 1752. Essex Institute, Salem, Mass.

——. Letter to John Phillips, November 19, 1759. Essex Institute, Salem, Mass.

——. Letter Book. Phillips Academy Library, Andover, Mass.

Tucker Family MSS. Vol. I (Essex County Innholders and Miscellaney, 1680–1812). Essex Institute, Salem, Mass.

PRINTED

Dane, John. "A Declaration of Remarkabell Provedenses in the Corse of My Lyfe," *NEHGR*, VIII (1854), 147–156.

Foster, Asa. "Diary of Capt. Asa Foster of Andover, Mass.,

Concerning Operations of the British Army in the French and
Indian War, 1758," *NEHGR*, LIV (1900), 183–188.

Miscellaneous

Barnard, John. *The Expectation of Man disappointed by the
Great God. A Sermon Preached at Andover South Parish;
Occasioned By the much lamented Death of that hopeful
Young Gentleman, Mr. Abiel Abbot; Who departed this life
on the 18th Day of May, 1739; in the 24th Year of his Age.*
Boston, 1739.

Paine, Thomas. *Common Sense and The Crisis.* New York, 1946.

Tocqueville, Alexis de. *Journey to America,* ed. J. P. Mayer.
New Haven, 1962.

SECONDARY SOURCES

Genealogies

Abbot, Abiel, and Ephraim Abbot. *A Genealogical Register of
the Descendants of George Abbot, of Andover, George Abbot,
of Rowley, Thomas Abbot, of Andover, Arthur Abbot, of
Ipswich, Robert Abbot, of Branford, Ct., and George Abbot,
of Norwalk, Ct.* Boston, 1847.

Abbott, Charles M. "Men and Rivers. George Abbott and his Kin
—on the Shawsheen, the Merrimac, the Souhegan, the Sandy,
the Kennebec, and the Charles." Watertown, 1953. Typed,
mimeographed copy in New England Historic Genealogical
Society, Boston.

Abbott, Charlotte Helen. Typed genealogies of 180 families in 56
looseleaf binders. Located in Memorial Library and Andover
Historical Society, Andover.

Abbott, Lemuel Abijah. *Descendants of George Abbott, of Row-
ley, Mass., of His Joint Descendants with George Abbott, Sr.,
of Andover, Mass., of the Descendants of Daniel Abbott, of
Providence, R.I.; of some of the Descendants of Capt. Thomas
Abbott, of Andover, Mass.; of George Abbott, of Norwalk,
Ct.; of Robert Abbott, of Branford, Ct.* N.p., 1906.

Aslett Family. Bound MSS. New England Historic Genealogical Society, Boston.

"Ballard Genealogy," *Essex Antiquarian*, VI (1902), 35.

Barker, Elizabeth Frye. *Barker Genealogy*. New York, 1927.

———. *Frye Genealogy*. New York, 1920.

Barker Family. Typed MSS. New England Historic Genealogical Society, Boston.

"Blanchard Genealogy," *Essex Antiquarian*, IX (1905), 26–32.

"Bradstreet Genealogy," *Essex Antiquarian*, XI (1907), 52–57.

Brigham, Willard I. Tyler. *The Tyler Genealogy. The Descendants of Job Tyler, of Andover, Massachusetts, 1619–1700.* N.p., 1912.

Burleigh, Charles. *The Genealogy and History of the Ingalls Family in America*. Malden, Mass., 1903.

Chandler, George. *The Chandler Family. The Descendants of William and Annis Chandler Who Settled in Roxbury, Mass., 1637.* Worcester, Mass., 1883.

De Forest, Louis Effingham. *Ballard and Allied Families*. New York, 1924.

"Descendants of Robert Barnard," *Essex Antiquarian*, VI (1902), 125.

Durrie, Daniel S. *A Genealogical History of the Holt Family in the United States: More Particularly the Descendants of Nicholas Holt of Newbury and Andover, Mass., 1634–1644, and of William Holt of New Haven, Conn.* Albany, N.Y., 1864.

Farlow, Charles Frederic. *Ballard Genealogy. William Ballard (1603–1639) of Lynn, Massachusetts and William Ballard (1617–1689) of Andover, Massachusetts and their Descendants.* Boston, 1911.

Farmer, John. *A Genealogical Register of the First Settlers of New England*. Lancaster, Mass., 1829.

Farnham, J. M. W. *Genealogy of the Farnham Family*. 2nd ed. Shanghai, China, 1888.

Field, Osgood. "A Contribution of the History of the Family of Osgood," *NEHGR*, XX (1866), 22–28.

Gatenby, Ethel M. Blanchard. "The Blanchard-Baker-Brown

Genealogy, 1639–1948." Typed MSS. New England Historic Genealogical Society, Boston.

Holman, Mary Lovering. *Ancestry of Charles Stimson Pillsbury and John Sargent Pillsbury*. 2 vols. Concord, N.H., 1938.

Holmes, Frank R. *Directory of the Ancestral Heads of New England Families 1620–1700*. New York, 1923.

Jackson, Annie Givin. *Genealogical Record of John Lovejoy of Andover, Massachusetts and of his Wife Mary Osgood of Ipswich, Massachusetts. Also of their Descendants Unto the Tenth Generation*. Denver, Colo., 1917.

Johnson, William W. *Johnson Genealogy: Records of the Descendants of John Johnson of Ipswich and Andover, Mass., 1635–1892*. North Greenfield, Wis., 1892.

Lovejoy, Clarence Earle. *The Lovejoy Genealogy With Biographies and History, 1460–1930*. N.p., 1930.

Moriarty, G. Andrews. "Ancestry of George Abbott of Andover, Mass.," *NEHGR*, LXXXV (1931), 79–86.

———. "Ancestry of William Chandler of Roxbury, Mass.," *NEHGR*, LXXXV (1931), 133–145.

———. "Stevens of Newbury and Andover, Mass.," *NEHGR*, LXXXV (1931), 396–401.

Osgood, Ira. *A Genealogy of the Descendants of John, Christopher, and William Osgood Who Came from England and Settled in New England Early in the Seventeenth Century*, ed. Eben Putnam. Salem, Mass., 1894.

Pierce, Frederick Clifton. *Foster Genealogy*. 2 vols. Chicago, 1899.

Russell, George Ely. "Descendants of William and Sarah (Emery) Russel of Andover, Mass., and Somers, Conn." Typed MSS (1951). New England Historic Genealogical Society, Boston.

———. "Russell Families of Seventeenth Century New England." Typed MSS (4 vols.). New England Historic Genealogical Society, Boston.

Robert Barnard of Andover, Mass., and His Descendants. Everett, Mass., 1899.

Savage, James, *A Genealogical Dictionary of the First Settlers of New England*. 4 vols. Boston, 1860–1862.

Local Histories

ANDOVER

Abbot, Abiel. *History of Andover from its Settlement to 1829.* Andover, Mass., 1829.

Bailey, Sarah Loring. *Historical Sketches of Andover (Comprising the Present Towns of North Andover and Andover), Massachusetts.* Boston, 1880.

Fuess, Claude M. *Andover—Symbol of New England: The Evolution of a Town.* Andover, Mass., 1959.

[Mooar, George.] *Historical Manual of the South Church in Andover, Mass.* Andover, Mass., 1859.

OTHER TOWNS

Innumerable local histories were useful in tracking the origins and migrations of Andover men and their families; the following list is a selection of those most directly related to this study.

Babson, John J. *History of the Town of Gloucester, Cape Ann, including the Town of Rockport.* Gloucester, Mass., 1860.

——. *Notes and Additions to the History of Gloucester.* Salem, Mass., 1891.

Bell, Charles. *Facts Relating to the Early History of Chester, N.H., from the Settlement in 1720, Until the Formation of the State Constitution in the Year 1784.* Concord, N.H., 1863.

——. *History of the Town of Exeter, New Hampshire.* Exeter, N.H., 1888.

Benedict, William A., and Hiram A. Tracy. *History of the Town of Sutton, Massachusetts, from 1704 to 1876.* Worcester, Mass., 1878.

Bouton, Nathaniel. *The History of Concord, from its First Grant in 1725, to the Organization of the City Government in 1853.* Concord, N.H., 1856.

Bowen, Clarence Winthrop. *The History of Woodstock, Connecticut; Genealogies of Woodstock Families.* 4 vols. Norwood, Mass., 1930.

Carter, N. F., and T. L. Fowler. *History of Pembroke, N.H., 1730–1895.* 2 vols. Concord, N.H., 1895.

Caswell, Lilley B. *The History of the Town of Royalston, Mass., 1762–1917.* Royalston, Mass., 1917.

Chase, Benjamin. *History of Old Chester, From 1719–1869.* Auburn, N.H., 1869.

Chase, George Wingate. *The History of Haverhill, Massachusetts, From Its First Settlement, in 1640, to the Year 1860.* Haverhill, Mass., 1861.

Coffin, Joshua. *A Sketch of the History of Newbury, Newburyport, and West Newbury, from 1635 to 1845.* Boston, 1845.

Currier, John J. *History of Newbury, Mass., 1635–1902.* Boston, 1902.

Dow, George Francis. *History of Topsfield, Mass.* Topsfield, Mass., 1940.

Gage, Thomas. *The History of Rowley, Anciently Including Bradford, Boxford, and Georgetown, from the Year 1639 to the Present Time.* Boston, 1840.

Hammond, Charles. *History of Union, Conn.* New Haven, 1893.

Hazen, Henry A. *History of Billerica, Mass., with a Genealogical Register.* Boston, 1883.

Howe, Joseph S. *Historical Sketch of the Town of Methuen, From Its Settlement to the Year 1876.* Methuen, Mass., 1876.

Hudson, Charles. *History of the Town of Marlborough, Middlesex County, Massachusetts, from Its First Settlement in 1657 to 1861.* Boston, 1862.

Hurd, Hamilton D. *History of Essex County, Massachusetts, With Biographical Sketches of Many of Its Pioneers and Prominent Men.* 2 vols. Philadelphia, 1888.

Larned, Ellen D. *History of Windham County, Connecticut.* 2 vols. Worcester, Mass., 1874–1880.

Mirick, B. L. *The History of Haverhill, Massachusetts.* Haverhill, Mass., 1832.

Paige, Lucius R. *History of Cambridge, Massachusetts, 1630–1877, With a Genealogical Register.* Boston, 1877.

——. *History of Hardwick, Mass., with a Genealogical Register.* Boston, 1883.

Perley, Sidney. *The History of Boxford, Essex County, Massachusetts, from the Earliest Settlement Known to the Present Time.* Boxford, Mass., 1880.

——. *The History of Salem, Massachusetts.* 3 vols. Salem, Mass., 1924–1926.

Waters, Thomas Franklin. *Ipswich in the Massachusetts Bay Colony.* 2 vols. Ipswich, Mass., 1905.

Waters, Wilson. *History of Chelmsford, Massachusetts.* Lowell, Mass., 1917.

Wheatland, Henry, *et al. Standard History of Essex County, Massachusetts, Embracing a History of the County From Its First Settlement to the Present Time, With a History and Description of its Towns and Cities.* Boston, 1878.

Worcester, Samuel T. *History of the Town of Hollis, New Hampshire, From Its First Settlement to the Year 1879.* Nashua, N.H., 1879.

General

Akagi, Roy H. *The Town Proprietors of the New England Colonies.* Philadelphia, 1924.

Andrews, Charles M. *The River Towns of Connecticut: A Study of Wethersfield, Hartford, and Windsor.* Baltimore, 1889.

Anshen, Ruth Nanda. *The Family: Its Function and Destiny.* New York, 1959.

Arensberg, Conrad M., and Solon T. Kimball. *Family and Community in Ireland.* 1940. Reprint. Gloucester, Mass., 1961.

Ariès, Philippe. *Centuries of Childhood: A Social History of Family Life,* trans. Robert Baldick. New York, 1962.

Bailyn, Bernard. *Education in the Forming of American Society: Needs and Opportunities for Study.* Chapel Hill, 1960.

——. *The New England Merchants in the Seventeenth Century.* Cambridge, Mass., 1955.

Battis, Emery. *Saints and Sectaries: Anne Hutchinson and the Antinomian Controversy in the Massachusetts Bay Colony.* Chapel Hill, 1962.

Berthoff, Rowland. "The American Social Order: A Conservative Hypothesis," *AHR*, LXV (1960), 495–514.

Bidwell, Percy Wells, and John I. Falconer. *History of Agriculture in the Northern United States, 1620–1860.* Washington, 1925.

Blake, John B. *Public Health in the Town of Boston, 1630–1822.* Cambridge, Mass., 1959.

Bloch, Marc. *French Rural History: An Essay on its Basic Characteristics,* trans. Janet Sondheimer. Berkeley, Calif., 1966.

Bott, Elizabeth. *Family and Social Network: Roles, Norms, and External Relationships in Ordinary Urban Families.* London, 1957.

Bridenbaugh, Carl. *Vexed and Troubled Englishmen, 1590–1642.* New York, 1968.

Bumsted, J. M., and J. T. Lemon, "New Approaches in Early American Studies: The Local Community in New England," *Social History,* II (1968), 98–112.

Bushman, Richard L. *From Puritan to Yankee: Character and the Social Order in Connecticut, 1690–1765.* Cambridge, Mass., 1967.

Calhoun, Arthur W. *A Social History of the American Family.* 3 vols. Cleveland, Ohio, 1917.

Campbell, Mildred. *The English Yeoman under Elizabeth and the Early Stuarts.* New Haven, 1942.

Caulfield, Ernest. "A History of the Terrible Epidemic, Vulgarly Called the Throat Distemper, as it Occurred in his Majesty's New England Colonies Between 1735 and 1740," *Yale Journal of Biology and Medicine,* XI (1938–1939), 219–272, 277–335.

———. "Some Common Diseases of Colonial Children," *Publications of the Colonial Society of Massachusetts,* XXXV (1942–1946), 4–65.

Chambers, J. D. *The Vale of Trent, 1670–1800: A Regional Study of Economic Change, EHR* Supplement no. 3 (1957).

Connell, K. H. "Land and Population in Ireland, 1780–1845," *EHR*, II (1950), 278–289.

———. "Peasant Marriage in Ireland: Its Structure and Development Since the Famine," *EHR*, XIV (1962), 502–523.

———. *Population of Ireland, 1750–1845.* Oxford, 1950.

Connor, Paul. "Patriarchy: Old World and New," *AQ*, XVII (1965), 48–62.

Cornwall, Julian. "Evidence of Population Mobility in the Seventeenth Century," *Bulletin of the Institute of Historical Research*, XL (1967), 143–152.

Davisson, William I. "Essex County Price Trends: Money and Markets in 17th Century Massachusetts," *EIHC*, CIII (1967), 144–185.

———. "Essex County Wealth Trends: Wealth and Economic Growth in 17th Century Massachusetts," *EIHC*, CIII (1967), 291–342.

Demos, John. "Families in Colonial Bristol, Rhode Island: An Exercise in Historical Demography," *WMQ*, XXV (1968), 40–57.

———. *A Little Commonwealth: Family Life in Plymouth Colony.* New York, 1970.

———. "Notes on Life in Plymouth Colony," *WMQ*, XXII (1965), 264–286.

Drake, Michael. "Marriage and Population Growth in Ireland, 1750–1845," *EHR*, XIV (1963), 301–313.

Duffy, John. *Epidemics in Colonial America.* Baton Rouge, La., 1953.

Dunn, Richard S. "The Barbados Census of 1680: Profile of the Richest Colony in English America," *WMQ*, XXVI (1969), 3–30.

———. *Puritans and Yankees: The Winthrop Dynasty of New England, 1630–1717.* Princeton, 1962.

Erikson, Erik H. *Childhood and Society.* New York, 1950.

Esler, Anthony. *The Aspiring Mind of the Elizabethan Younger Generation.* Durham, N.C., 1966.

Eversley, D. E. C. "Population, Economy and Society," in D. V.

Glass and D. E. C. Eversley, eds., *Population in History: Essays in Historical Demography* (Chicago, 1965), pp. 23–69.

———. "A Survey of Population in an Area of Worcestershire from 1660 to 1850 on the Basis of Parish Registers," *Population Studies*, X (1957), 253–279.

Fairchild, Byron. *Messrs. William Pepperrell: Merchants of Piscataqua.* Ithaca, N.Y., 1954.

Farber, Bernard, ed. *Kinship and Family Organization.* New York, 1966.

Finch, Mary E. *The Wealth of Five Northamptonshire Families, 1540–1640.* Publications of the Northamptonshire Record Society, vol. XIX. Oxford, 1956.

Firth, Raymond. "Family and Kinship in Industrial Society," in Paul Halmos, ed., *The Development of Industrial Societies.* Sociological Review Monograph no. 8 (1964), pp. 65–87.

Furstenberg, Frank F., Jr. "Industrialization and the American Family: A Look Backward," *American Sociological Review*, XXXI (1966), 326–337.

Gans, Herbert J. *The Urban Villagers: Group and Class in The Life of Italian–Americans.* Glencoe, Ill., 1962.

Glass, D. V., and D. E. C. Eversley, eds. *Population in History: Essays in Historical Demography.* Chicago, 1965.

Glick, Paul C. *American Families.* New York, 1957.

Goode, William J. *The Family.* Foundations of Modern Sociology Series, ed. Alex Inkeles. Englewood Cliffs, N.J., 1964.

———. *World Revolution and Family Patterns.* New York, 1963.

Goubert, Pierre. *Beauvais et le Beauvaisis de 1600 à 1730: Contribution à l'histoire sociale de la France du XVIIe siècle.* Paris, 1960.

———. "Legitimate Fecundity and Infant Mortality in France During the Eighteenth Century: A Comparison," *Daedalus*, Spring 1968, pp. 593–603.

———. "Recent Theories and Research in French Population Between 1500 and 1700," in D. V. Glass and D. E. C. Eversley, eds., *Population in History: Essays in Historical Demography* (Chicago, 1965), pp. 457–473.

Grant, Charles S. *Democracy in the Connecticut Frontier Town of Kent.* New York, 1961.

[Graubard, Stephen R., ed.] *Historical Population Studies, Daedalus,* Spring 1968, pp. 353–635.

Gray, Howard Levi. *English Field Systems.* Cambridge, Mass., 1915.

Greene, Jack P., ed. *The Diary of Colonel Landon Carter of Sabine Hall, 1752–1778.* 2 vols. Charlottesville, Va., 1965.

Greenfield, Sidney M. "Industrialization and the Family in Sociological Theory," *American Journal of Sociology,* LXVII (1961), 312–322.

Greven, Philip J., Jr. "Comments on 'Familial Politics: The Killing of the King, 1776,' by Winthrop D. Jordan." Paper delivered at the Organization of American Historians Meeting, April 27, 1967, Chicago, Ill.

———. "Family, Mobility, and Revivalism in Early America: Some Perspectives and Hypotheses." Mimeo. Paper delivered at the Southern Historical Association Meeting, November 7, 1968, New Orleans, La.

———. "Family Structure in Seventeenth-Century Andover, Massachusetts," *WMQ,* XXIII (1966), 234–256.

———. "Four Generations: A Study of Family Structure, Inheritance, and Mobility in Andover, Massachusetts, 1630–1750." Ph.D. diss., Harvard University, 1964.

———. "Historical Demography and Colonial America," *WMQ,* XXIV (1967), 438–454.

———. "An Historical Perspective on Family Structure." Mimeo. Paper delivered at the Social Science Research Council Conference on the History of the Family, October 26–27, 1967, Washington, D.C.

———. "Old Patterns in the New World: The Distribution of Land in 17th Century Andover," *EIHC,* CI (1965), 133–148.

Gutman, Robert. "Birth and Death Registration in Massachusetts, I: The Colonial Background, 1639–1800," *Millbank Memorial Fund Quarterly,* XXXVI (1958), 58–74.

Habakkuk, H. J. "English Population in the Eighteenth Century," *EHR*, VI (1953), 117–133.

——. "Family Structure and Economic Change in Nineteenth-Century Europe," *JEH*, XV (1955), 1–12.

Hajnal, J. "European Marriage Patterns in Perspective," in D. V. Glass and D. E. C. Eversley, eds., *Population in History: Essays in Historical Demography* (Chicago, 1965), pp. 101–143.

Handlin, Oscar. *The Americans: A New History of the People of the United States.* Boston, 1963.

——. *The Uprooted: The Epic Story of the Great Migrations that Made the American People.* Boston, 1951.

Heimert, Alan. *Religion and the American Mind from the Great Awakening to the Revolution.* Cambridge, Mass., 1966.

Henry, Louis. *Anciennes familles Genevoises: Étude démographique: XVIe–XXe siècle.* Travaux et documents d'Institut national d'études démographiques no. 26. Paris, 1956.

——. "The Population of France in the Eighteenth Century," in D. V. Glass and D. E. C. Eversley, eds., *Population in History: Essays in Historical Demography* (Chicago, 1965), pp. 434–456.

Hill, Christopher. *Society and Puritanism in Pre-revolutionary England.* 2nd ed. New York, 1967.

Hinton, R. W. K. "Husbands, Fathers, and Conquerors, II: Patriarchalism in Hobbes and Locke," *Political Studies*, XVI (1968), 55–67.

Holbrook, Stewart H. *The Yankee Exodus: An Account of Migration from New England.* New York, 1950.

Hollingsworth, T. H. *The Demography of the British Peerage.* Supplement to *Population Studies*, XVIII (1964).

Homans, George Caspar. *English Villagers of the Thirteenth Century.* 1941. Reprint. New York, 1960.

Hoskins, W. G. *Essays in Leicestershire History.* Liverpool, 1950.

——. *The Midland Peasant: The Economic and Social History of a Leicestershire Village.* London, 1957.

——. "The Population of an English Village, 1086–1801: A Study of Wigston Magna," in W. G. Hoskins, *Provincial England:*

Essays in Social and Economic History (London, 1963), ch. 10, pp. 181–208.

——. *Provincial England: Essays in Social and Economic History.* London, 1963.

Ironside, Charles Edward. *The Family in Colonial New York: A Sociological Study.* New York, 1942.

Jordan, Winthrop D. "Familial Politics: The Killing of the King, 1776." Paper delivered at the Organization of American Historians Meeting, April 27, 1967, Chicago, Ill.

Keim, C. Ray. "Primogeniture and Entail in Colonial Virginia," *WMQ,* XXV (1968), 545–586.

Kohl, Seena, and John W. Bennett. "Kinship, Succession, and the Migration of Young People in a Canadian Agricultural Community," *International Journal of Comparative Sociology,* VI (1965), 95–116.

Laslett, Peter. "The Gentry of Kent in 1640," *Cambridge Historical Journal,* IX (1948), 148–164.

——. *The World We Have Lost.* New York, 1965.

——, ed. *Patriarcha and Other Political Works of Sir Robert Filmer.* Oxford, 1949.

Laslett, Peter, and John Harrison. "Clayworth and Cogenhoe," in H. E. Bell and R. L. Ollard, eds., *Historical Essays, 1600–1750, Presented to David Ogg.* London, 1963.

Leach, Douglas Edward. *Flintlock and Tomahawk: New England in King Philip's War.* New York, 1958.

Lee, Everett S. "The Turner Thesis Re-examined," *AQ,* XIII (1961), 77–83.

Lee, Joseph. "Marriage and Population in Pre-famine Ireland," *EHR,* XXI (1968), 283–295.

Litwak, Eugene. "Geographical Mobility and Extended Family Cohesion," *American Sociological Review,* XXV (1960), 385–394.

——. "Occupational Mobility and Extended Family Cohesion," *American Sociological Review,* XXV (1960), 9–21.

Lockridge, Kenneth A. "Dedham, 1636–1736: The Anatomy of a Puritan Utopia." Ph.D. diss., Princeton University, 1965.

Lockridge, Kenneth A. "Land, Population and the Evolution of New England Society, 1630–1790," *Past and Present*, April 1968, 62–80.

——. "The Population of Dedham, Massachusetts, 1636–1736," *EHR*, XIX (1966), 318–344.

Lotka, Alfred J. "The Size of American Families in the Eighteenth Century and the Significance of the Empirical Constants in the Pearl-Reed Law of Population Growth," *Journal of the American Statistical Association*, XXII (1927), 154–170.

Main, Jackson Turner. *The Social Structure of Revolutionary America*. Princeton, 1965.

Matthews, Elmora Messer. *Neighbor and Kin: Life in a Tennessee Ridge Community*. Nashville, Tenn., 1965.

Matthews, Lois Kimball. *The Expansion of New England: The Spread of New England Settlement and Institutions to the Mississippi River, 1620–1865*. Boston, 1909.

Merrens, Harry Roy. *Colonial North Carolina in the Eighteenth Century: A Study in Historical Geography*. Chapel Hill, 1964.

Miller, Perry. *The New England Mind From Colony to Province*. Cambridge, Mass., 1953.

—— and Thomas Johnson. *The Puritans*. New York, 1938.

Mingay, G. E. "The Size of Farms in the Eighteenth Century," *EHR*, XIV (1962), 469–488.

Moller, Herbert. "Sex Composition and Correlated Culture Patterns of Colonial America," *WMQ*, II (1945), 113–153.

Monahan, Thomas P. *The Pattern of Age at Marriage in the United States*. 2 vols. Philadelphia, 1951.

Morgan, Edmund S. *The Puritan Family: Religion & Domestic Relations in Seventeenth-Century New England*. Rev. ed. New York, 1966.

——. *Virginians at Home: Family Life in the Eighteenth Century*. Chapel Hill, 1952.

Nettels, Curtis P. *The Roots of American Civilization*. New York, 1938.

Orwin, C. S. *The Open Fields*. Rev. ed. Oxford, 1954.

Parsons, Talcott. "The Kinship System of the Contemporary United States," *American Anthropologist*, XLV (1943), 22–38.
—— and Robert F. Bales. *Family, Socialization and Process.* Glencoe, Ill., 1955.

Perzel, Edward S. "Landholding in Ipswich," *EIHC*, CIV (1968), 303–328.

Potter, J. "The Growth of Population in America, 1700–1860," in D. V. Glass and D. E. C. Eversley, eds., *Population in History: Essays in Historical Demography* (Chicago, 1965), pp. 631–688.

Powell, Chilton L. "Marriage in Early New England," *New England Quarterly*, I (1928), 323–334.

Powell, Sumner Chilton. *Puritan Village: The Formation of a New England Town.* Middletown, Conn., 1963.

Pressat, Roland. *L'analyse démographique: Méthodes, résultats, applications.* Paris, 1961.

Ramsey, Robert W. *Carolina Cradle: Settlement of the Northwest Carolina Frontier, 1747–1762.* Chapel Hill, 1964.

Rich, E. E. "The Population of Elizabethan England," *EHR*, II (1950), 247–265.

Rosser, Colin, and Christopher Harris. *The Family and Social Change: A Study of Family and Kinship in a South Wales Town.* London, 1965.

Rothman, David J. "A Note on the Study of the Colonial Family," *WMQ*, XXIII (1966), 627–634.

Rutman, Darrett B. *Husbandmen of Plymouth: Farms and Villages in the Old Colony, 1620–1692.* Boston, 1967.
——. *Winthrop's Boston: Portrait of a Puritan Town, 1630–1649.* Chapel Hill, 1965.

Sachs, William S. "Agricultural Conditions in the Northern Colonies Before the Revolution," *JEH*, XIII (1953), 274–290.

Shipton, Clifford K. *Biographical Sketches of Those Who Attended Harvard College [Sibley's Harvard Graduates].* 14 vols. Boston, 1873–.

Sirjamaki, John. *The American Family in the Twentieth Century.* Cambridge, Mass., 1953.

Smith, James Morton, ed. *Seventeenth-Century America: Essays in Colonial History*. Chapel Hill, 1959.

Stephens, William N. *The Family in Cross Cultural Perspective*. New York, 1957.

Stone, Lawrence. *The Crisis of the Aristocracy, 1558–1641*. Oxford, 1965.

———. "Social Mobility in England, 1500–1700," *Past and Present*, April 1966, 16–55.

Sussman, Marvin B., and Lee G. Burchinal. "Kin Family Network: Unheralded Structure in Current Conceptualizations of Family Functioning," *Marriage and Family Living*, XXIV (1962), 231–240.

———. "Parental Aid to Married Children: Implications for Family Functioning," *Marriage and Family Living*, XXIV (1962), 320–332.

Sutherland, Stella H. *Population Distribution in Colonial America*. 1936. Reprint. New York, 1966.

Thernstrom, Stephan. *Poverty and Progress: Social Mobility in a Nineteenth Century City*. Cambridge, Mass., 1964.

Thirsk, Joan, ed. *The Agrarian History of England and Wales, 1500–1640*. Vol. IV. Cambridge, 1967.

Tocqueville, Alexis de. *Democracy in America*, ed. Phillips Bradley. 2 vols. New York, 1956.

Tranter, N. L. "Population and Social Structure in Bedfordshire Parish: The Cardington Listing of Inhabitants, 1782," *Population Studies*, XXI (1967), 261–281.

Tucker, G. S. L. "English Pre-industrial Population Trends," *EHR*, XVI (1963), 205–218.

Turner, Barbara Carpenter. *A History of Hampshire*. London, 1963.

Walcott, Robert. "Husbandry in Colonial New England," *New England Quarterly*, IX (1936), 218–252.

Walzer, Michael. *The Revolution of the Saints: A Study in the Origins of Radical Politics*. Cambridge, Mass., 1965.

Waters, John J., Jr. "Hingham, Massachusetts, 1631–1661: An

East Anglian Oligarchy in the New World," *Journal of Social History*, I (1968), 351–370.

——. *The Otis Family in Provincial and Revolutionary Massachusetts*. Chapel Hill, 1968.

Wertenbaker, Thomas Jefferson. *The First Americans, 1607–1690*. New York, 1929.

White, Philip L. *The Beekman Family of New York in Politics and Commerce, 1647–1877*. New York, 1956.

Williams, Robin M., Jr., *American Society: A Sociological Interpretation*. 2nd ed., rev. New York, 1960.

Williams, W. M. *The Sociology of an English Village: Gosforth*. London, 1956.

——. *A West Country Village, Ashworthy: Family, Kinship and Land*. London, 1963.

Wishy, Bernard. *The Child and the Republic: The Dawn of Modern American Child Nurture*. Philadelphia, 1968.

Wood, Gordon S. "Rhetoric and Reality in the American Revolution," *WMQ*, XXIII (1966), 3–32.

Wrigley, E. A. "Family Limitation in Pre-industrial England," *EHR*, XIX (1966), 82–109.

——. "Mortality in Pre-industrial England: The Example of Colyton, Devon, over Three Centuries," *Daedalus*, Spring 1968, pp. 546–580.

——. *Population and History*. London, 1969.

——. "A Simple Model of London's Importance in Changing English Society and Economy 1650–1750," *Past and Present*, July 1967, 44–70.

——, ed. *An Introduction to English Historical Demography from the Sixteenth to the Nineteenth Century*. New York, 1966.

Young, Michael, and Peter Willmott. *Family and Kinship in East London*. London, 1957.

Index

Faulkner family, 140, 215, 216, 219
Fertility index, 23, 24n, 104, 120,
    175, 183, 184, 185, 272
First and second generations, 19-101
Foster, Abraham, 69
Foster, Andrew, Sr., 46
Foster, Andrew, Jr., 46, 62n
Foster, Sarah, 160
Foster family, 140, 171, 215, 216,
    217, 219
Framingham, Mass., 159
France, 24, 113n, 191, 210
Frazier, Nathan, 214
Frye (Frie), Abiel, 233, 234
Frye, Isaac, 233
Frye, James, 135n, 136n
Frye, John, Sr., 46, 232-235
Frye, John, Jr., 62n, 233
Frye, Joseph, 234
Frye, Joshua, 233, 234
Frye (Frie), Nathan, 148n
Frye (Frie), Samuel, Sr., 148
Frye (Frie), Samuel, Jr., 148
Frye family, 140, 215, 216, 217, 221
Fuess, Claude M., 43n

Gans, Herbert J., 284n
Genealogy: as evidence, 4
    by Rev. Samuel Chandler, 256
    uses of, 4
Generational cycles, vii, 17, 17n-
    18n, 171, 180-181, 258, 274-275
    from first to second generation,
        37-39
    in Kent, Conn., 125-126n
Generational profiles, 22, 37-38
Generations: first and second, 19-99
    second and third, 101-172
    third and fourth, 173-258
    differences between, first and
        second, 22, 60-61, 62, 63-64,
        73, 130
    —second and third, 120, 124, 125-
        126, 136, 155
    —third and fourth, 175, 180-181,
        193, 197, 206, 222-223
    —second and fourth, 280-282
    —English and American, 270
    of families, 2
    of first settlers, 4, 48

of historians, vii-ix
    probate records for, 10-11
Glass, D. V., 6n, 17n, 23n, 32n, 105n,
    106n, 178n, 184n, 185n, 210n
Gloucester, Mass., 255
Goode, William J., 284n
Goodhue, Joseph, 81n
Gosforth, England, 75n
Goubert, Pierre, 24n, 191n
Grainger, Mary, 114
Grainger family, 219
Grant, Charles S., 9n, 17n, 42n, 48n,
    125n-126n, 158n, 162n, 177n,
    274n
Graves, Mark, 46
Gray, Howard Levi, 43n, 44n, 51n
Great Pond, 44, 87-88
Greene, Evarts N., 176n, 177n
Greenfield, Sidney M., 14n, 285n
Greenleigh, England, 285n
Greven, Philip J., Jr., 5n, 21n, 73n,
    267n, 281n
Grow, Thomas, 164n
Gutman, Robert, 6n

Habakkuk, H. J., 13n
Hajnal, J., 32n, 35n, 36n
Hampshire, England, 42, 44
Hampton, Conn., 167
Handlin, Oscar, 28n, 29n, 33n, 262n,
    264n
Hardwick, Mass., 159
Harrington, Virginia D., 176n, 177n
Harris, Christopher, 14n, 15n, 284n,
    285n
Harrison, John, 13n, 14n, 24n, 31n,
    40n, 97n, 106n, 266, 267n
Harvard College, 198, 240, 243, 251,
    252
Haverhill, Mass., 45, 52n, 56n, 64,
    139n, 170, 171, 198, 254
Heimert, Alan, 278n
Henry, Louis, 210n
Hill, Christopher, 277n
Hinckman, Thomas, 76
Hingham, Mass., 28n, 31n, 268n
Hinton, R. W. K., 282n
Historical perspectives on the fam-
    ily, 261-289
Hollingsworth, Richard, Sr., 90n
Hollingsworth, Richard, Jr., 90n